GW01150917

dBASE IV SQL
User's Guide

By Jack L. Hursch, Ph.D.
and
Carolyn J. Hursch, Ph.D.

ASHTON·TATE®

ISBN: 1-55519-052-9 (Ashton-Tate)
ISBN: 0-13-198755-0 (Brady Books)

Published by Tate Publishing, a division of Ashton-Tate, 20101 Hamilton Avenue, Torrance, California 90502-1319.

10 9 8 7 6 5 4 3 2 *89 90 91*

Printed in the United States of America; published simultaneously in Canada.

Disclaimer:
This product is designed to help you improve your computer use. However, the authors and publishers assume no responsibility whatsoever for the uses made of this material or for decisions based on its use and make no warranties, either express or implied, regarding the contents of this product, its merchantability, or its fitness for any particular purpose.

Neither the publishers nor anyone else who has been involved in the creation, production, or delivery of this product shall be liable for any direct, incidental, or consequential damages, such as, but not limited to, loss of anticipated profits or benefits resulting from its use or from any breach of any warranty. Some states do not allow the exclusion or limitation of direct, incidental, or consequential damages, so the above limitation may not apply to you. No dealer, company, or person is authorized to alter this disclaimer. Any representations to the contrary will not bind the author or publisher.

Acquisitions Editor: Larry Colker

Development Editor: David Rose

Editors: Ann B. Sloan, Denise Weatherwax

Technical Reviewers: Wendy Hoben, Paul Kennedy, Kwang-Ling Seh,

Graphics Production Supervisor: Lilo Kilstein

Cover Art: Robert Ross

Design Director: Thomas Clark

Editorial Asst.: Carole Krasowski-Hayes

Production Assistant: Juliette Robinson

This book was formatted and typeset with FullWrite Professional ™, an Ashton-Tate product. Final output was created on a Linotronic 300 laser typesetter.

Contents

1

Introduction

dBASE IV™ with SQL (Structured Query Language), the new dBASE® product, brings together the most widely used database management system for microcomputers with the most popular query language for use in a relational database.

Both the dBASE family of products from Ashton-Tate®, and SQL, based on IBM research, have a long history of development, during which each has been finely tuned to meet present-day needs. They are both easy to learn and efficient. dBASE IV—the combination of both products—represents the amalgamation of two separate lines of development, resulting in the most advanced relational database management system available today.

The SQL language is dynamic in that it can be adapted to the user's own situation. Considerations of speed and efficiency enter into the formulation of queries to the database; therefore, the precise form of a query will depend largely on the size and scope of each user's own material. Once the basic principles have been mastered, the ways in which a retrieval request can be presented to the database are limited only by the user's creativity.

This book emphasizes the use of SQL within the dBASE IV structure, both from the viewpoint of the casual user, as well as from the perspective of the programmer who must write special applications.

If you are familiar with other versions of dBASE products, you will find that dBASE IV is compatible with those versions, and that the addition of SQL will broaden the range of database operations now available to you.

If you are new to the dBASE family of products, you will be gratified by the ease of operation and speed of performance now available to you in dBASE IV.

1.1 ABOUT THIS BOOK

This book tells the whole story of SQL in dBASE IV, starting with the simplest concepts and gradually combining these with other concepts to form more complex operations. It should be used as a supplement to the documentation provided by Ashton-Tate with your copy of dBASE IV.

The book works through the SQL language, and shows examples of each command in a wide variety of applied situations. Chapters Two through Ten explain the structure and usage of SQL, while Chapter Eleven shows how to embed SQL in a procedural language. Chapter Twelve treats database design considerations. Following is a detailed description of each chapter.

The latter part of the current chapter gives you the basic definitions for the terms used, and lists the symbols and conventions that appear throughout the book.

Chapter Two gives an overview of the relationship between SQL and the dBASE programming language in dBASE IV. It's important for you to read this before going on, so that you will be clear on how SQL fits into the dBASE IV structure. The chapter explains how the various objects such as files, tables, catalogs, views, indexes, and programs in SQL relate to these concepts in dBASE IV.

Chapter Three presents the SQL data definition statements that are necessary to set up your database. Since all data in a relational database is arranged in tables, this chapter explains how to CREATE your tables initially, how to ALTER them if that becomes necessary, and how to DELETE unnecessary material by using the DROP command on databases, tables, views, synonyms and indexes.

Chapter Four explains and illustrates the SQL operators (arithmetic, comparison and logical), clauses (such as FROM, and WHERE), and expressions (such as cost + constant) that you will need to form SQL statements.

Chapter Five contains the instructions for LOADing data into your database, as well as UNLOADing it. This chapter also shows the usage of the SQL data manipulation commands INSERT, UPDATE, and DELETE that you will need to work with the information you have stored in the database tables.

Chapter Six illustrates many of the different ways of forming queries and subqueries in order to retrieve information from your database.

Chapter Seven explains the use of the SQL aggregate functions that can be used to average, sum, count, and find minimum and maximum values of column variables. It also defines and illustrates memory variables, especially the new dBASE ARRAYs of memory variables, and the dBASE IV dBASE functions that can be used in the SQL mode.

Since the ability to manipulate tables (using relational operations such as joins) in several different ways is one of the advantages of a relational database, Chapter Eight is devoted entirely to the subject of relational operators within the context of dBASE IV SQL.

Chapter Nine explains the features of dBASE IV SQL that provide security by restricting database access to those users who have been specifically GRANTed privileges of making changes. It also explains the use of views as security devices, and provides procedures for keeping the catalog current. It illustrates the use of the SQL data control statements, and also discusses maintaining database integrity through the transaction processing and ROLLBACK features.

Chapter Ten introduces dBASE IV commands that are useful in embedded SQL programming. In this chapter, you will find dBASE IV commands for controlling the flow of a program, dBASE IV commands for setting up the environment, user-defined functions, and a discussion of how to write your own program files using the MODIFY COMMAND of dBASE IV. It's important you read Chapter Ten before Chapter Eleven, since these dBASE commands provide the setting for embedding SQL in dBASE IV.

In Chapter Eleven, SQL's usefulness to the application developer is emphasized: specifically, the fact that it can be embedded in computer programs, thus simplifying the writing of programs to access the information in the database. Both new and former users of the dBASE programming language will profit from the examples and short utility programs in this chapter.

Chapter Twelve gives an overview of the design considerations you need to keep in mind when you set up your database. This chapter also discusses the principles behind relational databases, how tables can be related by keys and foreign keys, the four basic normal forms for tables, how to break down your tables, and why it is advisable to have your tables in normal form, thereby avoiding redundancy and update anomalies.

If database management systems are new to you, the Glossary will be of help in giving the meanings of terms in current usage in this field.

Appendix A contains a list of the SQL syntax and Runtime error messages, along with their causes and suggested remedies.

Appendix B lists all of the dBASE IV commands, and shows whether or not each can be used in SQL mode.

Appendix C lists all of the dBASE IV functions, shows which functions are allowed in SQL mode, and shows which of the dBASE functions can be used inside SQL commands and statements.

1.2 DEFINITIONS

In a relational database, certain common words have a specific meaning; therefore the relational terminology needs to be set forth here, since these terms will be referred to throughout this book. Definitions are given in the sections below.

1.2.1 Reserved Words

dBASE IV SQL contains a list of words that are used in SQL statements. These words are considered *reserved words*—meaning they cannot be used within your database management system to name databases, tables, views, synonyms, columns, or files. dBASE function names are also considered reserved words in SQL. The complete list of reserved words is contained in Figure 1-1.

Figure 1-1. SQL Reserved Words

ADD	DBDEFINE	LIKE	SMALLINT
ALL	DECIMAL	LIST	START
ALTER	DECLARE	LOAD	STOP
AND	DELETE	LOGICAL	SUM
ANY	DELIMITED	MAX	SYLK
AS	DESC	MIN	SYNONYM
ASC	DIF	NOT	TABLE
AVG	DISTINCT	NUMERIC	TEMP
BETWEEN	DROP	OF	TO
BLANK	EXISTS	ON	UNION
BY	FETCH	OPEN	UNIQUE
CHAR	FLOAT	OPTION	UNLOAD
CHECK	FOR	OR	UPDATE
CLOSE	FROM	ORDER	USER
CLUSTER	GRANT	PRIVILEGES	USING
COUNT	GROUP	PUBLIC	VALUES
CREATE	HAVING	REAL	VIEW
CURRENT	IN	REVOKE	WHERE
CURSOR	INDEX	ROLLBACK	WITH
DATA	INSERT	RUNSTATS	WKS
DATABASE	INTEGER	SAVE	WORK
DATE	INTO	SDF	All dBASE
DBCHECK	KEEP	SET	function names

1.2.2 Databases

A *database* is a named collection of tables, indexes, and application programs within a database management system. In dBASE IV SQL you may create and maintain as many databases as your DOS system will allow.

You start your database management system by creating a database (or by using one that has already been created). You must name each database in your system, keeping in mind that no database name can be a reserved word.

A database name:

- Must be a legal subdirectory name
- Must consist only of letters, numbers, and underscores
- Must begin with a letter
- Cannot be more than eight characters long

No two databases within your system can have the same name.

1.2.3 Base Tables

A *base table* is a named set of rows and columns, where each row and column position can contain a value. Base tables are usually just called *tables*, in contrast with views which are described in Section 1.2.6 below, and are called *virtual tables*.

A dBASE IV SQL table can have a maximum of 255 columns and a maximum of 1 billion rows. Its total width cannot exceed 4000 bytes, and the total amount of data stored in an individual table cannot exceed 2 billion bytes.

Table names must be legal dBASE .dbf file names. No two tables within the same database can have the same name, nor can a table name be the same as a view name or synonym within that database.

1.2.4 Columns

A dBASE IV SQL *column* is a part of a table, and contains data of only one type. You define the column datatype and width when you create the table. The types of data you can use in dBASE IV SQL are CHARACTER, DATE, DECIMAL, FLOAT, INTEGER, LOGICAL, NUMERIC, and SMALLINT. These datatypes are described in Figure 1-2.

Figure 1-2. dBASE IV SQL Datatypes

Datatype	Description
SMALLINT	Holds an integer with up to six digits (including sign). Values entered may range from -99,999 to 999,999.
INTEGER	Holds an integer containing up to 11 digits (including sign). Values entered may range from -9,999,999,999 to +99,999,999,999.
DECIMAL(x,y)	Holds a signed fixed decimal point number with x total digits (including sign) and y decimal places (significant digits to the right of the decimal point) where $x \leq 19$, $y \leq 18$, and $Y \leq x - 1$, e.g., DECIMAL (6,2) allows entry of an unsigned value up to 9999.99.
NUMERIC(x,y)	Holds a signed fixed decimal point number with x total digits (including sign and decimal point) and y decimal places (significant digits to the right of the decimal point). x may range from 1 to 20 and y may range from 0 to 18. y cannot be greater than x - 2. For example, NUMERIC(6,2) allows entry of an unsigned value up to 999.99 or signed values ranging between -99.99 and +999.99.
FLOAT(x,y)	Holds an x-digit floating point number with y decimal places. You may specify up to 20 total digits with up to 18 decimal places. The range of numbers is from 10-307 to 10+308.
CHAR(n)	Holds a character string of up to n characters. You must specify a length (a maximum of 254 characters). Values can be entered as a string constant, character type memory variable, or column. Character strings must be enclosed in single (') or double (") quotes.
DATE	Holds a date in the format mm/dd/yy. Values are entered from date memory variables or columns, or date strings converted with the dBASE CTOD() function, for example, CTOD("02/15/88") or {02/15/88}.
LOGICAL	Holds a single character, either T (for True) or F (for False). Values are entered from dBASE logical memory variables or columns, or by the constants .T., .t., .Y., .y., .F., .f., .N., and .n..

1.2.5 Rows

A *row* is a set of values corresponding to the column headings in a table. It represents one "record". There can be no more than one value in each column for any given row.

1.2.6 Fields

The intersection point of any column with any row is called a *field*, or a *cell*, or a *datum*. In a relational database this cell can contain only one value.

1.2.7 Views

A *view* is called a "virtual table" because it does not actually exist in the database, but appears to the user as though it does. It can be considered a *window* onto one or more base tables, containing any designated part (including all) of the data in the base table. It has exactly the same form as a base table, but—unlike a base table—only its definition is stored in the database.

1.3 SYMBOLS AND CONVENTIONS

The symbols that are part of the dBASE IV SQL language are explained as they appear in the chapters that follow. Details of the terms, symbols, and conventions used throughout this text to explain the dBASE IV SQL principles are given below.

1.3.1 Interactive SQL to Enter SQL Statements

Interactive SQL is the term used to designate the part of dBASE IV SQL where you enter one statement at a time at the prompt. To enter interactive SQL at the dot prompt you type the following:

```
SET SQL ON
```

SQL commands are usually written on multiple partial lines. To facilitate entering them in this form, you can press Ctrl-Home, which will give you an edit window. This edit window then allows you to type in partial lines. Press Ctrl-End remove the edit window and return you to the command line, where your multi-line command is now expanded into one line. To execute the command, press Return. dBASE IV inserts special characters to indicate returns and tabs, but these will not affect processing.

1.3.2 Embedded (Procedural) SQL to Run a Program Containing SQL Commands

Procedural SQL is the mode used to run a program, with embedded SQL commands. You enter it by typing DO <filename> at the dot prompt, where filename has a .prs file extension and contains a program with embedded SQL. Chapter Seven discusses functions and memory variables useful in procedural SQL. Chapters Ten and Eleven contain commands that can be used in procedural SQL.

1.3.3 Angle Brackets (< >) to Indicate What You Fill In

Angle brackets, < >, enclose a general term describing the specific term that you must fill in. For example, when you see:

<tablename>

this means that you need to fill in the name of a table in your database; thus, you may type:

Costs

(Note that you do not put the angle brackets around your table name when you fill it in.)

1.3.4 Square Brackets ([ ]) to Indicate an Optional Term

Square brackets, [ ], indicate that the term inside them is optional; you may choose to include it or not. For example,

```
SELECT <column_names>
FROM <clause>
[WHERE <clause>];
```

means that you have the option of adding a WHERE clause to the commands listed. (Don't put the square brackets around the enclosed term if you do choose to use it in an SQL statement.)

1.3.5 Ellipses (...) to Indicate Continuation.

An *ellipsis (...)* means that the same type of item is repeated. For example,

column 1, column 2, ... , column N

means that the numbered columns continue, no matter how many there are, until the last numbered column (N) appears.

1.3.6 SQL Commands in All Caps

All dBASE IV SQL commands will be shown in ALL CAPS, though you do not have to enter them that way when you use them. You may enter them in upper case letters (that is, all caps), lower case letters, or a combination of upper and lower case letters. Thus, you may enter the command SELECT as select, SELECT, or Select.

1.3.7 Initial Capital Letters for Table Names; Lower Case for Column Names

Throughout the text of this book, table names are entered with an initial capital letter and column names are entered in all lower case letters. For example:

Employee Table
containing columns: name, address, salary.

You may use your own conventions regarding upper and lower case for table and column names.

1.3.8 Slash (/) to Indicate that You Have a Choice

A slash (/) (or slashes) within an expression is used to indicate that you have a choice between two or more possibilities. For example, the notation (ALL/ANY) would mean that you may choose either one of the terms ALL or ANY.

1.3.9 Semicolon (;) as Terminator for SQL Statements

The *semicolon (;)* must be used to terminate all dBASE IV SQL statements.

NOTE: Do not use a semicolon to terminate dBASE IV statements that are not SQL statements. In dBASE IV, the semicolon (;) is used to continue dBASE commands from one line to another.

You can also use the semicolon (;) to continue dBASE IV commands in a .prs.

1.3.10 Result Tables

After you press Return to execute an SQL query, dBASE IV puts the answer to your query on the screen in the form of a table, called a *result table*. In this text, these result tables are given a figure number and name so that you can refer to them conveniently. However, the results that actually appear on your screen will not include any figure number or name. For the purposes of this text, results appear in the form shown in the Dummy Table, Figure 1-3.

Figure 1-3. Dummy Table

name	title	id_no	dept
Jones	acct	4532	acct
Smith	clerk	3801	sec
Brown	prog	8543	data

On your screen, the result table containing the information in Figure 1-3 would appear as follows:

name	**title**	**id_no**	**dept**
Jones	**acct**	**4532**	**acct**
Smith	**clerk**	**3801**	**sec**
Brown	**prog**	**8543**	**data**

1.3.11 Database Objects

The individual databases within your database management system, as well as the tables, views, indexes, synonyms, aliases, columns, and rows that you can create are all called *database objects*. When this term occurs, it refers to one or more of the entities listed above, with its exact meaning made clear by the context.

1.3.12 Target List

The term *target list* is used in this text to denote the list of columns you want to appear in the result table. The target list is entered directly after a SELECT command. For example, you enter:

SELECT <target list>

where:

<target list> is the list of column names to bedisplayed in the result table.

1.3.13 Navigation Keys

Some of the keys on your keyboard have special uses in dBASE IV SQL. In a few cases, reference may be made to these keys. Therefore, a chart of navigation and editing keys is included here as Figure 1-4, to define dBASE IV's references to your keyboard positions.

Figure 1-4. Navigation and Editing Keys

Key	Function
-> (Right arrow)	Moves cursor one character to right
<- (Left arrow)	Moves cursor one character to left
Up arrow	Moves cursor to previous line
Down arrow	Moves cursor to next line
Ctrl - Up arrow	Moves cursor to previous word in command
Ctrl- Down arrow	Moves cursor to next word in command
Home	Moves cursor to beginning of command line
End	Moves cursor to end of command line
Backspace	Deletes one character to left of cursor
Del	Deletes one character at cursor position
Ins	Switches modes between inserting and overwriting characters
Num Lock	Turns Numeric mode on and off (must be off for function keys on numeric keypad to operate)
Caps Lock	Switches automatic upper case mode on and off
F1 Help	Displays help for command if pressed after entry of SQL command keyword
Ctrl-Home	Opens a full-screen edit window
Ctrl-End	Closes a full-screen edit window, executes the command, and returns to the command line of either the dot prompt or the SQL dot prompt, depending from which environment you invoked the edit windows
Return	Carriage return. Executes the command displayed on the command line. Exception: when working in the edit window, you press Ctrl-End to execute the command displayed in the edit window.

2

Comparisons Between dBASE IV and SQL in dBASE IV

dBASE IV is a complete relational database system. In dBASE IV you can create a database containing many files (tables) of data, modify the files, and create reports, labels, and application programs.

While dBASE IV is similar to dBASE III PLUS, and most of the features of dBASE III PLUS are upwardly compatible with dBASE IV, dBASE IV has greatly extended and modified the capabilities of dBASE III PLUS, adding many new features to make it easier for you to use. One of the extensions of the capabilities of dBASE III PLUS is the addition of the SQL query language.

This book is about the SQL query language (Structured Query Language), as adapted by Ashton-Tate for use with dBASE IV. Because of its many useful features, SQL has become one of the most popular query languages for use with relational databases.

A *query language* is a language in which you can formulate questions about the database in such a way that the computer can find an answer. A good query language will allow you to do much more than formulate and get the answers to queries. It will also allow you to update rows, delete rows, create tables, drop tables, create indexes, drop indexes, and grant privileges to users.

In dBASE IV there are two modes: dBASE-only mode and dBASE/SQL mode. Interactively, a new dBASE SET command, SET SQL ON/OFF, enables you to switch between the modes. In the procedural interface where you run programs, on the other hand, the mode is determined by the file extension of the program file. Thus, if your program is a dBASE program with no SQL statements in it, the file extension must be .prg. If your program contains SQL statements, the file extension must be .prs.

In *dBASE-only mode*, all of the dBASE IV commands and activities are available. You can work on database files, formulate queries and views using Query By Example, create reports and labels, generate applications, and write and run dBASE programs using all of the dBASE IV commands.

In *dBASE/SQL mode*, you can write and execute SQL commands and run programs containing embedded SQL commands. Some of the dBASE IV commands and functions are not available in dBASE/SQL mode. For example, BROWSE is not available in dBASE/SQL mode. For a list of dBASE IV commands and functions available in dBASE/SQL mode, see Appendixes B and C. For more discussion of dBASE IV commands which can be used in SQL programs, see Chapter Ten. For a discussion of embedding SQL in programs, see Chapter Eleven.

In this chapter, we compare dBASE-only mode and dBASE/SQL mode in dBASE IV, so that you can decide which of the two modes is best for you to use in your database applications.

2.1 SQL Tables Versus dBASE Files

In SQL the data is kept in *tables*. In dBASE the data is kept in *files*. In dBASE IV, the underlying storage medium for both SQL tables and dBASE files is disk files with the .dbf file extension.

A table can be CREATEd in dBASE/SQL mode, and then used as a dBASE IV file in dBASE-only mode, by selecting it on the Data panel of the dBASE Control Center or from the dot prompt with the USE command. (For more information on the Control Center, see your Ashton-Tate dBASE IV documentation. On the other hand, you can use the CREATE/MODIFY STRUCTURE command, or you can choose **<create>** in the Data panel of the dBASE Control Center, to create a dBASE file, and then move it to whatever SQL database directory you choose, using either the dBASE IV or DOS COPY commands. Then you can import the file into that SQL database by SETting SQL ON and executing the SQL DBDEFINE <file name> command. (See Chapter Nine, Section 9.10 for more information about DBDEFINE.)

However, there are some restrictions on dBASE access to SQL-erected files. You cannot use the dBASE command MODIFY STRUCTURE, for example, on an SQL table.

2.2 SQL Catalogs Versus dBASE Catalogs

Catalogs play the role of providing you with information about your database. In dBASE/SQL mode, the *catalogs* are tables in the database which, besides providing you with information about the database, also are used by the system.

In dBASE-only mode, you have dBASE catalogs for each dBASE database. You can select the catalog you want on the Control Center screen. Every catalog contains the name and the description of the database files, indexes, views (QBE files), forms, reports, labels, and application programs that it contains. All of these files will be listed for you on the Control Center screen, where you can add new files or remove files from the catalog.

In dBASE/SQL mode, you CREATE a database in a directory of your choice. SQL then creates a set of catalog tables in that directory which will be in use after the database has been started. At that point you can query the catalog tables for information about the database. When you add objects to your SQL database, the catalog tables will be updated by the system to reflect these modifications.

The database itself is listed by SQL in the SQL master catalog table, named Sysdbs.dbf, which is in your SQL home directory. When you CREATE the database, it is activated for use until you either perform the STOP DATABASE command or START another database. See Chapter Nine, Section 9.6 for more information about the SQL catalog tables.

2.3 SQL Views Versus dBASE Views

In SQL, a *view* is defined by a CREATE VIEW statement which involves an SQL SELECT statement. The definition of the view is kept in the SQL database catalog tables. An SQL view can be accessed only with SQL commands. It can be used to UPDATE or DELETE from tables, provided the following conditions are satisfied:

- In the case of UPDATEs, the field being UPDATEd cannot be a calculated field.
- The view being UPDATEd or DELETEd from cannot be defined by an aggregate operator.
- The view definition must not contain more than one table in the FROM clause.
- The view definition must not contain a non-updatable view in the FROM clause.
- The view definition must not contain the keyword DISTINCT.
- The view definition must not contain a nested subquery whose FROM clause refers to the same base table on which the view is defined.

In dBASE IV, a view definition is kept in a .qbe file or a .vue file. It can be BROWSEd or EDITed with the dBASE BROWSE and EDIT commands.

If you plan to use a view in a situation where you will scan the rows of the view and make updates, it is best to use a dBASE view because of the availability of the BROWSE and EDIT commands.

If you are designing a program using SQL, you can use SQL views to control access to the data. By GRANTing privileges on views, you can control who will be allowed to run the program. SQL views cannot be used, as in dBASE IV, for forms, labels, and reports, because forms, labels, and reports require special dBASE files. However, you can use an SQL SELECT command with a SAVE TO TEMP ... KEEP clause to create a dBASE file for use with forms, labels, and reports.

2.4 SQL Indexes Versus dBASE Indexes

Both dBASE/SQL mode and dBASE-only mode can be used to create an .mdx index file. All dBASE/SQL mode indexes are "tags" in an .mdx file. For example, if you CREATE INDEX NUM on the Staff table, it will be in a file named STAFF.mdx.

In both SQL and dBASE-only modes, you can index a table or file on one or more columns, each in ascending or descending order (as long as you don't use both ascending and descending orders in the same index). In dBASE/SQL mode, you use the CREATE INDEX command to CREATE an index. (See Chapter Three, Section 3.6 for the CREATE INDEX command.) The difference is in your use of these indexes: in dBASE-only mode you can select the index that you want to use in retrieving database information, while in dBASE/SQL mode the index used is selected for you by the system.

A properly designed database will have many instances of two or more tables which are to be joined together for queries and reports. These tables will usually be joined on keys and foreign keys. To allow SQL to efficiently perform queries, you should maintain up-to-date, unique indexes on keys and non-unique indexes on foreign keys. For more information on design considerations, joins, keys, and foreign keys, see Chapter Eight.

2.5 dBASE IV Programs Versus SQL Programs

Before you begin to write SQL programs for dBASE IV, you need to consider the following points:

- dBASE IV programs and procedures can contain all dBASE IV commands and functions, but cannot contain any SQL statements.

- SQL programs and procedures can have SQL commands embedded in them, and can use most (but not all) of the dBASE IV commands and functions.

- Some of the dBASE IV functions which can be used in SQL can be embedded in SQL statements, but not all of them. (A list of the dBASE IV commands and functions indicating whether or not they can be used in dBASE/SQL mode, and whether or not they can be embedded in SQL statements, is given in Appendixes B and C.)

- dBASE IV distinguishes between dBASE programs and SQL programs by the file extension of the file containing the program. dBASE IV programs must have a .prg file extension, and SQL programs must have a .prs file extension.

- dBASE IV programs can call SQL programs, and vice versa.

dBASE IV will automatically switch to dBASE-only mode or dBASE/SQL mode, depending on the file extension of the program or procedure file. However, mixing dBASE programs and procedures with SQL programs and procedures requires extreme caution because:

- If you CREATE a STRUCTURE in dBASE-only mode, it will not be added to the SQL catalog, and SQL will not be able to use the resulting table until you apply a DBDEFINE command to it in dBASE/SQL mode.

- The SQL catalog tables are not updated in dBASE-only mode, and this can cause problems because the statistical information necessary for the system to determine the way in which an SQL command is executed may be wrong until you run RUNSTATS. (See Chapter Nine, Section 9.6.1 for more information about updating SQL catalog files.)

- Switching between dBASE-only mode and dBASE/SQL mode is time-consuming.

The advantages of programming in embedded SQL are:

- One SQL statement can do as much work as many dBASE IV commands; this results in simpler code, decreases the possibility of bugs, and makes the code easier to understand for programmers and non-programmers both.

- Designing programs is simpler in embedded SQL because you can think in terms of operations on one or more entire tables.

- Views and joins are easier to set up in SQL. If you want to BROWSE through a result table that you create with an SQL query, you can always use the SAVE TO TEMP clause with the KEEP option, and then BROWSE through the table in dBASE-only mode. This table will be automatically dropped from the SQL catalogs as soon as:

a.) SQL is set OFF

or

b.) a new database is started

or

c.) the .prs file in which it was created returns to the highest level .prs, or to a dot prompt.

2.6 CONCLUSIONS

dBASE-only mode in dBASE IV has many features which are extremely useful to the application developer, and are not available in SQL mode. You can use the BROWSE and EDIT commands. You can run forms, and print reports, and labels. You can use the Applications Generator, Apgen, to design your screens.

dBASE/SQL mode, on the other hand, is useful for writing easy-to-understand queries, updates, and deletions. You can also manipulate your database in an easy-to-understand way with SQL. You can easily CREATE tables, views, and synonyms. Embedded SQL makes it simple to write programs which include data definition and data manipulation.

In the opinion of the authors, a mixed approach to building applications is the best approach. Use dBASE-only mode for creating screens, writing reports, and creating labels. Use dBASE/SQL mode for quick and easy data definition and data manipulation.

3

How to CREATE, ALTER, and DROP Database Objects: Databases, Tables, Views, Indexes

dBASE IV SQL provides four commands for setting up a database, activating a database, deactivating a database, and eliminating a database. These are CREATE DATABASE, START DATABASE, STOP DATABASE, and DROP DATABASE, respectively. In addition there is a command, SHOW DATABASE, for seeing what databases are available.

This chapter will illustrate how to CREATE, START, STOP, DROP, and SHOW databases, how to CREATE, ALTER, and DROP tables, and how to CREATE and DROP views, synonyms, and indexes for your tables. It also explains the uses of tables, views, indexes, and synonyms.

3.1 HOW TO CREATE A DATABASE

Before you can perform any SQL commands, you must CREATE at least one database. To CREATE a database, type the following command:

CREATE DATABASE [path] <database name>;

where:

[path] is the absolute DOS path to the new database directory where the database tables will be kept.

<database name> is the name you give to the new database you are CREATing. The database name cannot be an SQL reserved word. (The list of SQL reserved words appears in Figure 1-1, Chapter One.).

The command:

CREATE DATABASE mybase;

will CREATE a database called mybase in the subdirectory mybase of your current directory (if the subdirectory does not already exist, the system will create it for you), and the system will display the message:

Database mybase created

When you CREATE a database, a set of catalog tables is created in the subdirectory set up to hold your database. (See Chapter Nine for information about the catalog tables.) In addition, an entry is made in the Sysdbs master catalog table in your SQL HOME directory, which includes the name of your database, your user name, the date the database was created, and the DOS directory path to your database.

When you use CREATE DATABASE, this activates the database for that session, so you don't need to use the START DATABASE command.

3.1.1 The START DATABASE Command

To START a database, you use the START DATABASE command. To START a database, the format is:

START DATABASE <database name>;

where:

<database name> is the name of a database previously created by using the CREATE DATABASE command. You cannot have more than one database STARTed at one time. If you wish to START a different database, just enter START DATABASE with the name of the new database. There is no need to stop the old database. If you leave SQL mode and then reenter it, the last database you were working on will automatically be reactivated for you. If you want a certain database to be automatically activated when you start dBASE and enter SQL mode, you can place the command SQLDATABASE = <database name> in your config.db file.

START DATABASE may be performed in both interactive and embedded modes.

3.1.2 The STOP DATABASE Command

If you decide to DROP a database, you must first STOP the database. To do so, simply enter the STOP DATABASE command, as follows:

```
STOP DATABASE;
```

There's no need to name the database being STOPped, since you can only STOP an active database, and you can only have one database active at a time.

STOP DATABASE may be performed in both interactive and embedded modes.

To enter another database (that has already been CREATEd), use the START DATABASE command shown in Section 3.1.1 above.

3.1.3 The DROP DATABASE Command

At some point, you might want to eliminate a database entirely because you have no further use for it. The format for removing a database from the system is:

```
DROP DATABASE <database name>;
```

You cannot DROP an active database; you must first STOP it with the STOP command. If you attempt to DROP an active database without STOPping it first, you will receive an error message.

The DROP DATABASE command removes those files associated with SQL objects and the SQL system catalog; it does not remove the subdirectory where the database resides, nor does it remove program or text files. The record of the database in the Sysdbs catalog table is also removed.

3.1.4 The SHOW DATABASE Command

You might want to know certain details about the databases that have already been CREATEd in an ongoing system. (For example, you may have forgotten the exact name of the database you want to use.) In this case, you can use the SHOW DATABASE command to give you information about all of the current databases.

Enter the SHOW DATABASE command in the following format:

```
SHOW DATABASE;
```

This command lists the name of each database, the DOS path to each database subdirectory, the user ID of the person who created the database, and the date the database was created. All of this information is stored in the Sysdbs master catalog table in the SQL HOME directory.

3.2 HOW TO CREATE TABLES

With SQL you can make two kinds of tables:

- Base tables: These are usually just called *tables*.

- Views: These are called *virtual tables* because, unlike base tables, only the view definition is stored. Also, as explained in Section 3.3, you cannot perform all the operations on views that you can perform on base tables.

After you have CREATEd them, base tables and views will look exactly the same on your screen, and can be queried in the same way. The reason for differentiating between them is that you must use different sets of commands to CREATE them, and you can't always UPDATE, INSERT INTO or DELETE FROM views as you can with base tables.

You CREATE a table by specifying its name and its column definition(s). You add the rows to the table later by using the INSERT command (discussed in Chapter Five).

To CREATE a base table, you must supply the information contained in the following general syntax:

```
CREATE TABLE <tablename>
    <(Column definition(s))>
```

where:

CREATE TABLE are SQL reserved words.

<tablename> is a name you choose that is no more than eight characters long, starting with a letter, and consisting of letters, numbers and underscores. You cannot use a dBASE IV SQL reserved word for a tablename. (The list of reserved words is shown in Figure 1-1, Chapter One.).

<(Column definition(s))> consist of the column name, along with the size and datatype for each column you want to have in the table. The complete syntax for CREATing a table is:

```
CREATE TABLE <tablename>
    <(column1 name         datatype (datasize),
    [column2 name          datatype (datasize),
    ...,
    columnN name           datatype (datasize)])>;
```

The datatype for each column must be specified in the CREATE statement, and the datasize, which specifies the maximum width of the column, must be stated for certain datatypes.

The types of data supported by SQL are CHAR, DATE, INTEGER, SMALLINT, DECIMAL, LOGICAL, FLOAT and NUMERIC. These datatypes are described in Figure 1-2 in Chapter One. For DATE, INTEGER, LOGICAL, and SMALLINT, you do not enter any datasize.

The entire group of column descriptions must be enclosed in parentheses.

Notice that each column description before the last column description must be followed by a comma, and the last column description—since it's the end of the SQL statement—must be terminated with a semicolon.

For example, to set up a table of suppliers, listing supplier names, part numbers, part names and price, you enter:

```
CREATE TABLE Supplier
    (Name           CHAR(30),
    Part_no         CHAR(12),
    Part_name       CHAR(15),
    Price           DECIMAL(6,2));
```

The above entry will give you a table where you can enter strings up to 30 characters long for the supplier's name, 12 CHAR spaces for the supplier's part number, and 15 CHAR spaces for the part name. For price, you must use the DECIMAL datatype. The numbers inside the parentheses specify that this DECIMAL column will allow for six digits, two of which are to the right of the decimal point.

Notice that CHAR spaces are used for the part number; this is because these numbers are merely labels and you don't intend to perform any arithmetic operations on them. Sometimes part numbers have letters attached to them. Using CHAR allows you to use both letters and numbers, but if you used INTEGER or SMALLINT datatype here, you could not include any letters in the part numbers.

Following is a summary of the rules for CREATing a table.

When you create a table...

You must:

- Limit the length of the table name to 8 characters.
- Start the tablename with a letter.

You can:

- Use any name you wish for the table except a reserved word.
- Use letters, numbers or underscores in a table name.

You cannot:

- Have two tables in the same database with the same name; nor can you have a table with the same name as a view or synonym in the same database.
- Put more than 255 columns in one table.
- CREATE a table that is more than 4000 bytes wide.
- Use reserved words for table names.,

3.2.1 Choosing Column Names

The rules for column names are similar to those for table names:

When you define a column..

You must:

- Limit the length of the column name to 10 characters.
- Start the column name with a letter.

You can:

- Use any name you wish for the column, except a reserved word.
- Use letters, numbers, or underscores in a column name.
- Use the same column name in two different tables.

You cannot:

- Use reserved words for column names.
- Have two columns in the same table with the same name.

3.2.2 How to ALTER Tables

If you find that you need to add another column in a table that you CREATEd sometime in the past, you can easily do this by using the ALTER command. All you need are the name of the table and the specifications for the new column.

The syntax for adding a column to a table is:

```
ALTER TABLE <table_name>

ADD <(column_name datatype(width)>;
```

For example, to add the suppliers' addresses to the Supplier Table CREATEd in Section 3.2 above, you would enter:

```
ALTER TABLE supplier

ADD (address CHAR(25));
```

This command adds the column name Address to the Supplier Table, and allows you to enter addresses consisting of 25 character strings in length.

Immediately after you add the new column, it will contain only blanks. Use the UPDATE command to fill the blanks for already existing rows.

You may add more than one column with the ALTER TABLE command. For example, you might want to add the salesman's name with whom you deal, as well as his phone number, on each supplier's record. To do this with one ALTER statement, you can enter:

```
ALTER TABLE Supplier

ADD (salesman  char(20),

     phone  char(12));
```

The above command will add two new columns to the Supplier Table: a salesman column where you can enter CHARacter strings of length 20, and a phone column where you can enter CHARacter strings of length 12. When you display the Supplier Table on your screen from now on, these two new columns will appear at the right of the previously existing columns.

Following is a summary of the rules for ALTERing tables:

To ALTER a table..

You must:

- Specify the name, datatype, and width of any new columns added.
- Place a comma after each column description in the ADD statement (if there is more than one column being added).
- Enclose the description of the column(s) added in parentheses.

You can:

- Add more than one column with the ALTER TABLE command, until you reach a total of 255 columns for the table.

You cannot:

- Delete or modify columns with the ALTER TABLE command.
- Fill in values in the new column(s) with the ALTER TABLE command.
- Use the ALTER command to add a column to a view.

3.2.3 How to DROP a Table From the Database

To remove a table from the database, use the DROP command, plus the name of the table. The syntax is:

```
DROP TABLE <table_name>;
```

For example, if you wish to get rid of a table (called Staff) you no longer use, enter:

```
DROP TABLE Staff;
```

CAUTION: Before you DROP a table from the database, you should consider the following: when you DROP a table, you also DROP all indexes, views, and synonyms defined on that table.

The only way to recover the data in a DROPped table is to CREATE the table again, and INSERT the data again (if you still have it!)

Following is a summary of the rules for DROPping a table:

To DROP a table...

You must:

- Name the table you want to DROP.
- Be certain you have no further use for the data in that table, or in the views defined on it.

You cannot:

- Restore the data in a DROPped table, except by re-CREATing the table and re-INSERTing the data.

3.3 VIEWS

A view is called a *virtual table* because it doesn't exist as such in the database. Only the view definition exists in the catalog table Sysviews. (See Chapter Nine for descriptions of all catalog tables.)

You CREATE a view by SELECTing specific rows and columns from a table that does exist in the database.

When you SELECT from a base table, dBASE IV SQL brings up the base tables as they exist in the database. By contrast, when you SELECT from a view, dBASE IV SQL looks at the view definition and then SELECTs the data you asked for from the result table of the view definition. However, information about this process will be of interest to you only if you are concerned with the procedural aspects of dBASE IV SQL; on your screen, a view looks just like a base table.

3.3.1 Reasons for CREATing Views

There are two principal reasons for CREATing views:

- Reducing redundancy.

  If a table is large, and you often work with only a limited number of its columns or rows, it may be cumbersome to repeatedly display the whole table on your screen. Also, it would be redundant to reproduce selected parts of that table in the database for specific purposes. For these reasons, you might want to SELECT out only the specific columns or rows that you need. The result (which will consist of columns and rows like any other table) is then called a *view*.

- Security.

  If many people use the database, you might want some of the information in it kept confidential. For example, you may have a table listing all company employees, their phone numbers, addresses, grade levels, and salaries. You might not want everyone to have access to salaries. In this case, you would CREATE a view of the Employee Table that includes all the rows but only the columns for names, addresses, and phone numbers. On the other hand, you might not want everyone who uses the database to have the home phone numbers of some executives. If so, the view could include all columns, but only for those rows containing names of personnel whose phone numbers are to be made public. This point is discussed further in Chapter Nine, which is devoted entirely to the security and integrity of the database.

In both of the above cases (one restricting the columns in the view, and one restricting the rows), you can ensure that the information in the table itself is not available to all employees, by GRANTing access to the table only to certain persons, and GRANTing access to the view to everyone else. (GRANTing access is discussed in Chapter Nine.) In this way, the complete table (of names, addresses, phone numbers, and salaries) is never available to employees whose work does not require them to use it.

3.3.2 How to CREATE a View

There are two parts to the statement for CREATing a view:

- a part giving the name of the view, and an optional list of the columns it will contain
- a part listing the columns to be SELECTed from the table, and naming the table containing those columns

The syntax for CREATing a view is:

```
CREATE VIEW <view_name>
   <([view_column_1, view_column_2, ... view_column_N)]>
AS SELECT <table_column_A, table_column_B, ...
   table_column_N>
FROM <table_name1, table_name2,...,table_nameN>
[WITH CHECK OPTION];
```

where:

CREATE VIEW are SQL reserved words.

<view_name> is the name you want the view to have.

AS SELECT (table_column_A, table_column_B, ...

table_column_N> is the list of columns you want to appear in the view.

FROM <table_name1, table_name2, ..., table_nameN> is the list of tables from which the SELECTed columns will be drawn.

[WITH CHECK OPTION] is an optional request you can make to the system, to check that no inappropriate UPDATEs or INSERTs are entered into the view at some later time.

If you do not include a list of view column names after the CREATE VIEW command, then your view will contain the column names listed after the SELECT command. In other words, your view column names will be the same as the column names in the underlying base table.

For example, to set up a view on the Employee Table (abbreviated to Emp in the database) where the column names in the view will be the same as those in the underlying table (i.e., the Employee Table), you must first decide on a name for the view, then list the columns after the SELECT command. Let's call the view Employees Limited (abbreviated to Emp_Ltd), and enter:

```
CREATE VIEW Emp_Ltd

AS SELECT name, address, title,

FROM Emp;
```

The above gives you a view with the three columns: name, address, title, from the Employee Table. It will be exactly the same as the view you would get if you entered:

```
CREATE VIEW Emp_Ltd

   (name, address, title,)

AS SELECT name, address, title

FROM Emp;
```

In some cases, you might want to use a view column name that is different from the original column name. For example, you might want to show a figure like "cost + 5 %" in the view in place of the column showing just "cost" in the table. In this case, you must show all of the view column names as you want them to appear in your view. (Performing an arithmetic computation on a column value turns that value into an *expression*. See Chapter Four for more details on expressions.)

The following example is a view from the Emp table, where you want the annual salary column in the table to become a monthly salary in the view, and you want the employees' addresses and grade levels eliminated from the view. The syntax for this is:

```
CREATE VIEW Salaries
   (name, monthly)
AS SELECT name, (salary / 12)
FROM Emp;
```

The above statement selects specific columns from the underlying table Employee. A view SELECTing only specified rows from a table requires the use of a WHERE clause (discussed in Chapter Four).

The syntax for CREATing a view that may SELECT fewer rows than exist in the complete table is:

```
CREATE VIEW <view_name>
   [(column_name_1, column_name_2, ... column_name_N)]
AS SELECT column_name_A, column_name_B ... column_name_N
FROM table_name
WHERE (condition = constant);
```

The CREATE VIEW statement containing a WHERE clause will not be discussed any further here, but see Chapter Four for a complete treatment of WHERE clauses.

Following is a summary of the rules for CREATing views.

When you CREATE a view...

You must:

- Give the view a name unique within the database with respect to all other views, tables, and synonyms.
- Limit the name of the view to an eight-character string containing letters, numbers, or underscores.
- Begin the view name with a letter.
- State the name(s) of the underlying table(s) from which the view columns are SELECTed.
- State the columns to be SELECTed from the base table(s).

- List the column names as they will appear in the view, if any column names are to be different from those being SELECTed from the base table(s).

You can:

- List the column names as they will appear in the view, even if they are the same as those being SELECTed from the base table.

- Add the words WITH CHECK OPTION to the view definition, and thereby ensure that no illegal UPDATEs or INSERTs get entered into the view.

You cannot:

- INSERT, UPDATE, or DELETE all views. For exceptions, see Sections 5.4.3, 5.5.1, and 5.6.1 in Chapter Five.

3.3.3 How to DROP a View

If you no longer have any use for a view you CREATEd, you may want to remove it. You can do this by using the DROP command followed by the name of the view. The syntax is:

```
DROP VIEW <view_name>;
```

For example, to DROP the view Emp_Ltd, enter:

```
DROP VIEW Emp_Ltd;
```

This will remove the view Emp_Ltd, but does not remove the Employee table from which you created the view, nor does it remove any index defined on it.

Following is a summary of the rules for DROPping views:

To DROP a view...

You must:

- Name the view after the DROP VIEW command.

You can:

- DROP a view without DROPping the table on which the view was defined.

You cannot:

- DROP a table by DROPping a view defined on that table.

3.4 HOW TO CREATE A SYNONYM

To reduce the amount of typing necessary, you can supply synonyms for frequently used tables or views.

The syntax for defining a synonym is:

```
CREATE SYNONYM <synonym name>
FOR <table or view name>;
```

where:

CREATE SYNONYM are SQL reserved words.

FOR <table or view name> is where you name the table or view for which you want to define a synonym.

For example, to define the synonym Emp to stand for the Employee Table, enter:

```
CREATE SYNONYM Emp

FOR Employee;
```

You can then define the synonym E_L for the view Emp_Ltd by entering:

```
CREATE SYNONYM E_L

FOR Emp_Ltd;
```

After defining the two synonyms above, you can refer to the Employee Table, in dBASE IV SQL commands, either as Employee or Emp, and you can refer to the view Employees Limited either as Emp_Ltd or as E_L.

Don't confuse synonyms with aliases; they are different objects and are used for different purposes. (Aliases are explained in Chapter Six.)

Following is a summary of the rules for defining a synonym:

To define a synonym...

You must:

- State the synonym name after the CREATE command.
- Name the table or view name (for which the synonym will be substituted) after the word FOR.

- Start the synonym name with a letter.
- Use a synonym name unique with respect to all other synonyms, tables, and views in the database.

You can:

- Use any CHAR string for the synonym name that is a letter, number, or underscore.
- Define a synonym for any table or view.

You cannot:

- Use a reserved word for a synonym name.

3.4.1 How to DROP a Synonym

To remove a synonym, you use the DROP command followed by the name of the synonym. The syntax is:

```
DROP SYNONYM <synonym name>;
```

For example, to remove the synonym E_L, enter:

```
DROP SYNONYM E_L;
```

3.5 INDEXES

An index is important to the operation of dBASE IV SQL because indexes are used to keep track of the location of rows within a database table. You specify what indexes you want to CREATE, but dBASE IV SQL decides which ones to use in retrieving data. It will automatically choose the most efficient index each time you enter an SQL statement.

3.5.1 CREATing an INDEX

You CREATE an INDEX by specifying the column name(s) on which you want the table INDEXed. You can put as many as 48 INDEX tags on any one table. An INDEX on an appropriate column(s) can speed up retrieval; however, keep in mind that the speed of the INSERT INTO, UPDATE, and DELETE functions usually goes down as the number of indexes goes up. This is because all of the indexes must be UPDATEd whenever an INSERT INTO, UPDATE, or DELETE is performed.

The syntax for CREATing an INDEX is:

```
CREATE [UNIQUE] INDEX <index name>
ON <table name>
(<column name> [[ASC]/DESC]
[,<column name> [[ASC]/DESC], ... ]);
```

where:

CREATE INDEX <index name> are SQL reserved words.

<index name> is the name you want the index to have.

[UNIQUE] is a reserved word that you have the option of specifying, that will force data values in the INDEXed column(s) to be unique. If these column values are not UNIQUE, then the INDEX will not be CREATEd, and an error message will appear on your screen.

ON <table name> is the name of the table containing the columns to be INDEXed.

<column name> indicates the column name(s) to be INDEXed.

[[ASC]/DESC] is an optional ordering you may specify to indicate that you want the rows of the data in the INDEXed column(s) in either ascending (ASC) or descending (DESC)order. Ascending is the default, so you don't need to specify it. However, you cannot mix ASC and DESC in the same index. Therefore, if the keyword DESC is specified, then it must be specified for all columns in that index. Indexes can use one or more columns, and can be based on all datatypes except LOGICAL.

For example, to CREATE an INDEX on the name column of the Supplier Table and ensure that the same name does not appear twice in the table, enter:

```
CREATE UNIQUE INDEX lastname

ON Supplier

(name ASC);
```

If you CREATE a UNIQUE INDEX, then dBASE IV SQL will check every INSERT and UPDATE entry to be sure that the values of the INDEXed column remain UNIQUE. (While these checks will ensure uniqueness, they can slow performance.)

The ascending (ASC) order of data in columns having characterdatatype follows the ASCII values. This means that upper case letters will be distinguished from lower case letters. For example, in the ASCII ordering, Dewey would come before deSoto.

To CREATE a UNIQUE INDEX in DESC order (going from largest amount to smallest) on the Price column of the Supplier Table, enter:

CREATE UNIQUE INDEX amount

ON Supplier

(price DESC);

You can only build indexes for tables, not for views. (But when you use a view, dBASE IV SQL may use the indexes based on the table from which the view is drawn.)

After you CREATE an INDEX, dBASE IV will record it in the catalog table Sysidxs. (Sysidxs and all other catalog tables are described in Chapter Nine.) You can look at the indexes already CREATEd by displaying columns from the Sysidxs table.

3.5.2 DROPping an INDEX

To eliminate an INDEX you no longer need, the command is:

DROP INDEX <index name>;

For example, you can DROP the Lastname INDEX on the Supplier table by entering:

DROP INDEX Lastname;

If a table is DROPped, an INDEX defined on that table is automatically DROPped. Therefore, if the Supplier Table had already been DROPped, you would not need to DROP the INDEX Lastname based on the Supplier Table, as it would have been dropped along with the table. (The converse is not true: DROPping an INDEX does not DROP the table on which it is defined.)

4

Operators, Clauses, Expressions, and Orders of Precedence in SQL Commands

To build SQL statements, you need connecting terms. These connecting terms are called *operators* (such as +, -, *, /, **), *clauses* (such as FROM and WHERE), and *expressions* (such as (cost * .25) or (salary * 12)). This chapter defines the terms that are supported by SQL, and gives you examples of how they are used.

SQL recognizes three different types of operators: *arithmetic*, *comparison*, and *logical*. dBASE IV SQL processes specified operations in the following order:

1. Arithmetic
2. Comparison
3. Logical.

In addition, within the sets of arithmetic and logical operations SQL will process operations in a predetermined order, unless you specify an order of precedence by the use of parentheses.

In this chapter, Sections 4.1 through 4.3 describe the operators and their default order of precedence, as well as the means for changing this precedence to suit your needs.

Sections 4.4 through 4.8 describe the clauses available in dBASE IV SQL. *Clauses* are those components of SQL statements that specify and/or restrict, group, order, or save the rows to be drawn from the database by a set of SQL commands. dBASE IV SQL recognizes the following clauses: FROM, WHERE, GROUP BY, HAVING, ORDER BY, FOR UPDATE OF, and SAVE TO TEMP.

Section 4.9 contains a description of the expressions supported by dBASE IV SQL, and shows how they are used.

The data shown in Figure 4-1 will be used throughout this chapter to illustrate the concepts defined.

Figure 4-1. The Employee Table

This table was created with the following column specifications:

name	CHAR(25)
yrs_serv	DECIMAL(2,1)
salary	SMALLINT
comm	SMALLINT
wrk_hrs	SMALLINT

name	yrs_serv	salary	comm	wrk_hrs
Beth White	2.5	2000	0	40
John Jones	1.5	1500	500	35
Dee Thomas	5.0	2500	1500	40
Loren Black	6.0	1875	300	20
Mary Gray	1.5	1950	1800	25
Thomas Doe	0.5	2500	900	40
Richard Roe	0.9	1300	0	40
Juli Sutton	9.0	3000	1750	20
Stan Baker	3.0	2500	2000	20
Michael Charles	1.3	1800	2500	25
James Alexander	1.5	1975	2500	30

4.1 ARITHMETIC OPERATORS

SQL supports the following arithmetic operators:

- Addition (+)
- Subtraction (-)
- Division (/)

- Multiplication (*)
- Exponentiation (** or ^)

These operators are used with constants in the WHERE clause of an SQL command, as in the following examples:

WHERE (cost * .30) = price

WHERE (salary + comm) = income

If in your SQL statement you do not specify the order in which you want these operations to be performed, SQL will perform them in the following sequence:

prefix +
prefix -
exponent (** or ^)
Multiply (*)
Divide (/)
Add(+),
Subtract (-)
left to right

However, by using parentheses, you can specify to SQL the order in which you want the operations to be performed.

For example, suppose you have the following expression to be evaluated:

A + B - C / 3*15

If you enter the expression as shown above, SQL will evaluate it as follows:

the sum of A + B
less
the quantity: (C divided by 3 times 15).

However, by using parentheses as follows:

(A + B - C) / (3 * 15)

you can force SQL to evaluate it this way:

the sum of (A + B - C)
divided by (3 times 15).

Try this experiment: Assign the numbers 1, 2, and 3 in that order to the constants A, B, and C to prove to yourself that the results would be different in these two cases. The result of the first computation will be 44/15, whereas the result of the second computation will be the quantity 0/45.

4.2 COMPARISON OPERATORS

SQL supports the comparison operators shown in Figure 4-2, below.

Figure 4-2. Comparison Operators

Symbol	Meaning
>	greater than
<	less than
=	equals
>=	greater than or equal to
<=	less than or equal to
<>	not equal to
!=	not equal to
!>	not greater than
!<	not less than

These comparison operators are used in WHERE clauses to compare the rows being SELECTed with a constant, as well as in HAVING clauses to designate rows being GROUPed.

For example:

```
WHERE price = 10
HAVING AVG(cost) !> 50000
WHERE  title <> 'manager'
WHERE  salary BETWEEN 3000 AND 5000
WHERE  city != 'Denver'
HAVING  MAX(income) <= 3000
WHERE   age !> 60
```

4.3 LOGICAL OPERATORS

SQL supports the three logical operators AND, OR, and NOT. You use these operators to modify search conditions in the WHERE clause, and thus limit the number of rows returned by the result. (These operators are also discussed in terms of the relational model in Chapter Eight, Section 8.2.)

The following sections show how to use each logical operator.

4.3.1 How to Use the Logical Operator AND

Suppose you are about to give bonuses to some of your employees, and you decide to award bonuses only to persons who have been with the company more than 2 years, and whose commissions for this year are more than $1,000. In this case you want the WHERE clause to pick out only those employee records (that is, only those rows of the Employee Table) satisfying both of these conditions.

Use the WHERE clause to SELECT the entry "greater than 2" from the column "Years of Service", and the AND operator to add the condition "equal to or greater than $1,000" from the Commission column, as follows:

```
SELECT name, yrs_serv, comm

FROM  Emp

WHERE yrs_serv > 2,

AND   comm >= 1000;
```

The Result Table shown in Figure 4-3 is the result of a query using the above WHERE clause to retrieve data from the table shown in Figure 4-1.

Figure 4-3. Bonus Recipients 1

name	yrs_serv	comm
Dee Thomas	5.0	1500
Juli Sutton	9.0	1750
Stan Baker	3.0	2000

You could add more conditions by using more AND statements. For example, you might also require the bonus recipient to be a part-time employee. In that case, add the third condition with another AND.

```
SELECT  yrs_serv, wrk_hrs, comm
FROM  Emp
WHERE yrs_serv > 2,
AND   comm >= 1000,
AND   wrk_hrs < 40;
```

The result of using the two ANDs in a query directed to the data shown in Figure 4-1 is shown in the result table in Figure 4-4.

Figure 4-4. Bonus Recipients 2

name	yrs_serv	wrk_hrs	comm
Juli Sutton	9.0	20	1750
Stan Baker	3.0	20	2000

4.3.2 How to Use the Logical Operator OR

Suppose that, in the example cited in Section 4.3.1 above, bonus recipients are to be employees who satisfy any one or more of the three conditions stipulated. In this case, you would use two OR operators instead of the two AND operators.

```
SELECT yrs_serv, comm, wrk_hrs
FROM  Emp
WHERE yrs_serv > 2
OR   comm >= 1000
OR   wrk_hrs < 40;
```

The result of using this WHERE clause in a query to the data in Figure 4-1 will be the result table in Figure 4-5.

Figure 4-5. Bonus Recipients 3

name	yrs_serv	comm	wrk_hrs
Beth White	2.5	0	40
John Jones	1.5	500	35
Dee Thomas	5.0	1500	40
Loren Black	6.0	300	20
Mary Gray	1.5	1800	25
Juli Sutton	9.0	1750	20
Stan Baker	3.0	2000	20
Michael Charles	1.3	2500	25
James Alexander	1.5	2500	30

Notice that the number of people SELECTed by the OR operator is much larger than the number SELECTed by the AND operator, and includes every row that was in the group covered by the AND operator. This is because when you use OR, any one or more of the conditions can be true, or all may be true. Thus, the OR includes everybody in the AND list who fulfill all conditions, as well as those personnel who are not in the AND list because they satisfy only one or two of the conditions.

4.3.3 How to Use AND and OR Together

When you mix AND and OR conditions in the same WHERE clause, some confusion may result. To eliminate the confusion, use parentheses to set off your *alternative conditions* (the ones that may be substituted for others) from your *mandatory conditions*.

For example, consider the following WHERE clause:

```
WHERE yrs_serv > 2,
OR comm >= 1000 AND wrk_hrs < 40
```

Does this mean that:

- the employee must have more than 2 years of service and work less than 40 hours,

OR

- the employee must show a commission equal to or greater than $1,000?

Or, does it mean:

- the employee must either have 2 years of service and commission equal to or greater than $1,000,

  OR

- the employee must work only part-time?

The question is: which conditions are alternative (may be substituted for others), and which are mandatory? There is no way to tell from the position of the OR and AND following the WHERE. In cases like this, SQL will make a decision based on its built-in order of precedence rules (listed in Section 4.3.5), but this may not give you the results you intend.

Therefore, use parentheses to clarify your intention. For example:

```
WHERE yrs_serv > 2,
OR (comm> >= 1000 AND wrk_hrs < 40);
```

The above means that employees have to meet at least one of the following two conditions:

- Years of service are greater than 2
- Commission is at least $1,000, and work is part-time

If the above WHERE clause were part of a query directed to the data in the table shown in Figure 4-1, the result would be as shown in the Result Table in Figure 4-6:

Figure 4-6. Bonus Recipients 4

name	yrs_serv	comm	wrk_hrs
Beth White	2.5	0	40
Dee Thomas	5.0	1500	40
Loren Black	6.0	300	20
Mary Gray	1.5	1800	25
Juli Sutton	9.0	1750	20
Stan Baker	3.0	2000	20
Michael Charles	1.3	2500	25
James Alexander	1.5	2500	30

The other possibility can be entered as:

```
WHERE (yrs_serv > 2 OR comm >= 1000)
AND   wrk_hrs < 40;
```

which means that they must meet both of the two following conditions:

- Years of service are greater than 2, or commission is greater than 1,000
- Work hours are less than 40

If the above WHERE clause were part of a query directed to the data in the table shown in Figure 4-1, the result would appear as shown in the result table in Figure 4-7:

Figure 4-7. Bonus Recipients 5

name	yrs_serv	comm	wrk_hrs
Mary Gray	1.5	1800	25
Loren Black	6.0	300	20
Juli Sutton	9.0	1750	20
Stan Baker	3.0	2000	20
Michael Charles	1.3	2500	25
James Alexander	1.5	2500	30

Parentheses are the only way to make your meaning clear when using both ANDs and ORs in a WHERE clause. With a large database, you will never know that you've been misinterpreted, until it's too late. If there is any possibility for confusion, use parentheses liberally .

4.3.4 How To Use the Logical Operator NOT

To have a logical operator NOT in dBASE IV SQL might seem superfluous, since you already have the symbols != and <>, each of which is translated "not equal". However, there are certain situations where you cannot use either != or <>. This is where the NOT comes in.

NOT is used to modify the operators BETWEEN, LIKE, IN, and EXISTS. Details are discussed in the following sections in the current chapter:

NOT BETWEEN — Section 4.4.2.2

NOT IN — Section 4.4.2.3

NOT LIKE — Section 4.4.2.4

NOT EXISTS — Section 4.4.2.7

You can also use NOT to limit a search condition by combining it with AND or OR. This usage will exclude certain rows. For example, you might want to give bonuses to employees who have been with the company for more than 2 years and have earned commissions of more than $2,000, but not if they work less than full time. The WHERE clause for these conditions is:

```
WHERE yrs_serv > 2,
AND   comm >= 2000,
AND NOT work_hrs < 40;
```

Note that the NOT comes directly after the AND, not after "work_hrs." This is because NOT cannot be part of a predicate. (A *predicate* is a search condition that can be evaluated to True or False.) In other words, the predicate in this example is "work_hrs < 40," and you cannot insert the word NOT within a predicate. Instead, you must negate the entire predicate by putting the NOT outside of it.

4.3.5 Order of Precedence for Logical Operators

In the absence of any other directions, SQL will follow this order of precedence in processing logical operators:

( )

NOT

AND

OR

left to right

The above listing again emphasizes that you need to use parentheses to override SQL's built-in order of precedence for AND, OR, and NOT.

4.4 CLAUSES

dBASE IV SQL supports the following clauses in SELECT statements:

FROM

WHERE

GROUP BY

HAVING

ORDER BY

SAVE TO TEMP

Each of these are discussed in the sections that follow.

4.4.1 The FROM Clause

The FROM clause identifies the table(s) or view(s) from which the rows will be drawn to satisfy the search condition.

The syntax is:

```
FROM <tablename> [alias]
     [,<table name> [alias] ...]
```

where:

FROM is a keyword.

<table name> is the name of a table, synonym, or view to be used in the SELECT statement.

<alias> is an optional name that can be used in place of the table, synonym, or view name in the SELECT and WHERE clauses. Aliases are used for

distinguishing tables in correlated subqueries and in self-joins. (Joins are explained in Chapter Eight.)

For example, if you want to work with the Employee Table, your FROM clause would be:

```
FROM Employee
```

Synonyms for tables or views may be used in the FROM clause; for example, if your synonym for the Employee table is Emp, then your FROM clause would be:

```
FROM Emp
```

To include aliases in the FROM clause (for example, the designation Staff1 and Staff2 as aliases for the Employee Table), you would enter:

```
FROM Employee Staff1, Employee Staff2
```

The FROM clause must appear in every SQL query; it must also appear in DELETE statements; it may appear in UPDATE statements.

4.4.2 The WHERE Clause

The WHERE clause specifies the search condition(s) to be satisfied by the rows SELECTed from the table(s) named in the FROM clause.

There are eight different search conditions that can occur in dBASE IV SQL. They are:

- Simple Comparison
- BETWEEN Comparison
- IN Comparison
- LIKE Comparison
- Simple Comparison With Subquery
- IN Comparison With Subquery
- EXISTS Condition With Subquery
- Join Condition.

The use of each of these search conditions with the WHERE clause is explained in the following sections.

The syntax for all conditions is:

WHERE <search condition>

4.4.2.1 SIMPLE COMPARISON. In a simple comparison occurring in an SQL statement, you compare a value on the left of a comparison operator with a value on the right of the comparison operator.

The syntax is:

<column name or expression> <comparison operator> <column name or expression>

where:

<column name> names the column containing the values to be compared,

<expression> is a constant, memory variable, dBASE function, or column name,

<comparison operator> is one of the comparison operators discussed in Section 4.2 above.

For example, to SELECT only those employees (i.e., rows) where the value in the salary column is greater than 2500, enter the following WHERE clause:

WHERE salary > 2500

The datatypes must be the same in the column values represented by the column name on one side of the comparison operator, and the expression or column name on the other side.

4.4.2.2 BETWEEN...AND... COMPARISON CONDITION. The BETWEEN...AND... comparison condition restricts the SELECTed rows to those rows falling between two values. The syntax for using the BETWEEN ... AND ... comparison condition in an SQL statement is:

<expression1> [NOT] BETWEEN
<low expression2> AND <high expression3>

where:

<expression1> is the expression (usually a column) containing the values to be tested.

NOT is an optional keyword that reverses the sense of the BETWEEN condition. In other words, it causes the rows with values outside the BETWEEN... AND range to be SELECTed.

BETWEEN...AND... is the comparison condition.

<expression2> is any combination of constants, host variables, dBASE functions, memvars, or column names defining the lower bound of the range of values to be SELECTed.

<high value> is any combination of constants, host variables, dBASE functions, memvars, or column names defining the upper bound of the range of values to be SELECTed.

NOTE: The BETWEEN...AND...comparison condition includes the beginning and end points of the designated range.

The expressions used in a BETWEEN ... AND ... condition may be of any data type except LOGICAL.

For example, you can set up a query to SELECT salaries within the range $500 to $2,000, by entering the following as part of an SQL statement:

```
BETWEEN 500 AND 2000
```

This includes all values starting with 500, up to and including the value 2000.

Or, you can SELECT all rows containing dates between one fiscal period and the next, by entering:

```
BETWEEN CTOD('03/01/88') AND CTOD('02/01/89')
```

where:

CTOD() is the dBASE character-to-date conversion function. It must be used whenever you want a date (which is a character string) to be used as a dBASE IV DATE data type.

Or, you can SELECT house numbers in a certain area of town by restricting the rows to those containing values in a specified range, by entering:

```
WHERE VAL house_no

BETWEEN 830 AND 1045
```

where:

house_no is a CHARacter data type column.

Or, you can SELECT sections of the alphabet by specifying a range in the alphabet, and entering:

BETWEEN 'A' AND 'L'

In each of the above cases, the values you put on each side of the AND must have the same datatype.

When you use the reserved word NOT with the BETWEEN...AND... comparison condition, the syntax is:

NOT BETWEEN <low value> AND <high value>

For example, you may enter:

NOT BETWEEN 19 AND 24

This means that rows containing the values 19, 20, 21, 22, 23, and 24 will not be returned in the result table.

All of the restrictions on use of the BETWEEN comparison condition apply to the use of the NOT BETWEEN comparison condition.

4.4.2.3 The IN Comparison Condition. The IN Comparison condition restricts the rows being SELECTed to those rows where the column values are in the list presented in the SQL statement. The syntax is:

WHERE <column name> IN (<value list>)

where:

<column name> names the column containing the values to be compared with the value list,

<value list> is a list of constant values, enclosed in parentheses, with each value separated from the others by a comma.

For example, to SELECT from the Employee Table rows containing only specific numbers of years of service, enter an SQL statement containing the following IN comparison condition:

WHERE yrs_serv IN (2, 4, 6, 8)

If you specify this condition, rows listing employees with 3, 5, or 7 years of service will not be SELECTed.

To SELECT only specific salary figures, enter an SQL statement containing the following IN comparison condition:

WHERE salary IN (500, 1500, 2000)

With the above condition, only the rows for employees earning 500, 1500, or 2000 will be SELECTed.

As another example, to SELECT suppliers from specific locations, enter an SQL statement containing the following IN comparison condition:

WHERE city IN ('Boston', 'New York', 'Wilmington')

The reserved word NOT can be used with the IN comparison condition. The syntax is:

WHERE <column name> NOT IN (<value list>)

For example:

WHERE city NOT IN ('Dallas', 'Chicago', 'Boston')

The restrictions on the use of the NOT IN comparison condition are the same as those for the IN comparison condition.

For another use of the IN comparison condition, see Section 4.4.2.5, IN Comparison With Subquery.

<u>4.4.2.4 The LIKE Comparison Condition.</u> The LIKE comparison condition restricts the rows SELECTed to those with column values matching a specified search string, or a search string containing either one, or both, of the two wildcards supported by dBASE IV SQL.

The syntax is:

WHERE <column name> LIKE <'search string'>

where:

<column name> names the column containing the values to be compared with a search string.

<'search string'> is a string enclosed in single or double quotes that may be any one of the following, or a combination of all three:

- a character string
- •) a character string containing the percent wildcard (%) to indicate an indeterminate number (including zero) of unspecified characters
- a character string containing the underscore wildcard (_) to indicate individual unspecified characters.
- a memory variable is also an allowed syntax if the memvar is of CHAR type. Wildcards % and _ may be used in the memvar itself.

CAUTION: If the dBASE wildcard characters asterisk (*) or question-mark (?) are used in the LIKE comparison condition, they will be ignored by SQL.

If you need to find the records of all the employees named "Smith", you can do so by using the LIKE comparison in an SQL query as follows:

WHERE name LIKE "Smith"

If you want to find the records of all employees who have "smith" as a part of their surname (e.g., Arrowsmith, Goldsmithson), you can use the LIKE comparison with the percent (%) wildcard to indicate that the "smith" may occur anywhere in the string:

WHERE name LIKE "%smith%"

However, since LIKE is case-sensitive (that is, it will only search for the word with the same upper and lower case that you specify), the above WHERE clause would not find employees where the "smith" occurred at the beginning of the last name, such as Smithson. To overcome this problem, you can use the dBASE function UPPER, and enter the clause as follows:

WHERE UPPER (name) LIKE '%SMITH%'

The above will convert all small letters in the character string to capital letters. See Chapter Seven for a discussion and listing of UPPER and other dBASE functions that can be used in interactive SQL mode.

The above comparison statement will also take care of retrieving any employee named simply "Smith", since the % wildcard indicates any number of unspecified characters including zero.

If you are looking for the record of an employee named "Johnson", and know that there are exactly three letters after the "John", but are not sure whether the name is spelled "Johnsen", "Johnsan", or "Johnson", then you can use the underscore (_) wild card by entering:

WHERE name LIKE "Johns_n"

Or you can use three underscores, as in the following entry:

WHERE name LIKE "John_ _ _"

The SQL reserved word NOT can be used with the LIKE comparison condition. The syntax is:

WHERE <column name> NOT LIKE <search string>

For example, if you want to retrieve all supplier records except those in Chicago, Toledo, and Kokomo, you can use the NOT LIKE condition in your SQL query to exclude suppliers in those cities by entering:

WHERE city NOT LIKE "%o"

Notice that the above comparison condition will also exclude any suppliers who happen to be in Buffalo, San Francisco, or Orlando (or in any other cities ending with "o"), since in this case the percent (%) wildcard indicates an unspecified number of characters in a string ending with "o". Therefore, this wildcard combined with NOT should be used cautiously, because you will have no record of which rows were excluded from the retrieval.

All of the points made above regarding the LIKE comparison condition also hold for the NOT LIKE comparison condition.

4.4.2.5 IN COMPARISON WITH SUBQUERY. The IN comparison, when used with a subquery, restricts the rows SELECTed to those that satisfy the results of the second SELECT statement in an SQL command. In other words, the subquery (which starts with the second SELECT statement in the command) takes the place of the <value list> shown with the IN comparison in Section 4.4.2.3. The syntax is:

WHERE <column name> IN (<subquery>)

where:

<column name> names the column containing the values to be compared with the results of the subquery;

<subquery> is any SQL command starting with a SELECT statement after the first SELECT statement. (Subqueries are discussed in greater detail in Chapter Six.)

For example, suppose you have the Employee Table containing, among other things, employee names and identification numbers (id_no), and you have another table called Tax File containing id numbers and salaries. If you want the names of employees who receive more than $50,000, enter:

```
SELECT name
FROM   Employee
WHERE  id_no IN
    (SELECT id_no
    FROM   Tax_File
    WHERE  salary >= 50000);
```

4.4.2.6 COMPARISON USING ANY OR ALL WITH A SUBQUERY. You can make a comparison using the SQL reserved words ANY or ALL by setting up a subquery. The syntax is:

<column name> <comparison operator> [ANY or ALL] (<subquery>)

where:

<column name> names the column containing the values to be compared with the result of the subquery.

<comparison operator> is any one of the comparison operators described in Sections 4.1 through 4.3 above.

<subquery> is any command starting with a SELECT statement appearing after the first SELECT statement that you have entered to return a set of values.

ANY is an SQL reserved word which provides that a row will be returned if the comparison is true for any of the values returned by the subquery.

ALL is an SQL reserved word which provides that a row will be retrieved if the comparison is true for all values retrieved by the subquery.

For example,

WHERE salary < ANY (<subquery>);

WHERE salary > ALL (<subquery>);

4.4.2.7 COMPARISON USING THE EXISTS CONDITION WITH A SUBQUERY. The EXISTS condition restricts the rows SELECTed to those where a subquery returns one or more rows. The syntax is:

WHERE EXISTS (<subquery>)

The EXISTS condition is used with a correlated subquery, that is, where the subquery contains a reference to a column in the main query. (Correlated subqueries are discussed in Chapter Six, Section 6.4.3.)

The logical operator NOT can be used with EXISTS in this same type of query. The syntax is:

WHERE NOT EXISTS (<subquery>)

Note that the NOT goes before EXISTS, rather than directly before the subquery.

For a detailed discussion of correlated subqueries and the use of the EXISTS condition, see Chapter Six.

4.4.2.8 COMPARISON USING THE JOIN CONDITION. The join condition restricts the rows to be retrieved to those satisfying a condition common to two (or more) column values in different tables or in a self-join. The syntax is:

<column name 1> <comparison operator> <column name 2>

where:

<column name 1> and <column name 2> are two distinct columns.

<comparison operator> is any one of the operators shown in Figure 4-2.

You will find a complete discussion of joins (an important part of SQL), as well as the join condition in the WHERE clause, in Chapter Eight.

4.4.3 The GROUP BY Clause

The GROUP BY clause puts those rows that have the same value together in a specified column. The result table then shows a single value for each group of rows. GROUP BY is usually used when there is one or more aggregate functions in the SELECT statement; such aggregate functions then apply to the column values within the group rather than to each value in the column.

You may GROUP BY more than one column in a single SELECT statement, but you cannot GROUP BY any derived columns.

The total concatenated length of the columns listed in the GROUP BY column list cannot exceed 100 bytes.

The syntax for GROUP BY is:

GROUP BY <column list>

where:

<column list> is a list of the column name(s) by which you want SQL to group the rows SELECTed.

For example, suppose that (as the owner of a tool shop) you have an Inventory Table of tools on hand, with columns for suppliers, supplier locations, tool names, cost of each tool, and the number of each on hand, as shown in Figure 4-8A.

Figure 4-8A. Inventory

Suppliers	Location	Tool	Cost	Number
Acme	Boston	wrench	3.00	50
ABC	NY	hammer	2.00	40
Durable	Phila	pliers	3.00	150
Fasttool	Dallas	wrench	4.00	15
XYZ	Chicago	pliers	2.00	100
Smartool	Spokane	lathe	40.00	15
Fasttool	Dallas	screwdriver	1.00	250
ABC	NY	wrench	3.00	15
D & B	Stockton	lathe	25.00	20
XYZ	Chicago	hammer	5.00	30
Acme	Boston	screwdriver	3.00	40

You might want to know the value of your present inventory, GROUPed BY type of part. To find this value, enter:

```
SELECT tool_name, SUM(cost)
FROM   Inv
GROUP  BY tool_name;
```

The result table will be in the form shown in Figure 4-8B.

Figure 4-8B. Value of Present Inventory

tool name	SUM(cost)
Wrench	255
Hammer	230
Pliers	650
Screwdrivers	370
Lathes	1100

The SUMs shown in Figure 4-8B are the sum of the cost of wrenches supplied by all suppliers, the SUM of the cost of all hammers, and so on. In other words, this Figure shows the total cost of the total on hand of each type of tool in your Inventory Table, regardless of which supplier it came from.

Note that the tools are not necessarily in alphabetical order. In fact, their order will be random, since GROUP BY does not do any ordering. To alphabetize the tool names in the result table, you need to use the ORDER BY command, discussed in Section 4.7.

Every column named in the SELECT command must be mentioned in the GROUP BY clause, unless it is the argument to an aggregate function. (This point is explained in greater detail in Chapter Seven, where each aggregate function is defined.)

4.4.4 The HAVING Clause

The HAVING clause specifies a search condition for a group, just as a WHERE clause specifies a search condition for individual values. HAVING is usually preceded by a GROUP BY clause. If it is not preceded by GROUP BY, then the entire result table is considered a group. Also, if HAVING appears without a GROUP BY clause, then all column names appearing in the SELECT clause must be arguments to SQL aggregate functions.

You cannot put correlated references in a HAVING clause subquery.

The syntax for the HAVING clause is:

HAVING <search condition>

where:

HAVING is a keyword

<search condition> specifies a condition that each group must satisfy in order to appear in the result table.

For example, if (using the example in Section 4.5 above) you wanted to list only those types of tools with an average value of $1 or more, you could use the HAVING clause to do this.

Enter:

```
SELECT  tool_name, SUM(cost)
FROM    Inv
GROUP BY  tool_name
HAVING    AVG(cost) >= 1.00;
```

This statement would exclude from the result table any type of tool whose average cost was less than $1.

4.4.5 The ORDER BY Clause

The ORDER BY clause specifies the order in which the SELECTed rows will be displayed on your screen. The syntax is:

ORDER BY <column name> / <integer> [ASC/DESC]
    [,<column name> / <integer> [ASC/DESC], ...]

where:

<column name> names the column containing the values to be ordered.

<integer> is a constant indicating the left-to-right order of the columns in the SELECT statement.

ASC is an optional SQL reserved word indicating that the ordering must be in ascending order, from lowest to highest. If the ordering is alphabetical, then ASC indicates that earlier letters of the alphabet will come before later letters. If you do not specify either ascending or descending order, then the ordering will be ASC, as that is the default setting. (Keep in mind that in ASCII, capital letters have a different code from lower case letters; therefore Z will not be in the same position as z, and Z will come before a.)

DESC is an optional SQL reserved word indicating that the ordering must be in descending order, from highest to lowest. If the ordering is alphabetical, then DESC indicates that later letters of the alphabet will come before earlier letters.

You may ORDER BY more than one column. To do so, list the columns by which you want the result table ORDERed. dBASE IVwill order first on the first one you list, then within that ORDERing, will order the second one you list, and so on.

For example, if you want to order personnel first by hrs_wrk in DESCending order, then by name alphabetically in ASCending order, you would enter this in the ORDER BY clause as the last item in the SQL statement as follows:

```
SELECT name, wrk_hrs
FROM   Employee
ORDER BY wrk_hrs DESC, name;
```

Note that you do not need to enter the ASC for ascending order since ASC is the default, but you do need to enter DESC for descending in order to change the default setting.

The above query will produce the result table shown in Figure 4-9.

Figure 4-9. Hours Worked

name	wrk_hrs
Beth White	40
Dee Thomas	40
Richard Roe	40
Thomas Doe	40
John Jones	35
James Alexander	30
Mary Gray	25
Michael Charles	25
Juli Sutton	20
Loren Black	20
Stan Baker	20

Notice that in Figure 4-9, the names are alphabetized on the first letter of the first name rather than the last. This is because the names appear that way in the original table, i.e., with the first name as the beginning of the character string. To ORDER BY the first letter of the last name, you need to either list the employees by last name first in the table in Figure 4-1, or make "lastname" a separate column and enter it after the ORDER BY in the SQL statement.

You can ORDER BY a column's relative position in the SELECT statement by using a number to indicate its position in the column list.

For example:

```
SELECT      name, yrs_serv, salary
FROM        Employee
WHERE       wrk_hrs >= 30
ORDER BY    2;
```

Using the data in Figure 4-1, the result table for the above query would be as shown in Figure 4-10.

Figure 4-10. Years of Service

name	yrs_serv	salary
Thomas Doe	0.5	2500
Richard Roe	0.9	1300
John Jones	1.5	1500
James Alexander	1.5	1975
Beth White	2.5	2000
Dee Thomas	5.0	2500

4.4.6 The SAVE TO TEMP Clause

You can save the results of a SELECT statement as a temporary table by using the SAVE TO TEMP clause. You can then use this temporary table to generate reports and forms in dBASE mode.

The syntax is:

```
SAVE TO TEMP <table name>
    [(column name, column name ...)] [KEEP] ;
```

where:

SAVE TO TEMP are keywords

<table name> is the name you are giving the table that will hold the results being saved.

<column name> is the name of the column(s) that will go into the TEMP table. If the SELECT statement lists columns with the same names, or derived columns, the SAVE TO TEMP column list must be explicitly defined. Otherwise an error will occur.

[KEEP] is an optional keyword that will save the table as a database file after SET SQL OFF, STOP DATABASE, CREATE DATABASE, or DROP DATABASE. If you use KEEP, the table will be copied as a .dbf file into the user directory when the table is dropped from the system catalog. Then .dbf dBASE report forms can be used with it at any time to create reports.

During the rest of the SQL session, you can access a temporary table with SQL commands, but—unless you specify KEEP—it will only persist until SET SQL OFF (or until the .prs in which it was created returns to the dBASE or SQL dot prompt).

Even if you do specify KEEP, the temporary table will no longer exist as an SQL table when you re-enter SQL. However, you can use DBDEFINE to convert the saved .dbf into an SQL table.

NOTE: You cannot use SAVE TO TEMP to create a temporary table if the SELECT statement contains FOR UPDATE OF or INTO clauses.

4.5 EXPRESSIONS

An *expression* is any combination of columns, operators, constants, and dBASE functions that returns a numeric or character value. You can use expressions to provide descriptive column information, to define a new calculated column in the SELECT clause, to define conditions in a WHERE clause, and to define ORDER BY, GROUP BY, and HAVING clauses.

An expression can contain a combination of columns, arithmetic operators, dBASE functions, constants, and memory variables. (The use of dBASE IV functions and memory variables in expressions is explained in Chapter Seven.)

Aggregate functions cannot be nested. (Aggregate functions are discussed in Chapter Seven.) For example, the following is an illegal expression:

```
AVG (SUM(cost))
```

A constant expression can be used in a SELECT command to insert descriptive column information in the result table; to do so, place a comma after the column name, and add the expression in quotes.

You can use a variable expression in a SELECT command to define a new, "calculated column" in the result table. The calculated column will be based upon an existing column in the base table.

For example, although monthly salaries are listed in your Employee Table, you might need an annual figure for a specific purpose. You can make this change by using a variable expression (salary*12) for the calculated column, and a constant expression (annual) to follow the calculated column values. To do so, enter:

```
SELECT name, salary*12, "(annual)"
```

```
FROM   Employee;
```

You can put an expression in the WHERE clause. For example:

```
WHERE salary*12 < 20000
```

dBASE functions and memory variables can be used in expressions. Appendix C contains a list of the dBASE functions available for use in SQL statements; Chapter Seven explains how to use them, as well as how to use memory variables in expressions.

5

Manipulating Data: Loading, Unloading, Inserting, Updating, and Deleting

As soon as the base tables are set up, you can load in data from other sources, add new rows to the original data, update column values, and delete rows. All of these operations come under the general class of *data manipulation*, and are discussed in the sections that follow. Forming queries and subqueries to retrieve information from the database are also data manipulation operations, but because these are large topics in themselves, they are discussed separately in Chapter Six.

This chapter explains and illustrates LOADing DATA, UNLOADing DATA, transaction processing, and the INSERT, UPDATE and DELETE commands. Later chapters show how these data manipulation commands can be used in conjunction with other SQL statements to query the database, to optimize retrieval, and to perform more complicated operations.

5.1 HOW TO LOAD DATA INTO THE DATABASE

To load .dbf files created in dBASE mode into SQL, you use the DBDEFINE command discussed in Section 9.10.3 of Chapter 9. You can also use the LOAD DATA command.

The LOAD DATA command is used to LOAD tables in dBASE IV with data generated by programs from other software vendors (for example, MultiPlan by Microsoft). The syntax for the LOAD DATA command is:

LOAD DATA FROM [path]<filename>
INTO TABLE <table name>
[[TYPE] {SDF/DIF/WKS/FW2/RPD/DBASEII/SYLK/DELIMITED}
[WITH {BLANK/<expC>]}];

where:

<path> is the directory path to the file from which data are to be loaded. For example, if the file is in the MM subdirectory of the directory named Microsft, then the path is \Microsft\MM.

<filename> is the filename. Thus, if the file is named foo in the MM subdirectory of the Microsft directory, the command begins: LOAD DATA FROM \Microsft\MM\foo INTO TABLE ..

[TYPE] is optional, but if it is omitted, it is assumed that the file is a .dbf file. The TYPEs allowed and their meanings are:

- SDF — standard data format
- DIF — DIF spreadsheet format
- WKS — Lotus 1-2-3 spreadsheet file
- SYLK — Microsoft MultiPlan spreadsheet file
- FW2 — Framework II™ file
- RPD — RapidFile
- DBASEII — dBASE II file.
- DELIMITED — Delimited foreign files have variable length records, with the fields separated by a specified character (such as a comma), called a *delimiter*. Records are separated by carriage return line feeds.

WITH BLANK are reserved words if the TYPE is DELIMITED with blank.

WITH <expC> is required if the TYPE is DELIMITED with other than blank.

The datatypes, field widths, and field names must match for the LOAD command.

5.2 HOW TO UNLOAD DATA FROM THE DATABASE

The UNLOAD DATA command is used to UNLOAD tables in dBASE IV to other tables in dBASE IV, or to files like those generated by programs from other software vendors, such as Microsoft's MultiPlan. The syntax for the UNLOAD DATA command is:

```
UNLOAD DATA TO [path] <file name>
FROM TABLE <table name>
[TYPE {SDF/DIF/WKS/SYLK/FW2/RPD/DBASEII/DELIMITED
[WITH {BLANK/<expC>}]}];
```

where:

<path> is the directory path to the file to be unloaded into. For example, if the file is in the MM subdirectory of the Microsft directory, then the path is \Microsft\MM.

<filename> is the filename. Thus, if the filename is foo in the MM subdirectory of the Microsft directory, the command begins: UNLOAD DATA TO \Microsft\MM\foo FROM TABLE.

[TYPE] is optional, but if it is omitted, it is assumed that the file is a .dbf file. The TYPEs allowed, and the meaning of each, is as follows:

- SDF — system data format
- DIF — DIF spreadsheet format
- WKS — Lotus 1-2-3 spreadsheet file
- SYLK — Microsoft MultiPlan spreadsheet file
- FW2 — Framework II file
- RPD — RapidFile
- DBASEII — dBASE II file
- DELIMITED — Delimited foreign files have variable length records, with the fields separated by a specified character (such as a comma), called a *delimiter*. Records are separated by carriage return line feeds.

WITH BLANK are required keywords if the TYPE is DELIMITED with blank.

WITH <expC> is required if the TYPE is DELIMITED with other than blank.

5.3 TRANSACTION PROCESSING

Sometimes you will engage in an operation on the database that must be performed in several steps. For example, the sale of goods might require not only the recording of the sale income, but also a reduction in the amount of those goods from inventory. If both parts of the transaction are not accomplished in the same work session, your company will show more goods on hand than it actually has.

In a single-user system, there's a danger that because of an interruption you may forget to perform some of the necessary steps. In a multi-user system, on the other hand, someone else may be changing part of the data while you are performing the steps. In both cases, the integrity of the data will be threatened or destroyed.

dBASE IV SQL provides a means whereby you can be sure that either all or none of the SQL steps you intend to enter are recorded. Either way, the integrity of the database will be maintained.

An operation requiring several steps is called a *transaction*, and safeguards should be used whenever you perform it. To serve as safeguard, dBASE IV provides the command BEGIN TRANSACTION to indicate the start of an operation requiring several steps. When you complete all the steps and your work is ready to be recorded in the database, you use the command END TRANSACTION. If an interruption of any kind occurs after you have entered BEGIN TRANSACTION but before you have entered END TRANSACTION, all the changes you have made can be rolled back with the ROLLBACK command (see Chapter Nine, Section 9.7) so that the database will remain as it was before you started the series of steps. This prevents an incomplete transaction from being entered into the database.

The following dBASE commands may NOT be used during a transaction:

- CLEAR ALL
- CLOSE ALL/DATABASE/INDEX
- DELETE FILE
- ERASE
- MODIFY STRUCTURE
- INSERT

- PACK
- RENAME
- ZAP

Attempting to use any of these commands during a transaction will result in an error message.

In addition, the following dBASE IV commands are not allowed during a transaction if they result in the closing of a file:

- CREATE [FROM]
- INDEX ON
- SET CATALOG TO
- SET INDEX TO
- USE

Since the above commands are not allowed in SQL mode, the conclusion is that during a transaction you cannot use the following SQL commands.

- All CREATE commands
- All DROP commands
- ALTER TABLE
- GRANT
- REVOKE
- DBCHECK
- DBDEFINE
- RUNSTATS

For a listing of commands allowed in dBASE IV SQL, see Appendix B.

5.4 HOW TO INSERT NEW ROWS INTO THE DATABASE

The INSERT command is used to put rows, or parts of rows into tables (see Section 5.4.1 regarding parts of rows). There are two general forms for this command:

Form (1)

This form is used for inserting a single row. The syntax is:

```
INSERT INTO  <tablename>
      [(column list)]
VALUES  (<value list>);
```

where:

INSERT INTO are SQL reserved words.

<tablename> names the table into which values are to be INSERTed.

[(<column list>)] is an optional listing of the columns that INSERT will UPDATE. If you use a column list, it must name the columns, separated from each other by a comma, into which the new values will be INSERTed. This column list defines the order in which the values are expected to appear in the value list or in the result of the SELECT statement. If you do not use the column list, then the values in the value list are assumed to be in the same order as they are in the table definition.

(<value list>) is a list of the values, separated by commas, and with each character value enclosed in single or double quotes, that are to be INSERTed into the columns.

As stated above, Form (1) is used when INSERTing a single row or part of a single row.

For example, if you want to add a new supplier to your Supplier Table, enter:

```
INSERT INTO Supplier
      (name, part#, part_name, price)
VALUES (`nutool', '234A3', 'wrench', 24.95);
```

The above SQL statement will INSERT the new supplier Nutool, the part No. 234A3, the part name wrench, at a price of $24.95, into the Supplier Table.

Form (2)

This form is used to INSERT multiple rows. The syntax is:

```
INSERT INTO <tablename>
      [(<column list>)]
<SELECT statement>;
```

where:

INSERT INTO are SQL reserved words.

<tablename> names the table into which values are to be INSERTed

[(<column list>)] is an optional listing of the columns that INSERT will UPDATE. If you use a column list, it must name the columns, separated from each other by a comma, into which the new values will be INSERTed. This column list will define the order in which the values are expected to appear in the value list or in the result of the SELECT statement. If you do not use the column list, then the values are assumed to be in the same order as they are in the table definition.

<SELECT statement> is a SELECT statement that will SELECT rows that are to be INSERTed into the table named after the INSERT INTO command.

As stated above, Form (2) is generally used when multiple rows are being INSERTed, usually from some other table that has the same columns.

For example: If you have a table of old suppliers which you intend to drop, but you want to keep the information on all the suppliers of wrenches, you can put it into your current Supplier Table with the Form (2) INSERT command by entering:

```
INSERT INTO Supplier
SELECT *
FROM  Old_Supp
WHERE part_name = 'wrench';
```

The above command would enter into your current Supplier Table all the suppliers of wrenches listed in the Old Supplier Table. This assumes that the Old Supplier Table has the same column names as the current Supplier Table. If not, then you need to INSERT the rows by using the column names.

For example, if Old_Supp has columns name, address, city, phone, and part_name, and Supplier has columns part_name, name, city, and address, you enter the following command:

```
INSERT INTO Supplier
SELECT part_name, name, city, address
FROM Old_Supp
WHERE part_name = 'wrench';
```

Any value INSERTed must match the datatype of the column into which you are making the INSERTion.

CHARacter values INSERTed must be enclosed in single quotes. NUMerical values should not be enclosed in quotes.

If values are being INSERTed into all columns in the table (i.e., if complete rows are being INSERTed), then column names do not have to be listed after the tablename. However, the column values being inserted must appear in the same order as the order of the column names when the table was created, with no omitted values. In this case, the syntax is:

```
INSERT INTO <tablename>
VALUES (value1, value2, value3, ... );
```

For example, to insert a a new full-time employee, Jonna Wright, with a salary of $1,000 a month, into the Employee Table created in Chapter Four, and to fill in all columns in the table, enter:

```
INSERT INTO  Emp
VALUES  ('Jonna Wright,' 0,  1000, 0, 40);
```

The above command INSERTs a row that stores the following information in the Employee Table, the synonym for which is Emp: Jonna Wright, with no years of service, receives a salary of $1,000 a month; she has no commission, and will work 40 hours a week.

5.4.1 INSERTing Parts of Single Rows

If you are inserting *parts of rows*—that is, fewer column values than the number of columns in the table—then you must either specify column names, or insert a blank value for the column(s) where you are not making an INSERT. In this case, the syntax is:

```
INSERT INTO <tablename>
      (column 1 name, column N name)
VALUES  (value1, valueN);
```

or:

```
INSERT INTO <tablename>
VALUES  (value1, blank,valueN);
```

For example, you can INSERT some of the information for a new employee (even though you do not know his salary at this time), as follows:

```
INSERT INTO Emp
name, yrs_serv, comm, wrk_hrs)
VALUES ('Norman_Charles', 0, 0, 40);
```

where the columns being filled are specified after the INSERT INTO <tablename>;

or:

```
INSERT
INTO Emp
VALUES ('Norman_Charles', 0, 0.00, 0, 40 );
```

where no columns are specified after INSERT, but all columns are accounted for after VALUES (in the left-to-right order in which they were originally placed in the table), and they are represented either by a specific value or by a default value. In the case of a character data type, the default is all blanks; in the case of a numeric data type, the default is 0, and in the case of a logical data type, the default is .F.

Both of the entries above indicate that you know Charles' name, he has zero years of service, you do not know his salary, he has no commission, and he works 40 hours a week.

If a column value is specified, and no values are listed for unspecified columns, then SQL will assume that every column is to be filled with a value, and will insert default values in place of any unspecified column values.

Omitting column names in the INSERT statement can cause problems if the number or order of the column names has changed since they were listed in the original CREATE TABLE statement. Assuming the number and order of column names is an especially risky thing to do within an application program.

5.4.2 INSERTing Multiple Rows, or Parts of Multiple Rows

The multiple row INSERT statement shown in Section 5.4 above SELECTs information already present in one table and INSERTs it INTO another table.

For example, if you are no longer doing business with Chicago suppliers, and want to pull them out of your current Supplier Table yet retain their records, you can CREATE a new table called Former Suppliers (FS), and put the Chicago suppliers in it. You do this with two separate commands.

The first command CREATEs the new table FS:

```
CREATE TABLE FS
     (name,        CHAR(10)
     part_no       NUM(5)
     price         NUM(10));
```

The second command INSERTS rows into the new table from the old table:

```
INSERT INTO FS (name, part_no, price)
SELECT name, part_no, price
FROM Supplier
WHERE city = 'Chicago';
```

The above does not remove the Chicago suppliers from the current Supplier Table, however; it merely copies their records into the FS table. To remove the Chicago suppliers from the current Supplier Table, you must use the DELETE command discussed in Section 5.6 below.

When you INSERT rows INTO a table, these rows will then appear in any view based on that table if they satisfy the WHERE clause in the view definition.

5.4.3 INSERTing Values INTO Views

When you INSERT a row into a view, it will also be INSERTed into the table on which the view is based. Therefore, there are six special rules you need to observe when INSERTing values into views. These rules are:

You cannot INSERT rows into a view if the view:

- Is defined on more than one table
- Contains an aggregate function
- Contains a GROUP BY clause
- Contains DISTINCT in the SELECT statement
- Includes a SELECT statement with a subquery, and the subquery is on the same table as the one on which the view is defined
- Contains a column derived from an expression.
- Is defined on another, non-updatable view

If the view does not contain any of the six items listed above, you can INSERT INTO it just as you would INSERT INTO a table unless it was CREATEd with CHECK OPTION, which checks inserts as well as updates and rejects them if not within the view definition.

Following is a summary of the rules for INSERTing rows:

To INSERT rows...

You must:

- Use either Form (1) or Form (2) (shown in Section 5.4) to INSERT rows or parts of rows INTO a table or view.
- Match the datatype of existing columns with row data being INSERTED INTO a table or view.
- Enclose CHARacter values being INSERTed in single or double quotes.
- Separate column names in the INSERT INTO statement with commas.

You can:

- Use the INSERT INTO command to transfer multiple rows of data from one table to another.
- Transfer multiple rows of data from one table to another.
- Eliminate the use of column names in the INSERT INTO command if complete rows (all columns) are being INSERTed, and if column values are in the same order as in the base table.
- INSERT parts of single rows INTO tables or views if you specify column names for INSERTed data, or INSERT BLANKS for columns where you are not INSERTing data, and if you place data in the same left-to-right order as in the base table.

You cannot:

- INSERT INTO a view if the view falls into any one or more of the six categories listed in Section 5.4.3.

5.5 HOW TO UPDATE A ROW OR A TABLE

The UPDATE command is used to change values in existing rows. The syntax is:

```
UPDATE <tablename>
SET  <column1 = newvalue>,
     [<column2 = newvalue>],
     ...
     [<columnN = newvalue>]
[WHERE  <condition>];
```

When you use the SET clause with the UPDATE command, it indicates which columns are to be updated, and what the new values in those columns will be. You use it to impose a condition on all rows specified in the WHERE clause. This avoids your having to UPDATE each row individually.

For example, if you decide that all part-time employees can work no more or less than 20 hours, enter the following command to make this change:

```
UPDATE Emp
SET wrk_hrs = 20
WHERE wrk_hrs != 40;
```

The UPDATE command affects all the rows that meet the condition stated in the WHERE clause.

If the WHERE clause is omitted, all rows will be updated.

For example, if the above UPDATE contained only the following data:

```
UPDATE Emp
SET wrk_hrs = 20;
```

then every employee listed in the Employee Table would have his/her work hours changed to 20, regardless of what values this column had before the UPDATE.

You can UPDATE several rows at once by specifying conditions in the WHERE clause that will apply to those rows.

As shown above in the general form of the UPDATE command, you can UPDATE several columns in each row with a single UPDATE command by listing those columns after the word SET.

For example, suppose you wanted to give all full-time employees in your Employee Table a 10% raise. You can do this with one command as follows:

```
UPDATE Emp
SET salary = (1.1 * salary)
WHERE wrk_hrs = 40;
```

The WHERE clause in an UPDATE command may contain a subquery. For example:

```
UPDATE tablename
SET salary = (1.1 * salary)
WHERE commission =
      (subquery)
```

Detailed information on subqueries is given in Section 6.4 of Chapter Six.

When you UPDATE a row or a table, the UPDATEs you have performed will then appear in any view based on that table.

5.5.1 How To UPDATE a View

When you UPDATE rows in a view, the UPDATEs you have performed will appear in the table on which the view is based. Therefore, special rules apply when you UPDATE views; this results in the fact that some views cannot be UPDATEd. The same six rules apply to UPDATing that were stated regarding INSERTing INTO views (see Section 5.4.3 above). If a view definition contains any of the six items listed in that section, then it cannot be UPDATEd.

If a view does not contain any of the items specified in the six rules shown in Section 5.4.3 under INSERTing, then the view can be UPDATEd just as you would UPDATE a table--unless it was CREATEd WITH CHECK OPTION.

Following is a summary of the rules for UPDATing rows:

To UPDATE rows...

You must:

- Specify rows to be UPDATEd by a condition in the WHERE clause, if you do not want the UPDATE to apply to all rows of the table or view.

You can:

- UPDATE either single or multiple rows with the UPDATE SET command.
- UPDATE specific columns by listing the columns to be UPDATEd after the word SET in the UPDATE command.

You cannot:

- UPDATE a view if it falls into any one or more of the six categories listed in Section 5.4.3.

5.6 HOW TO DELETE ROWS FROM A TABLE

To remove rows from a table or view, use the DELETE command. The syntax for DELETing from a table is:

```
DELETE
FROM <tablename>
[WHERE <condition>];
```

When you DELETE rows from a table, those rows are also DELETEd from any views based on that table.

Because you cannot delete partial rows, it is not necessary to include the column names.

The condition you state in the WHERE clause will determine which rows are DELETEd.

If you want to DELETE one row from a table, specify a condition in the WHERE clause applying to just that row. For example:

```
DELETE
FROM Emp
WHERE name = 'Jones';
```

To delete several rows from a table (all with one command), specify the condition common to all of the rows. For example:

```
DELETE
FROM Emp
WHERE wrk_hrs < 40;
```

To delete all the rows from a table (all with one command), omit the WHERE clause and enter only the following command:

```
DELETE
FROM <tablename>;
```

When you use this command, it removes all of the rows from the table, leaving only the column specifications and tablename. Note that this is different from the DROP command, which removes the table name and column specifications as well as all of the rows.

5.6.1 How to DELETE Rows From a View

When you DELETE rows from a view, those rows are also DELETEd from the table on which the view is based.

The syntax for DELETing from a view (subject to the special rules explained below) is as follows:

```
DELETE
FROM <viewname>
WHERE <condition>;
```

As with INSERTing and UPDATing, when you DELETE rows from a view, these rows will be DELETEd from the table on which the view is based. Therefore, special rules apply: Namely, the first five rules shown in Section 5.4.3 under INSERTing also apply to DELETing from views. If the view contains any of the items listed in those five rules, then you cannot DELETE rows from that view.

If the view does not contain any of the items specified in the first five rules listed in Section 5.4.3, then you can DELETE rows from the view just as you would DELETE rows from a table.

Following is a summary of the rules for DELETing rows:

To DELETE rows...

You must:

- Specify a condition in the WHERE clause if you are DELETing less than all rows from a table.

You can:

- DELETE individual rows or specified groups of rows with the DELETE command.

You cannot:

- DELETE partial rows from a table or view.
- Use the DELETE command to remove an entire database, table, view, or synonym from the system. (To remove a complete database, table, synonym, view, or index, use the DROP command discussed in Chapter Three.)
- DELETE rows from a view if the view falls into any one or more of the first five categories listed in Section 5.4.3.

6

Queries and Subqueries: Using SELECT

Every query and every subquery that you make to your database includes the SQL SELECT command. The SELECT clause is always followed by FROM.

The SELECT clause lists the column(s) or expressions from which you want to retrieve information, and the FROM clause refers to the table(s) containing these columns or expressions.

The sections that follow will illustrate the use of SELECT...FROM... in conjunction with the many clauses, expressions, and functions that can be combined with this command (in both simple and complex form) to provide you with fast retrieval of the information you have stored in your database.

For the purposes of this chapter, tables will be used from a fictional museum database: Figure 6-1 provides the Exhibit Table, listing the works currently on display. Figure 6-2, the Assets Table, is a table listing all art objects owned by the museum, including those on loan, being restored, or not yet on display. Figure 6-3, the Donors Table, lists the people who have donated either art objects or cash to the museum over the last 25 years. The specifications for columns used to create each table are shown at the top of each figure.

Figure 6-1. Exhibit Table

Note: This table was created with the following column specifications:

title	CHAR(20)
gallery	CHAR(1)
condition	NUMERIC(6,0)
value_code	NUMERIC(5,2)

title	gallery	condition	value_code
Nightwatch	A	1	12.00
Le Dejeuner	C	3	6.50
Baigneuses	C	2	2.30
Parliament	D	1	2.56
Impression	D	2	2.80
Argenteuil	D	4	3.00
Archers Banquet	A	5	5.00
Melancholy	A	1	4.70
Blue Boy	B	3	4.20
Soldier	A	4	3.80
Becquigny	B	1	2.75

Figure 6-2. Assets Table

Note: This table was created with the following column specifications:

name	CHAR(15)
title	CHAR(20)
status	CHAR(10)
condition	NUMERIC(6,0)
value_code	NUMERIC(5,2)

name	title	status	condition	value_code
Rodin	Thinker	On Loan	1	3.38
Michaelangelo	David	On Loan	2	9.67
Titian	Madonna	On Loan	4	1.34
Bosch	Temptation	Restor	5	1.00
El Greco	Resurrection	Restor	5	2.05
Correggio	Madonna	Restor	6	7.60
Rembrandt	Danae	Restor	5	9.50
Rembrandt	Nightwatch	Exhibit	1	12.00
Renoir	Le Dejeuner	Exhibit	3	6.50
Cezanne	Baigneuses	Exhibit	2	2.30
Monet	Parliament	Exhibit	1	2.56
Monet	Impression	Exhibit	2	2.80
Monet	Argenteuil	Exhibit	4	3.00
Hals	Archers Banquet	Exhibit	5	5.00
Durer	Melancholy	Exhibit	1	4.70
Gainsborough	Blue Boy	Exhibit	3	4.20
Rousseau	Becquigny	Exhibit	1	2.75

Figure 6-3. Donors Table

Note: This table was created with the following column specifications:

name	CHAR(15)
address	CHAR(15)
gift	CHAR(20)
don_date	DATE

name	address	gift	don_date
B Jones	New York	cash	01/01/75
D Smith	Boston	Argenteuil	03/05/79
R Black	Amsterdam	Nightwatch	04/04/85
C Jones	San Diego	cash	09/18/76
Z Fisher	Seattle	cash	10/01/69
R Browne	Chicago	David	09/02/81
B Fox	Chicago	cash	04/03/84
D Bario	Oshkosh	Thinker	02/28/77
L Walters	Oshkosh	cash	09/09/86

6.1 SIMPLE QUERY

When you need to retrieve information from your database, you use the SELECT command. The simplest form of this command is the keyword SELECT, followed by the column names containing the information you want, followed by FROM and the name of the table(s) containing those columns. The syntax is:

```
SELECT <columnname1, columnname2,..., columnnameN>
FROM <tablename>;
```

For example, you can retrieve the donor names and the amount of each donation by entering:

```
SELECT name, gift
FROM  Donors;
```

Figure 6-4 shows the result table for the above SQL statement.

Figure 6-4. Donor Names and Gifts

name	**gift**
B Jones	cash
D Smith	Argenteuil
R Black	Nightwatch
C Jones	cash
Z Fisher	cash
R Browne	David
B Fox	cash
D Bario	Thinker
L Walters	cash

If you want to retrieve information from all columns in a table, you can do this without having to list every column after the SELECT command by entering an asterisk (*) immediately after the SELECT. This tells SQL that you want all columns from the table named after the FROM. The syntax is:

```
SELECT *
FROM <tablename>;
```

For example, to display the entire Donors Table on your screen, enter:

```
SELECT *FROM Donors;
```

The result table for the above SQL statement will return all columns and all rows in the Donors Table. It will be exactly the same as the base table Donors shown in Figure 6-3.

You can also use the asterisk (*) to return all columns from a table, but only certain rows. This requires use of the WHERE clause, and is discussed in Section 6.2 below.

6.2 QUERY TO RETRIEVE ONLY SPECIFIED ROWS

If you want only certain rows in the columns you specify, you can restrict the retrieval to the rows you want by adding a condition to the SELECT statement in a WHERE clause. (WHERE clauses are discussed in detail in Chapter Four.) The syntax for doing this is:

```
SELECT <columnname1, columnname2, ... columnnameN>
FROM <tablename>
WHERE <condition>;
```

For example, if you want to retrieve all columns of the Donors Table, but only for those donors who live in Chicago, enter:

```
SELECT *
FROM Donors
WHERE address = 'Chicago';
```

The result table for the above SQL statement is shown in Figure 6-5.

Figure 6-5. Chicago Donors

name	address	gift	don_date
K Browne	Chicago	David	09/02/81
B Fox	Chicago	cash	04/03/84

Or, if you want a list of just the names and addresses of those donors who gave cash rather than an art object, enter:

```
SELECT name, address
FROM Donors
WHERE gift = 'cash';
```

Figure 6-6 shows the result table for the above SQL statement.

Figure 6-6. Names and Addresses of Cash Donors

name	address
B Jones	New York
C Jones	San Diego
Z Fisher	Seattle
B Fox	Chicago
L Walters	Oshkosh

If you want to retrieve all columns of the Donors Table, but only for donors who contributed cash, use the asterisk (*) to indicate "all columns", and enter:

```
SELECT *
FROM Donors
WHERE gift = 'cash';
```

Figure 6-7 shows the result table for the above SQL query.

Figure 6-7. All Data on Cash Donors

name	address	gift	don_date
B Jones	New York	cash	01/01/75
C Jones	San Diego	cash	09/18/76
Z Fisher	Seattle	cash	10/01/69
B Fox	Chicago	cash	04/03/84
L Walters	Oshkosh	cash	09/09/86

6.3 QUERY WITH MORE THAN ONE CONDITION

You can further restrict or enlarge the number of rows returned by adding other conditions to your WHERE clause. You can do this in different ways, depending on what result you want.

The logical operators discussed in Chapter Four are useful for specifying more closely the result you want. The AND operator—by making your query more specific—will usually decrease the number of rows returned. The OR operator may increase the number returned while broadening its scope. The NOT operator may either increase or decrease the number of rows returned, depending on the contents of your database.

Examples of the use of the logical operators AND and OR are shown in Sections 6.3.1 through 6.3.3. The use of NOT is shown in Section 6.3.6.

6.3.1 Query Using AND

You use the AND operator to make your request more specific. The syntax is:

```
SELECT <columnname(s)>
FROM <tablename>
WHERE <condition 1>
AND <condition 2>
...
AND <condition N>;
```

For example, if you want to retrieve the names and addresses of those donors who gave cash, live in Chicago, and donated their gift prior to 1985, enter:

```
SELECT name, address, don_date
FROM Donors
WHERE address = 'Chicago'
AND   gift = 'cash'
AND   don_date < CTOD('01/01/85');
```

Figure 6-8 shows the result table for the above query.

Figure 6-8. Chicago Cash Donors Prior to 01/01/85

name	address	don_date
B Fox	Chicago	04/03/84

The only rows returned will be those rows that meet all of the conditions specified by the WHERE clause, plus all of the AND clauses.

6.3.2 Query Using OR

Use the logical operator OR to add one or more alternate conditions to the query. The syntax is:

```
SELECT <columnname(s)>
FROM <tablename>
WHERE <condition 1>
OR <condition 2>
...
OR <condition N>;
```

For example, if you want to know the names of donors who live either in New York, Chicago, or Boston, enter:

```
SELECT name, address
FROM Donors
WHERE address = 'New York'
OR address = 'Chicago'
OR address = 'Boston';
```

The result table for the above query is shown in Figure 6-9.

Figure 6-9. Donors Living in New York, Chicago, or Boston

name	address
B Jones	New York
D Smith	Boston
R Browne	Chicago
B Fox	Chicago

You can also retrieve the above information by using the IN clause. (See Section 6.3.6 below.)

6.3.3 Query Using Both AND and OR

You can combine the logical operators AND and OR in a single query. For example, if you want a list of donors who live in either New York or Chicago and gave cash, enter:

```
SELECT  name, address
FROM  Donors
WHERE  gift = 'cash'
AND  (address = 'Chicago'
OR  address = 'New York');
```

The above query will produce the result table shown in Figure 6-10.

Figure 6-10. Cash Donors Living in New York or Chicago

name	address
B Jones	New York
B Fox	Chicago

When combining AND and OR in a single query, you should always consider the following:

CAUTION: SQL processes logical comparison operators in a predetermined order of precedence, unless you make clear the order you intend. (Order of precedence for logical comparison operators is shown in Chapter Four, Section 4.3.5.)

In view of the above caution, you must enter the above command as follows:

```
SELECT  name, address
FROM  Donors
WHERE  gift = 'cash'
AND  (address = 'New_York' OR address = 'Chicago');
```

The result table for the above query will be that shown in Figure 6-10.

As discussed in Chapter Four, Section 4.3.5, if there is any possibility that your query can be interpreted in more than one way by dBASE IV SQL, you should use parentheses. For example, in the above query the use of parentheses reduces the query to only one possible interpretation.

6.3.4 Query Using BETWEEN...AND...

The comparison operator BETWEEN...AND... can be used in a query where the rows you want to SELECT contain values within a certain range. It can be used to designate a range of numbers, letters or dates.

When combined with the NOT keyword, BETWEEN... AND ... can be used to SELECT values outside of a range rather than inside the range. (See Section 6.3.7 below for examples of the use of NOT BEWEEN...AND... .)

For example, if you want to SELECT all the art objects on exhibit whose condition is between 3 and 5 so that you can send these deteriorating pieces out for restoration, you should enter:

```
SELECT title, gallery
FROM  Exhibit
WHERE  condition BETWEEN '3' AND '5';
```

The result table for this query is shown in Figure 6-11.

Figure 6-11. Exhibits in Condition 3 Through 5

name	gallery
Le Dejeuner	C
Argenteuil	D
Archers Banquet	A
Blue Boy	B
Soldier	A

Or, you may want a list of donors who made contributions between the years 1979 and 1983. To obtain this, enter:

```
SELECT *
FROM  Donors
WHERE  don_date BETWEEN CTOD('01/01/79') AND CTOD('12/31/83');
```

The result table for this query is shown in Figure 6-12.

Figure 6-12. Donations Between 01/01/79 and 12/31/83

name	address	gift	don_date
D Smith	Boston	Argenteuil	03/05/79
R Browne	Chicago	David	09/02/81

6.3.5 Query Using LIKE

You may need information on a painting where the spelling of the title varies, and you are not sure how it is spelled in the database. Instead of attempting a spelling which may not be correct, you can query the database for the letters you are certain of, and then use the percent (%) or underscore (_) wildcard for the letters you are not certain about. (Use of the wildcards is discussed in detail in Section 4.4.2.4 in Chapter Four.)

For example, the Monet painting named "Argenteuil" could be searched for by entering:

```
SELECT *
FROM Assets
WHERE title LIKE 'Argent%';
```

The above query indicates that you do not know how many letters there are after the "Argent", and that you do not know what those letters are.

The result table for the above query would contain all art objects with titles containing zero or more letters after the "Argent."

6.3.6 Query Using IN

In Section 6.3.2 above, the OR was used to increase the scope of the WHERE clause. However, if the additional condition refers to the same column as the preceding condition, it may be easier to make a list of the conditions, and use the reserved word IN.

For example, if you are searching for donors located in any one of several specific cities, enter:

```
SELECT name, address
FROM Donors
WHERE address IN ('Boston', 'New_York', 'Chicago');
```

This will give the same result as that produced by adding ORs after the WHERE clause. The result table for the above query will be exactly the same as the result table in Figure 6-9.

6.3.7 Query Using NOT

The reserved word NOT can be used in a query with all of the above operators. The syntax is:

```
SELECT <column name(s)>
FROM <table name(s)>
WHERE NOT <condition>;
```

For example, for the queries shown in preceding sections, if you wanted to exclude the previously SELECTed rows, you would use NOT as follows in the WHERE clauses:

```
SELECT *
FROM Donors
WHERE don_date NOT BETWEEN CTOD('01/01/79') AND
    CTOD('12/31/83');

SELECT *
FROM Assets
WHERE title NOT LIKE 'Argent%';

SELECT *
FROM Donors
WHERE address NOT IN ('New York', 'Boston', 'Chicago');
```

You cannot use NOT to change the direction of an equals (=) sign. Instead, you must use one of the forms of "not equal to" supported by dBASE IV SQL, such as !=, or <>. For example:

WHERE address NOT = 'Chicago' is an illegal form.

WHERE address <> 'Chicago' is a legal form.

WHERE address != 'Chicago' is a legal form.

6.4 SUBQUERIES

A *subquery* is any SELECT statement after the initial SELECT. It is sometimes called a *subSELECT*. Subqueries are used to retrieve information necessary to satisfy the condition(s) in the main SELECT statement. (The subquery is often called the *inner SELECT*, while the main query is called the *outer SELECT*.) The syntax for a subquery is:

```
SELECT <columnname1, columnname2, ..., columnnameN>
FROM <tablename>
WHERE <expression> <comparison>
    (<subquery>)
```

where:

SELECT is an SQL reserved word. In this case, it is the start of the main query.

<columnname1, columnname2, ..., columnnameN> is the list of column names in the main query.

FROM <tablename> shows the name of the table from which the columns in the main query will be drawn.

WHERE <expression> is the expression (usually a column) whose values will be compared against the result of the subquery.

<comparison> is a comparison operator.

<subquery> is a SELECT statement that will return a value or set of values for the search condition in the main query. The subquery itself is formed in the same way the main query is formed, except that the subquery cannot contain an ORDER BY, SAVE TO TEMP, or FOR UPDATE OF clause.

dBASE IV SQL evaluates the subquery first, then evaluates the main query, applying to it the result of the subquery (except in the case of a correlated subquery, where the subquery will be evaluated for each row of the main query).

6.4.1 Subquery following IN or NOT IN

You can use a subquery (after the operators IN or NOT IN) in place of the list of column values shown in Section 6.4 above. When used this way, the result of the subquery supplies the value list needed by the main query. The syntax is:

```
WHERE <columnname> [NOT] IN (<subquery>);
```

For example, if you want the names of the artists whose works were donated, enter:

```
SELECT name
FROM  Assets
WHERE  title IN
(SELECT gift
FROM  Donors
WHERE  gift <> 'cash');
```

The result table for the above query is shown in Figure 6-13.

Figure 6-13. Donated Works

name
Rodin
Michaelangelo
Rembrandt
Monet

Using the above subquery is simpler than entering a command listing all the donated titles, even with the limited size of our sample museum database. Given any medium- or large-sized database, the task of listing all cases might be forbidding.

6.4.2 Subquery Following ANY or ALL

The reserved word ANY can be used to restrict the results returned by a subquery to those rows satisfying a comparison condition. ANY specifies that a row will be SELECTed by the main query if the comparison is true for any values returned by the subquery.

For example, you might want to remove for restoration any art objects now on exhibition if their state deteriorates to the point where it is as bad or worse than any of your present assets (with higher-numbered conditions signifying a more pressing need for restoration). In this example, the worst state among the present assets not already being restored is Condition 5.

To select the art objects on exhibition that are in need of repair, you set up a query and subquery as follows:

```
SELECT  Exhibit.title, condition
FROM  Exhibit
WHERE  title = ANY
    (SELECT  Assets.title
    FROM  Assets
    WHERE  condition >= '5'
    AND  status <> 'Restor');
```

Note that in the above query, the title column in the outer SELECT is qualified by the table name from which that column is drawn, i.e., "Exhibit.title", and the title column in the inner SELECT is also qualified by the table name from which it is drawn, i.e., "Assets.title". In this case, it is not absolutely necessary to qualify the column name by indicating the table containing the column, but it is done here for illustrative purposes. In some cases, however, it is necessary to do so.

You can't go wrong by making the table name explicit; it is a safeguard in cases where there is a possibility of doubt or confusion. The use of aliases (explained in Section 6.4.4 in this chapter), is another way of avoiding confusion when using subqueries.

Any art objects listed in the Assets Table that are now on exhibit in Condition 5 or greater will appear in the result table as shown in Figure 6-14.

Figure 6-14. Art Objects Needing Restoration

title	condition
Archers Banquet	5

By contrast, when you use the reserved word ALL with a subquery, a row will be returned only if the comparison is true for all values returned by the subquery.

For example, you might want to renovate the pieces in the exhibition only if they are in worse condition than those on loan. To find out if there are any such pieces, enter:

```
SELECT title
FROM  Exhibit
    WHERE  condition > ALL
    (SELECT condition
    FROM  Assets
    WHERE  status = 'On Loan');
```

The result table is given in Figure 6-15. It shows that only the exhibit "Archers Banquet" is in worse condition than any of the art objects on loan.

Figure 6-15. Exhibited Art Objects in Worse Condition Than Those on Loan

title
Archers Banquet

6.4.3 Correlated Subqueries

In some subqueries, the subquery is executed once, and the system passes the resulting value to the main query where it is used by the WHERE clause. You can also have a subquery that is executed repeatedly: once for each row considered for selection by the main query. This is called a *correlated subquery*.

For example, you might want to know which titles on exhibit are valued above the average for the gallery in which they are displayed. You can set up a correlated subquery to calculate this. (Correlated subqueries usually use aliases, explained in Section 6.4.4.) To do so, you would enter:

```
SELECT title, gallery, value_code
FROM  Exhibit
WHERE  value_code >
(<average value in title's gallery>);
```

where:

(<average value in title's gallery>) is a subquery that computes the average value in a gallery after the main query "tells" the subquery the gallery's identification letter.

Since the above query will refer to the same table in both the main query and the subquery, the best way to handle it is with the help of an alias name for the table. This allows you to use the Exhibit Table in the subquery for one purpose (to compute the average value of the objects in the gallery), and using the same Exhibit Table in the main query for a different purpose (to pick out the value of individual objects in a gallery and test them against the average value).

6.4.4 Subquery Using Aliases

The query "Which titles on exhibit are valued above the average for the gallery in which they are displayed?" (presented in Section 6.4.3) is best handled by assigning the alias EX1 to the Exhibit Table in the main query, and the alias EX2 to the Exhibit Table in the subquery.

After you assign the aliases, the complete query is:

```
SELECT  title, gallery, value_code
FROM  Exhibit Ex1
WHERE  value_code >
      (SELECT  AVG(value_code)
      FROM  Exhibit Ex2
      WHERE  Ex1.gallery = Ex2.gallery);
```

where:

AVG(value_code) is an aggregate function which (in this case) computes an average value code for each gallery. (All aggregate functions supported by dBASE IV SQL are defined and illustrated in Chapter Seven.)

Ex1 is an alias for the table of Exhibit in the main query.

Ex2 is an alias for the table of Exhibit in the subquery.

The subquery returns the average of the value_code for the gallery in which the painting (in the current row of the Ex1 copy of the Exhibit Table) is displayed. This average is obtained from the Ex2 copy of the Exhibit Table. This average is compared with the value_code of the painting (in the current row of the Ex1 copy of the Exhibit Table) to determine whether or not the values of title, gallery, and value_code will occur in the result table.

The result table for the above query is shown in Figure 6-16.

Figure 6-16. Exhibited Pieces with Value Codes Above the Average for Gallery

title	gallery	value_code
Nightwatch	A	12.00
Blue Boy	B	4.20
Le Dejeuner	C	6.50
Impression	D	2.80
Argenteuil	D	3.00

Note that the result table does not show the average for each gallery. This is because the average is merely used in the computation; it does not appear as one of the columns to be displayed. It cannot be listed as a column to be displayed because the displayed columns all list single-row values, whereas AVG(value_code) results in a value for a group of rows (one value per gallery). These two cannot be mixed in a SELECT statement unless the row-value columns are each referred to in a GROUP BY command.

Obviously, it would not be possible to show the average for each gallery, as well as the "above average" art objects, all in the same table. To show the average value for each gallery requires the following SELECT statement:

```
SELECT gallery, AVG(value_code)
FROM   Exhibit
GROUP BY gallery;
```

The SQL aggregate function AVG(value) in the above query is an SQL aggregate function that will return one value—the average value—for each gallery. (Aggregate functions are discussed in Chapter Seven.)

The result table for the above query is shown in Figure 6-17.

Figure 6-17. Average Value Code for Galleries

gallery	AVG(value_code)
A	6.38
B	3.48
C	4.40
D	2.79

6.4.5 Subquery Following EXISTS or NOT EXISTS

The reserved words EXISTS and NOT EXISTS are usually used with a correlated subquery, as explained in Section 6.4.3 above.

You can use EXISTS wherever the IN comparison operator can be used, but the converse is not true.

For example, you could use EXISTS in the example shown in Section 6.4.1, and get the same result as if you used IN. To do so, enter:

```
SELECT name
FROM   Assets
WHERE  EXISTS

       (SELECT gift
       FROM   Donors
       WHERE  Assets.title = gift;
```

The result table for the above query will be exactly the same as that shown in Figure 6-13 above.

6.4.6 Multiple Subqueries in the Same Query

dBASE IV SQL allows subqueries to be nested within each other. However, in most cases *nested subqueries*, or *nested SELECTs*, as these are called, become hard to interpret (or to enter correctly) after the first two or three. You might find it more efficient to break the group down into a series of queries, each containing only one or two subqueries. dBASE IV will process the innermost subquery first, then the next higher up, and so on until it gets to the main query for processing.

For example, list the names of those donors who gave an art object that is now in a gallery containing a Ter Borch. The following query, containing three nested subqueries, will return the correct result:

```
SELECT name
    FROM  Donors
        WHERE  EXISTS
            (SELECT  gallery
            FROM     Exhibit E1
            WHERE    Donors.gift = E1.title
            AND EXISTS
                (SELECT Assets.title, gallery
                FROM Exhibit E2
                WHERE E2.gallery  = E1.gallery
                AND  E2.title = Assets.title
                AND  Assets.name = 'Ter Borch'));
```

The result table for the above query is shown in Figure 6-18.

Figure 6-18. Donations in the Same Gallery with a Ter Borch

name
R Black

You can continue to add qualifications to the query by adding subqueries, but to do so might have little more than exercise value. It would probably be more efficient (after this point) to write a succession of simpler queries, especially since processing time increases rapidly as the number of subqueries increases.

There is an endless variety of possibilities for creating queries and subqueries. This chapter has illustrated the most common usages. Succeeding chapters will illustrate more complex forms, and will incorporate some of the permitted dBASE commands and functions into the SQL statements.

7

Aggregate Functions, Memory Variables, and dBASE IV Functions

In this chapter you will become acquainted with aggregate functions, memory variables, and dBASE IV functions that can be used in SQL.

Aggregate functions are used in SELECT statements to indicate the column(s) SELECTed when you want to get summary values computed over groups of rows.

You can use memory variables and dBASE IV functions (with certain exceptions) in the WHERE clauses of SQL SELECT, INSERT, DELETE, and UPDATE commands. In the cases of INSERT and UPDATE, memory variables and dBASE IV functions frequently provide the values to be INSERTed and the values for UPDATE. In Chapter Eleven, you will see the utility of memory variables in embedded SQL, where values rom tables can be SELECTed INTO and FETCHed INTO memory variables.

7.1 AGGREGATE FUNCTIONS: AVERAGE, COUNT, MIN, MAX, SUM

Certain SQL commands operate on a group of rows, and return a single value. These are called *aggregate* (or *built-in*, or *group*) *functions*, and are listed in Figure 7-1.

Figure 7-1. The Aggregate Functions

Function	Description
AVG	operates on a group of rows and obtains an average value for the group.
COUNT (DISTINCT<column name>	counts the number of rows having distinct values in a specified column, eliminating duplicates, and returns a single value.
COUNT(*)	counts the number of rows in a table, and returns a single value, without eliminating duplicates.
MAX	selects and returns the highest column value in a group of rows.
MIN	selects and returns the lowest column value in a group of rows.
SUM	adds the specified column values in a group of rows, and returns a single value.

The aggregate function is placed in the SELECT command. The result is displayed in the form of a table with a single column containing one row.

For example, to obtain the SUM of all salaries in the Employee Table, enter:

```
SELECT SUM(salary)
FROM   Emp;
```

The result table will contain a single value, such as the following:

SUM 1
52,363.00

Aggregate functions can appear in the main query or in a subquery. They may also be used in conjunction with comparison operators and value expressions.

In a query you cannot mix individual and aggregated values. There are two ways to aggregate values: aggregate functions and GROUP BY. Thus, if an aggregate function is applied to one of the columns SELECTed, then an aggregate function (not necessarily the same aggregate function) must be applied to all other columns SELECTed—unless the query contains a GROUP BY clause. You can include an individual value column in the SELECT if you are GROUPing BY that column.

For example, the following query will give you an error message:

```
SELECT title, AVG(salary)
FROM   Emp;
```

But you will get a valid result with this query:

```
SELECT  title, AVG(salary)
FROM   Emp
GROUP BY  title;
```

You can use more than one aggregate function in a SELECT statement. For example, the following query combines all six functions:

```
SELECT AVG(salary), MIN(salary), MAX(salary), SUM(salary),
     COUNT(DISTINCT salary), COUNT(*)
FROM   Employee;
```

The above command will return the average, minimum and maximum salary, the total of all salaries, the number of different salaries (eliminating duplicates), and the number of salaries listed (which will be the number of rows in the Employee Table, whether or not every row has an entry in the salary column).

The syntax and rules for using each of the dBASE IV SQL aggregate functions are explained in the sections that follow.

7.1.1 How to Use the Average (AVG) Function

If the AVG function is used, then the column to which it is applied must not be of character or logical datatype. The result of AVG always contains two decimal places. To eliminate duplicate values before averaging, you can use the DISTINCT keyword. (See Section 7.1.2.)

For example, to find the average salary of all employees of the company, enter:

```
SELECT AVG(salary)
FROM   Emp;
```

The result will be a table with one column and one row, such as:

AVG
3025.45

You could also find the average of a specified group or a number of groups, all by using one command. For example, if you want to find the average salary of accountants, enter:

```
SELECT AVG(salary)
FROM   Emp
WHERE  title = 'accountant';
```

If you want to find the average of each of several types of classifications within a column, you could enter several individual queries—but it is more efficient to do it with one query, using both the AVG function and the GROUP BY clause.

For example, you can find the average salary of many different job classifications, by entering:

```
SELECT title, AVG(salary)
FROM    Emp
GROUP BY  title;
```

The result will be in the following form:

title	AVG1
Secretary	900
Accountant	1500
Salesman	2000

7.1.2 How to Use The COUNT (DISTINCT <column name>) Function

The COUNT function must be followed by the specification DISTINCT and a column name, or by an asterisk (*). (COUNT DISTINCT <column name>) eliminates duplicate rows. (Note that the same is not true of COUNT(*), which is discussed in Section 7.1.3.) Specifically, the rows that duplicate a column value already COUNTed are eliminated before the function is applied.

For example, if you need to know how many suppliers you are currently using, you enter:

```
SELECT COUNT (DISTINCT <name>)
FROM  Supplier;
```

The result will be a number indicating the number of different supplier names occuring in the name column of the Supplier Table. All duplicate entries for any one supplier will be eliminated before the COUNT(DISTINCT) function is applied.

7.1.3 COUNT(*)

By contrast with COUNT(DISTINCT), if you were to query the Supplier Table with COUNT(*), it would list the total number of supplier names in the table—disregarding the fact that some suppliers may supply several parts, and thus may be listed more than once. Therefore, you can get a very different result by using COUNT(*) than by using COUNT(DISTINCT ( )).

7.1.4 SUM

The SUM function adds the values in the specified column, and, as with all aggregate functions, returns a single value. The column must contain NUMERIC values. The DISTINCT keyword can be used with SUM to eliminate duplicate values.

You can use the SUM function, for example, to find the total company expenditure for salaries. Enter:

```
SELECT  SUM(salary)
FROM    Emp;
```

Here again, as illustrated in Section 7.1, you cannot mix individual values with aggregate values in the same SELECT statement, unless you are GROUPing BY the individual values. For example, if you want to find the total expenditure for each classification of employee, the following query is illegal, and will give you an error message:

```
SELECT title, SUM(salary)
FROM   Emp;
```

The following query is legal, and will give you a result table showing the SUM of salaries for each job title in your Employee Table:

```
SELECT title, SUM(salary)
FROM   Emp
GROUP BY title;
```

7.1.5 MAX and MIN

The MAX function returns the largest value in a column; the MIN function returns the smallest value in a column. The specification DISTINCT is meaningless with these two functions, and therefore should not be used.

As an example, you can determine the highest-priced part listed by the suppliers in your Supplier Table by entering:

```
SELECT part_name, MAX(price)
FROM   Supplier
GROUP BY  part_name;
```

The above query will tell you the price of the most expensive part for each different part name.

7.2 MEMORY VARIABLES

Memory variables in dBASE IV are similar to variables in other programming languages, except that their type is determined by storing in them a value of a certain type.

The number of memory variables allowed in dBASE IV is 2048, an increase from the limit of 256 allowed in previous versions of dBASE products. The amount of space for memory variables is allocated when dBASE IV starts up. Therefore, you need to place two commands in the config.db file to control the number of memory variables you can have and the space allocated for them. Enter these commands as follows:

mvarsize=nn

mvcount=cc

where:

nn is a number between 1 and 64, with 6 being the default. It is the amount of space in K bytes allocated for memory variables.

cc is a number between 256 and 2048, which is the number of memory variable "slots" that are to be maintained. Memory variables and each array element occupy one of these slots.

Memory variables are useful for holding values while they are checked for validity, and before they are entered in a database table. Memory variables can also be used to transfer values to subprograms or procedures, as in the case of the parameter list of a DO statement.

Another use of memory variables is as substitutes for values in an SQL statement. See Section 7.2.4 for a discussion of the use of memory variables in WHERE clauses.

There are two formats for storing a value in a memory variable. One is the STORE command, with the following format:

STORE <expression> TO <memory variable list>

where:

<expression> is a number, or a string of characters surrounded by single or double quotes, or .T., or .F. for the logical values True or False, respectively.

<memory variable list> is a list of memory variable names. All of the memory variables in the list will have the expression value stored in them.

The other format for storing a value in a memory variable is:

<memory variable name> = <expression>

where:

<memory variable name> is the name given to some memory variable.

<expression> is the same as in the case of the STORE command.

Space is saved for the memory variables at the time that a value is stored in the memory variable.

SQLCNT and SQLCODE are two very useful memory variables. Their values are determined by the status of the last SQL operation. See Section 11.1.

7.2.1 Arrays of Memory Variables

In dBASE IV, arrays of memory variables can be declared by means of the DECLARE command:

DECLARE <array name>[<integer>[,<integer>]]

(Note that the outer square brackets are not optional.)

where:

<array name> is the name you want to give to your array.

<integer> is an integer such as 10 or 20.

You can declare several arrays, separated by commas, with a DECLARE command. For example:

DECLARE m_date[30,12], m_employee[40], m_parts[50]

The above command tells dBASE IV to save space for the following: an ARRAY 30 by 12 of memory variables named m_date, an ARRAY of 40 memory variables named m_employee, and an ARRAY of 50 memory variables named m_parts.

Only one- and two-dimensional arrays are allowed. The type of the memory variables in an array can vary for members of the array, and is determined by substitution as in the case of ordinary memory variables.

For example, you can enter:

```
DECLARE m_dates[25], m_names[2,13], m_ss_nos[50]
```

or

```
DECLARE m_dates[30,15],m_nuggets[30,30]
```

The maximum size of an ARRAY is 1023. For example you cannot have ARRAY m_names[40,40], since that would reserve 1600 locations, exceeding the limit of 1023.

ARRAY type memory varaibles may be indexed by other memory variables, or by any valid expression whose result falls within the limits of the ARRAY.

7.2.2 PUBLIC and PRIVATE Memory Variables

PUBLIC memory variables are global and can be used by any other program. They are not released when the program ends. The format for PUBLIC is:

```
PUBLIC <memory variable list>/ARRAY <array definition list>
```

where:

<memory variable list> is a list of memory variables.

<array definition list> is a list of array variables.

PRIVATE memory variables can have the same names as the memory variables in a calling program, without affecting the variables in the calling program. When control is returned to the calling program, the PRIVATE memory variables are RELEASed.

The format for PRIVATE is the same as the format for PUBLIC, except that PRIVATE can also be declared with the following format:

```
PRIVATE ALL [LIKE/EXCEPT <skeleton>]
```

Further details on LIKE, EXCEPT, and skeleton are given in Section 7.2.3 below.

7.2.3 The CLEAR MEMORY, RELEASE, SAVE, and RESTORE Commands

Since memory variables tend to pile up in memory, there are several ways of removing them. They can simply be removed by means of the CLEAR MEMORY and RELEASE commands, or they can be SAVEd to a file and RESTORED from the file at a later time.

The CLEAR MEMORY command releases all memory variables.

The RELEASE command is more selective. The format for RELEASE is:

RELEASE <memory variable list> /[ALL [LIKE/EXCEPT<skeleton>]]

where:

<memory variable list> is a list of memory variables to be released.

<skeleton> is a part of a character string, with wildcards replacing some of the letters. LIKE and EXCEPT allow you to use a skeleton name with the question mark (?) and asterisk (*) wild cards, where ? stands for one unknown letter, and * stands for an unknown character string.

In interactive dBASE IV, RELEASE ALL removes all memory variables. In programs, it only removes PRIVATE memory variables. You cannot use RELEASE ALL in dBASE/SQL mode.

The SAVE command has the following format:

SAVE TO <filename> [ALL LIKE/EXCEPT <skeleton>]

where:

<filename> is the name of a file in the current directory where the memory variables are to be SAVEd. If no file extension is given, dBASE IV adds the file extension .mem to the file name.

If [ALL LIKE/EXCEPT <skeleton>] is omitted, all memory variables are SAVEd.

[ALL LIKE/EXCEPT <skeleton>] allows the use of wild cards, as in the case of RELEASE.

The RESTORE command has the format:

RESTORE FROM <filename> [ADDITIVE]

where:

<filename> is the name of a file where memory variables have been SAVEd. If a file name extension is omitted, the file name extension is assumed to be .mem.

ADDITIVE is used to keep all of the current memory variables. If ADDITIVE does not appear, then all current memory variables are RELEASEd upon performance of the RESTORE command.

7.2.4 Using Memory Variables in dBASE IV SQL WHERE Clauses

Memory variables can be used anywhere in SQL statements that you could use a constant. As an example, see the following SELECT statement:

```
SELECT name
FROM   Emp
WHERE  city = 'Chicago';
```

You could replace 'Chicago' in the WHERE clause above with a character string-type memory variable which has 'Chicago' stored in it, as in the following example:

```
m_city = 'Chicago'

SELECT  name
FROM    Emp
WHERE   city = m_city;
```

However, you cannot use memory variables in any of the data definition statements, such as CREATE TABLE or CREATE INDEX.

Another way in which memory variables can be used in dBASE IV SQL is in the INSERT statement. Memory variables can be used in an INSERT for the VALUES. For example:

```
INSERT INTO Sales (Emp_id,Item,No_sold)
VALUES (m_id,m_item,10);
```

where:

m_id and m_item are memory variables containing the values you want to INSERT into the Sales Table.

7.3 DBASE FUNCTIONS IN DBASE IV SQL MODE

dBASE IV provides functions which operate on memory variables, and can be used in SQL statements. The functions treated here are divided into four groups: arithmetic, date and time, character string, and SOUNDEX. The rest of the dBASE IV functions appear in Appendix C.

In the following sections, expC and expN will stand for expressions or memory variables of CHARacter type and NUMeric type respectively.

7.3.1 Arithmetic Functions

Arithmetic functions are useful in engineering applications, and for modifying memory variables for comparisons. There are trigonometric functions such as SIN() and COS(), which return the sine and cosine of angles in radians; and there are other useful functions such as ABS(), which returns the absolute value of a numeric variable. The complete list of arithmetic functions available in dBASE IV /SQL mode is shown in Figure 7-2.

Figure 7-2. Arithmetic Functions

Function	Description
ABS()	Absolute value
ACOS()	Returns arc cosine in radians
ASIN()	Returns arc sine in radians
ATAN()	Returns arc tangent in radians
ATN2(<expN1>,<expN2>)	Where <expN1> is a cosine of a particular angle, and <expN2> is the sine of a particular angle. ATN2() returns a floating point number representing the angle in radians in the range -PI() to PI().
CEILING()	Smallest integer greater than or equal to value
COS()	Cosine
DTOR()	Converts degrees to radians
EXP()	e to the x power
FIXED()	Converts floating point to fixed point
FLOAT()	Converts fixed point to floating point
FLOOR()	Largest integer less than
INT()	Converts to integer by truncating decimals
LOG(<expN>)	Natural logarithm to base e where <expN> is a numeric like 2.45
LOG10()	Logarithm to base 10
MOD(<expN1>,<expN2>)	Divides <expN1> by <expN2> and returns the largest integer less than or equal to the remainder with the sign of <expN2>
PI()	Circumference of a circle dividedby the diameter
RAND([<expN>])	Where <expN> is an integer. RAND() returns a random number between 0.0 and 1.0. If <expN> is used, a new random number sequence is started. Otherwise, RAND() returns the next number in the current random number sequence. For more details, see your Language Reference manual.
ROUND(<expN1>,<expN2>)	Rounds off <expN1> to <expN2> decimal places
RTOD()	Radians to degrees
SIGN()	Returns the sign of a number
SIN(<expN>)	Returns sine from angle in radians
SQRT()	Square root
TAN()	Returns tangent from angle in radians

7.3.2 Date and Time Functions

The date and time functions provided by dBASE IV have many uses. Among these are finding rows in tables where a date column is within a certain range. The date data type has a form which is not easy to work with, because it is the number of days since some fixed beginning date. Therefore, there are functions for converting date to various character formats, and there are other functions for converting character format dates to the date data type. The entire list of these functions appears in Figure 7-3.

Figure 7-3. Date and Time Functions

Function	Description
CDOW()	Day of week
CMONTH(	Returns name of month from a date
CTOD()	Character to date conversion
DATE()	System date
DAY()	Number of the day of the month
DMY()	Converts to DD/Mon/YY
DOW()	Day of the week
DTOC()	Date to character string format MM/DD/YY
DTOS	Returns the ANSI date
MDY()	Converts date to format Mon DD YY
MONTH()	Returns number of month in a date
TIME()	Returns system clock time in the format hh:mm:ss
YEAR()	Returns year from date expression

7.3.3 CHARacter String Functions

CHARacter string functions are useful for manipulating strings. dBASE IV provides functions for converting numeric data types to character data types and vice versa, and for manipulating CHARacter strings by inserting CHARacter strings in other CHARacter strings, or by removing substrings. The entire list of these functions is contained in Figure 7-4.

Figure 7-4. Character String Functions

Function	Description
ASC()	Returns ASCII value of leftmost character in a character string
AT(<expC>,<expC>)	Returns beginning position of first character string in second character string
CHR(<expN>)	Returns a character from an ASCII code value
LEFT(<expC>,<expN>)	Returns <expN> characters from a character string, <expC> starting with the first character on the left
LEN(<expC>)	Returns the number of characters in a character string where <expC> is either a character string or a character type memory variable
LOWER()	Converts a character string to all lower case letters
LTRIM()	Removes leading blanks from a character string
REPLICATE(<expC>, <expN>)	Replicates the character string <expC> <expN> times
RIGHT(<expC>,<expN>)	Returns the last <expN> characters from the right of the character string <expC>
RTRIM(<expC>)	Removes trailing blanks from the character string <expC>
SPACE(<expN>)	Returns <expN> blanks as a character string
STR(<expN>[,<length>] [,<decimal places>])	Converts the number <expN> to a character string of length <length> with <decimal places> decimal places. If you specify length less than the number of digits to the left of the decimal, dBASE IV returns asterisks.
STUFF(<expC1>,<expC2>) <start position>, <number of characters>, <expC2>)	Returns <expC1> with <number of characters> removed starting at <start position> and replaced with <expC2>
SUBSTR(<expC>, <starting position> [,<number of characters>])	Returns <number of characters> starting at the <starting position> from the character string <expC>.
TRIM(<expC>)	Returns <expC> with trailing blanks removed
UPPER(<expC>)	Returns <expC> with all lower case letters converted to upper case.
VAL(<expC>)	Converts the character string <expC> to a number. If <expC> is non-numeric, zero will be returned.

7.3.4 SOUNDEX Functions

SOUNDEX functions are used to find CHARacter strings which sound alike but are spelled differently. dBASE IV uses a special algorithm for finding SOUNDEX codes, which are computed by the SOUNDEX function. dBASE IV also provides a function for finding the difference in the SOUNDEX code between two different character strings. The SOUNDEX functions appear in Figure 7-5.

Figure 7-5. Soundex Functions

Function	Description
SOUNDEX(<expC>)	SOUNDEX provides a 4-character code by means of the following algorithm: 1. Retain the first letter of the character string and drop all occurrences of a, e, h, i, o, u, w, and y. 2. Assign numbers to the remaining letters according to the following table: b f p v — 1 c g j k q s x z — 2 d t — 3 l — 4 m n — 5 r — 6 3. If two or more characters with the same code were adjacent before step 1, omit all but the first. 4. If there are more than 3 digits, drop all but the first three. If there are less than three digits, add zeros to give three digits.
DIFFERENCE(<expC1>,<expC2>)	Where <expC1> and <expC2> are two character strings. The outcome of the DIFFERENCE() is an integer between (and including) zero and four. If the two character strings match, DIFFERENCE() returns four. If no character of <expC1> matches a character of <expC2>, DIFFERENCE() returns zero. For more details, refer to your *Language Reference* manual.

7.3.5 Transaction Functions

There are two functions related to transactions that can be used in an SQL program, but cannot be used in an SQL statement. They are shown in Figure 7-6.

Figure 7-6. Transaction Functions

Function	Description
COMPLETED()	When a BEGIN TRANSACTION command has been executed, and until an END TRANSACTION command is executed, this function returns .F. Otherwise, COMPLETED() returns .T.
ROLLBACK()	Ordinarily, ROLLBACK() returns .T. When a ROLLBACK command is executed, the ROLLBACK() function returns .F. until the ROLLBACK is successfully completed.

7.4 COMMENT

The functions and memory variables presented in this chapter are especially useful in dBASE IV embedded SQL. Some of these uses are illustrated in Chapter Eleven, which deals with embedded SQL.

8

Operations on Tables

This chapter treats the operations that can be performed on tables in terms of the relational algebra upon which these operations are based. It discusses and illustrates projection, Boolean (set) operators, and joins. You can find more information on this subject in the references at the end of this chapter. The tables in Figures 8.1, 8.2, and 8.3 will be used to illustrate some of the examples in this chapter.

Figure 8-1. Salesman Table

Note: This table was created with the following column specifications:

id_no	CHAR(4)
name	CHAR(15)
address	CHAR(20)
phone	CHAR(8)

id_no	**name**	**address**	**phone**
1000	Joe James	1201 Adams St.	832 4509
1001	Bill Cray	1011 Marion St.	486 2100
1002	John Smith	1812 Kearney St.	211 9875

Figure 8-2. Sales Table

Note: This table was created with the following column specifications:

id_no	CHAR(4)
item	CHAR(10)
no_sold	NUMERIC(2,0)

id_no	item	no_sold
1001	Furnace	50
1000	Radio	10
1000	Stove	5
1001	Stove	6

Figure 8-3. Join of Salesman & Sales Tables on id_no

id_no	name	address	phone	item	no_sold
1000	Joe James	1201 Adams St	832 4509	Radio	10
1000	Joe James	1201 Adams St.	832 4509	Stove	5
1001	Bill Cray	1011 Marion St.	486 2100	Furnace	50
1001	Bill Cray	1011 Marion St.	486 2100	Stove	6

8.1 PROJECTION

Projection is a simple operation on a table whereby you select a subset of the columns. In SQL queries the columns to be selected are always named immediately following the SELECT. What is actually happening when you list these columns is that you are choosing the projection that you want displayed in the result table.

When you SELECT <column list> FROM <table> with the SQL SELECT command, you are "projecting the <table> on the <column list>." For example, you may project the above join of the Sales and Salesman Tables on the columns called name, item, and no_sold to obtain the table shown in Figure 8-4.

Figure 8-4. Projection of the Join of Salesman & Sales Tables

name	item	no_sold
Joe James	Radio	10
Joe James	Stove	5
Bill Cray	Furnace	50
Bill Cray	Stove	6

8.2 SET OPERATIONS

The set operations on tables are *union, intersection,* and *minus*. Each of these operates on two tables where all the column data types match.

The *union* of two tables is a table containing all the rows of both the tables you started with. The *intersection* of two tables is a table containing only the rows the two tables have in common. One table *minus* another table is the table you get by taking all the rows in the first table which are not in the second table.

dBASE IV SQL has a reserved word, UNION, for the union of two result tables, but does not have any intersection or minus. However, union, intersection and minus can all be achieved by use of the logical connectors AND, OR, and NOT, and the logical quantifier EXISTS with a subquery, in the WHERE clause. The basics of AND, OR, and NOT have been explained in Chapter Four. EXISTS with subqueries was discussed in Chapter Six.

For an example of union, intersection, and minus, consider the two classroom tables in Figures 8-5 and 8-6.

Figure 8-5. Classes1

Note: This table was created with the following column specifications:

subject	CHAR(10)
number	NUMERIC(3,0)
room	NUMERIC(3,0)
starts	CHAR(5)
ends	CHAR(5)
credits	NUMERIC(1,0)

subject	number	room	starts	ends	credits
dBASE	100	102	10:00	10:50	5
Physics	105	103	14:00	14:50	3
Math	103	205	16:00	17:30	4
French	260	415	15:00	16:30	5

Figure 8-6. Classes2

Note: This table was created with the following column specifications:

subject	CHAR(10)
number	NUMERIC(3,0)
room	NUMERIC(3,0)
starts	CHAR(5)
ends	CHAR(5)
credits	NUMERIC(1,0)

subject	number	room	starts	ends	credits
Chemistry	300	117	09:00	10:30	4
dBASE	100	102	10:00	10:50	5
Math	103	205	16:00	17:30	4
Geology	204	318	13:00	13:50	3

Because dBASEIV does not have a time, datatype, starts, and ends are character fields of width five.

The union of the two tables is shown in Figure 8-7.

Figure 8-7. Classes1 Union Classes2

subject	number	room	starts	ends	credits
dBASE	100	102	10:00	10:50	5
Physics	105	103	14:00	14:50	3
Math	103	205	16:00	17:30	4
French	260	415	15:00	16:30	5
Chemistry	300	117	9:00	10:30	4
Geology	204	318	13:00	13:50	3

Classes1 UNION Classes2 can be obtained by the following SELECTstatement:

```
SELECT *
FROM Classes1
UNION
SELECT *
FROM Classes2
```

The intersection of the two tables in Figures 8-5 and 8-6 is shown in Figure 8-8.

Figure 8-8. Classes1 Intersection Classes2

subject	number	room	starts	ends	credits
dBASE	100	102	10:00	10:50	5
Math	103	205	16:00	17:30	4

Classes1 intersection Classes2 may be obtained by means of the following SELECT statement:

```
SELECT *
FROM Classes1
WHERE EXISTS
    (SELECT *
    FROM Classes2
    WHERE Classes2.subject = Classes1.subject
    AND Classes2.number = Classes1.number
    AND Classes2.room = Classes1.room
    AND Classes2.starts = Classes1.starts
    AND Classes2.ends = Classes1.ends
    AND Classes2.credits = Classes1.credits);
```

The table in Figure 8-5 minus the table in Figure 8-6 is shown in Figure 8-9.

Figure 8-9. Classes1 Minus Classes2

subject	number	room	starts	ends	credits
Physics	105	103	14:00	14:50	3
French	260	415	15:00	16:30	5

Classes1 minus Classes2 can be obtained by means of the following SELECT statement:

```
SELECT *
FROM Classes1
WHERE NOT EXISTS
    (SELECT *
    FROM Classes2
    WHERE Classes2.subject = Classes1.subject
    AND Classes2.number = Classes1.number
    AND Classes2.room = Classes1.room
    AND Classes2.starts = Classes1.starts
    AND Classes2.ends = Classes1.ends
    AND Classes2.credits = Classes1.credits);
```

Given two result tables obtained from the same table (with each result table derived from a SELECT statement having at least one condition in the WHERE clause), the union, intersection, and difference can be obtained by use of OR, AND, and NOT applied to the conditions in the WHERE clauses. Thus, the union of the two result tables can be obtained by combining the conditions for the two result tables with an OR. The intersection of the two result tables can be obtained by combining the conditions with an AND, and the difference of the two result tables can be obtained by combining the conditions with an AND NOT.

For example, using the Sales Table of Figure 8-2, if you have the two queries:

```
SELECT *
FROM Sales
WHERE id_no = 1000;
```

and

```
SELECT *
FROM Sales
WHERE item = 'stove';
```

then you can obtain the UNION of the result tables by the following query:

```
SELECT *
FROM Sales
WHERE id_no = 1000 OR item = 'stove';
```

You can obtain the intersection of the two result tables with the query:

```
SELECT *
FROM Sales
WHERE id_no = 1000 AND item = 'stove';
```

You can obtain the difference of the two result tables with the query:

```
SELECT *
FROM Sales
WHERE id_no = 1000 AND NOT item = 'stove';
```

8.3 JOINS

A *key* is a column (or set of columns) in a table which determines the other columns. A *foreign key* is a column or set of columns in a table which is a key in some other table. For more details about keys, see Chapter Twelve.

If you have two tables related by a key in one table, which is a foreign key in the other, you can combine the two tables on the basis of the key and foreign key. You simply need to concatenate or join the rows of the table containing the foreign key with the rows of the table containing the key, where the key and the foreign key match. If the key and the foreign key are the only columns the two tables have in common, the resulting table is called the *natural join* or the *join on <name of key column>*. The natural join is useful for combining tables on common columns, not just key columns. See Section 8.3.2 for more discussion of the natural join.

For example, the join on id_no of the Salesman and Sales Tables in Figures 8-1 and 8-2, respectively, is shown in Figure 8-3.

Notice that, since there is no row in the Sales Table with id_no equal to 1002, there is no row in the join table with that id_no either.

The *join*, then, is an operation which is performed on two or more tables in a relational database. Joining tables is an operation in the relational algebra which you can use to bring the information from two or more tables together in a result table. There are many types of joins: *equijoins, natural joins, theta joins,* and *self joins*. All of these are useful, and will be treated in the sections that follow.

8.3.1 Equijoins

Given two tables, and a selected pair of columns (one from each of the two tables), such that both members of the pair have the same data type, you can form a new table by concatenating those rows of the two tables where the selected column in the first table equals the selected column in the second table. The resulting table is called the equijoin (on the pair of columns). For example, you can form the equijoin of the Salesman Table in Figure 8-1 and the Sales Table in Figure 8-2 on the pair of id_no columns. The result is shown in Figure 8-10:

Figure 8-10. Equijoin of Salesman and Sales Tables on id_no

id_no	name	address	phone	id_no	item	no_sold
1001	Bill Cray	1011 Marion St.	486 2100	1001	Furnace	50
1000	Joe James	1201 Adams St.	832 4509	1000	Radio	10
1000	Joe James	1201 Adams St.	832 4509	1000	Stove	5
1001	Bill Cray	1011 Marion St.	486 2100	1001	Stove	6

Notice that the id_no column occurs twice, once for its occurrence in the Salesman table and once for its occurrence in the Sales table. Also notice that the row of the Salesman table with John Smith in it never occurs in the result table at all since there is no occurrence of id_no equal to 1002 in the Sales Table.

The SQL query for the above equijoin result table is:

```
SELECT *
FROM Salesman, Sales
WHERE Salesman.id_no = Sales.id_no;
```

General rules for joins are:

- The selected pair of columns being joined on need not have the same name.
- There can be more than one selected pair of columns to be joined on.
- By using more selected pairs, there can be more than two tables joined.

A join query (except in the case of the Cartesian product described in the next paragraph) always has at least one condition in the WHERE clause which involves columns from two tables. Whenever there is such a condition, a join is being performed.

The *Cartesian product* of two tables is a table whose columns are the union of the columns in both of the tables, and whose rows are the concatenation of every row of the second table with every row of the first table.

For example the Cartesian product of the Salesman Table (Figure 8-1) with the Sales Table (Figure 8-2) is shown in Figure 8-11.

Figure 8-11. Cartesian Product of Salesman Table with Sales Table

id_no	name	address	phone	id_no	item	no_sold
1000	Joe James	1201 Adams St.	832 4509	1001	Furnace	50
1000	Joe James	1201 Adams St.	832 4509	1000	Radio	10
1000	Joe James	1201 Adams St.	832 4509	1000	Stove	5
1000	Joe James	1201 Adams St.	832 4509	1001	Stove	6
1001	Bill Cray	1011 Marion St.	486 2100	1001	Furnace	50
1001	Bill Cray	1011 Marion St.	486 2100	1000	Radio	10
1001	Bill Cray	1011 Marion St.	486 2100	1000	Stove	5
1001	Bill Cray	1011 Marion St.	486 2100	1001	Stove	6
1002	John Smith	1812 Kearney St.	211 9875	1001	Furnace	50
1002	John Smith	1812 Kearney St.	211 9875	1000	Radio	10
1002	John Smith	1812 Kearney St.	211 9875	1000	Stove	5
1002	John Smith	1812 Kearney St.	211 9875	1001	Stove	6

It is exceedingly unlikely that you will ever want the Cartesian product. However, we include it—for conceptual purposes—as an extreme case of the equijoin. The SQL SELECT statement to obtain the Cartesian product in Figure 8-11 is:

```
SELECT *
FROM Salesman, Sales;
```

8.3.2 Natural Joins

You can use the natural join to bring tables together on columns which they have in common. The *natural join* is like the equijoin except that:

- The pairs of columns joined on must have the same name.
- All pairs of columns with the same name must be joined on.
- Duplicate columns must be eliminated from the result.

For example, the natural join of the Salesman Table in Figure 8-1 and the Sales Table in Figure 8-2 is shown in Figure 8-12.

Figure 8-12. Join of Salesman and Sales Tables on id_no

id_no	name	address	phone	item	no_sold
1000	Joe James	1201 Adams St.	832 4509	Radio	10
1000	Joe James	1201 Adams St.	832 4509	Stove	5
1001	Bill Cray	1011 Marion St.	486 2100	Furnace	50
1001	Bill Cray	1011 Marion St.	486 2100	Stove	6

The SQL command to do this is:

```
SELECT Salesman.id_no, name, address, phone, item, no_sold
FROM Salesman, Sales
WHERE Salesman.id_no = Sales.id_no;
```

Notice that the natural join is the projection on id_no, name, address, phone, item, and no_sold of the table in Figure 8-10.

The WHERE clause of the SQL SELECT command for the natural join must have enough equality conditions to make the common pairs of columns match.

For example, consider the Salary Table as shown in Figure 8-13:

Figure 8-13. Salary Table

Note: This table was created with the following column specifications:

id_no	CHAR(4)
salary	NUMERIC(5,0)

id_no	salary
1000	20000
1001	26000
1002	27000

Then, the natural join of the Salesman, Sales, and Salary Tables results in the table in Figure 8-14.

Figure 8-14. Natural Join of Salesman, Sales, and Salary Tables

id_no	name	address	phone	item	no_sold	salary
1000	Joe James	1201 Adams St.	832 4509	Radio	10	20000
1000	Joe James	1201 Adams St.	832 4509	Stove	5	20000
1001	Bill Cray	1011 Marion St.	486 2100	Furnace	50	26000
1001	Bill Cray	1011 Marion St.	486 2100	Stove	6	26000

The SQL query for the table in Figure 8-14 is:

```
SELECT Salesman.id_no, name, address, phone, item, no_sold, salary
FROM Salesman, Sales, Salary
WHERE Salesman.id_no = Sales.id_no
AND Sales.id_no = Salary.id_no;
```

The above query actually has three conditions. The third is Salesman.id_no = Salary.id_no, but the two given in the WHERE clause imply the third.

The equijoin with the three conditions given would have three occurrences of the id_no column, and is obtained by the query:

```
SELECT *
FROM Salesman, Sales, Salary
WHERE Salesman.id_no = Sales.id_no
AND Sales.id_no = Salary.id_no;
```

The natural join is obtained by eliminating duplicate columns from the equijoin.

The order in which the rows are displayed on the screen is not relevant to relational algebra. However, the SQL clauses ORDER BY and GROUP BY allow you to order and group the rows in a way that will be useful to you. (ORDER BY and GROUP BY are discussed in Chapter Four, Sections 4.5 and 4.7.)

For a slightly more complicated example, suppose you have three tables. The first has columns A, B, C, and D; the second has columns A, C, and E; and the third has columns A, B, and E. In this case, the SQL query for the natural join is:

```
SELECT Table1.A, Table1.B, Table1.C, D, Table2.E
FROM Table1, Table2, Table3
WHERE Table1.A = Table2.A AND Table2.A = Table3.A
AND Table1.B = Table3.B AND Table1.C = Table2.C
AND Table2.E = Table3.E;
```

8.3.3 Theta Joins

Equijoins based on the equals (=) comparison operator are a special case of the *theta join*. The theta join generalizes the equijoin to any comparison operator.

Suppose you want to find two classes from among those in the tables in Figures 8-5 and 8-6, such that one of them begins within half an hour of the time the other ends. In this case, the following theta join query will result in a table containing all such pairs of classes:

```
SELECT Classes1.subject, Classes2.subject
FROM Classes1, Classes2
WHERE (val(substr(Classes2.starts,1,2)) * 60) +
          val(substr(Classes2.starts,4,2))
BETWEEN (val(substr(Classes1.ends,1,2)) * 60) +
          val(substr(Classes1.ends,4,2))
AND (val(substr(Classes1.ends,1,2)) * 60) +
      val(substr(Classes1.ends,4,2)) + 30
UNION
SELECT Classes2.subject, Classes1.subject
FROM Classes2, Classes1
WHERE (val(substr(Classes1.starts,1,2)) * 60) +
          val(substr(Classes1.starts,4,2))
BETWEEN  (val(substr(Classes2.ends,1,2)) * 60) +
          val(substr(Classes2.ends,4,2))
AND (val(substr(Classes2.ends,1,2)) * 60) +
      val(substr(Classes2.ends,4,2)) + 30;
```

The above query uses the dBASE IV functions val and substr to obtain the number of minutes from the beginning of the day. Substr(...,1,2) picks out the hours, and substr(...,4,2) picks out the minutes. Val converts these substrings to numeric datatype for use in the comparisons.

The result table is shown in Figure 8-15.

Figure 8-15. Classes Within 30 Minutes of Each Other

Subject	Subject
Geology	Physics

8.3.4 Self-Joins

Self-joins are used to join together different rows in the same table. For example, suppose you run a dating service and have a table, Dating, with columns named age, sex, name, city, main_int, where the main_int column contains the main interest of the individual. You want to find those individuals of opposite sex, of the same age, who have the same main interest. Then the following SQL self-join query is appropriate for matching individuals:

```
SELECT Male.name, Female.name
FROM Dating Male, Dating Female
WHERE Male.Sex = 'Male' AND Female.Sex = 'Female'
AND Male.Age = Female.Age AND Male.City = Female.City
AND Male.Main_int = Female.Main_int;
```

Male and Female in the above query are aliases. (See Chapter Six, Section 6.4.4 for a discussion of aliases.) Self-joins are achieved by means of aliases, one for each copy of the table to be self-joined. Each row of the result table will contain the names of two individuals of the opposite sex who are of the same age, live in the same city, and have the same main interest.

An example of a self-theta-join can be constructed from the Classes Table, Figure 8-16, where the columns are subject, room_no, start_t (for start time), and finish_t (for finish time). As in the case of the tables Classes1 and Classes2 above, Start_t and finish_t are character fields of width five.

Figure 8-16. Classes Table

Note: This table was created with the following column specifications:

subject	CHAR(14)
room_no	CHAR(3)
start_t	CHAR(5)
finish_t	CHAR(5)

subject	room_no	start_t	finish_t
Chemistry 101	200	08:00	08:50
Math 102	205	08:00	09:50
Physics 200	300	09:00	10:00

If you want to take two classes that do not conflict, you can form the self-theta-join where start_t is greater than finish_t. The SQL query for this is:

```
SELECT First.subject, Second.subject
FROM Classes First, Classes Second
WHERE (val(substr(First.finish_t,1,2)) * 60) +
      val(substr(First.finish_t,4,2)) <
      (val(substr(Second.start_t,1,2)) * 60) +
      val(substr(Second.start_t,4,2));
```

The result table is given in Figure 8-17.

Figure 8-17. Classes That Do Not Conflict

First.subject	Second.subject
Chemistry 101	Physics 200

References:

Date, C. J. *An Introduction to Database Systems*, Vol. 1, 4th Edition. Menlo Park, CA: Addison-Wesley, 1986.

Korth, Henry F., and Silberschatz, Abraham. *Database System Concepts*. New York: McGraw-Hill, 1986.

Maier, David. *The Theory of Relational Databases*. Rockville, MD: Computer Science Press, 1983.

9

Security and Integrity Measures

If there is a need to keep your data secure, dBASE IV can be set up so that only a database administrator can give users the right to use the databases, tables, and views in dBASE IV SQL. There are several levels of such privileges, ranging all the way from merely looking at the contents of specific views, to privileges of UPDATing, INSERTing and DROPping database objects, and the right to GRANT privileges to other persons.

dBASE IV includes an extensive security system, called PROTECT. This system is optional, and can be used in a single-user or multi-user environment. PROTECT is a menu-driven command that can be invoked from inside dBASE IV by the system administrator in charge of security.

When the PROTECT system is in effect, all users must use an assigned password to gain access to dBASE IV in dBASE mode. After logging in successfully, users can perform only those operations at levels for which they have been assigned access.

For SQL users, the two commands GRANT and REVOKE will give and take back privileges in SQL mode. These two SQL authorization commands use the same user IDs for each person as the PROTECT command. GRANT and REVOKE can only be used to further restrict privileges given by the PROTECT command; they do not override restrictions specified in dBASE mode by the PROTECT command.

When the PROTECT security system is not in use, the SQL authorization commands GRANT and REVOKE can be used without resulting in an error, but they will have no effect.

9.1 EFFECT OF THE dBASE IV PROTECT UTILITY ON SQL OPERATIONS

The dBASE IV PROTECT utility contains three different types of security, two of which affect SQL operations. These types of security are:

- *Log-in,* in which you define the user name and password, thus giving you control over who has access to dBASE IV. The user is identified by the assigned name and password throughout dBASE IV, including SQL mode. User IDs are recorded in the SQL catalog file called Sysauth for table and view privileges, and in the SQL catalog file Syscolau for column UPDATing privileges.

- *File and Field Access,* in which you define access levels to dBASE files and fields. This type of security does not have any effect on SQL operations.

- *Data Encryption,* which allows for automatic encryption and decryption of data entered in the database. This affects your ability to use the DBDEFINE command to bring dBASE files into SQL, as well as your ability to read SQL files from dBASE-only mode. Data encryption and decryption and use of the DBDEFINE command in this context are described in Sections 9.3.5 and 9.4 .

9.2 THE SQL DATABASE ADMINISTRATOR

A special "super-user" called the *SQL Database Administrator* (SQLDBA) must be appointed to handle administrative responsibilities, which include security. To set up this super-user, you create the log-in name SQLDBA with the PROTECT command in dBASE mode. SQLDBA then becomes the ID of the person who will hold that position. As discussed below, most of the authorization restrictions do not apply to the SQLDBA.

The SQLDBA can GRANT and REVOKE privileges to other users on tables, views, indexes, and synonyms at any time. Only the SQLDBA can DROP objects that he/she did not CREATE.

Only the SQLDBA can directly UPDATE SQL system catalogs using SQL commands, since the read-only restriction on these catalogs does not apply to the SQLDBA. But not even the SQLDBA can use the ALTER TABLE command to change the structure of the SQL system catalogs.

9.3 SQL SECURITY AND INTEGRITY

To avoid unauthorized changing of SQL data, specific privileges can be GRANTed, such as UPDATE or INSERT, while withholding the privilege of ALTERing or DELETing data. Restricting privileges is explained in Section 9.3.2.

In a large organization, if a database object is to be open to all users, it is simpler to GRANT privileges to all users at once by GRANTing to the keyword PUBLIC. This procedure is explained in Section 9.3.3.

Your database may contain sensitive information that should be kept confidential. Yet it may be necessary for some employees to work with certain non-sensitive columns and rows in the table containing confidential data. In such a case, you can keep the sensitive material confidential by GRANTing only the necessary privileges on a view of the table instead of on the entire table. This procedure is explained in Section 9.3.4.

At some point, it may be necessary for you to REVOKE the privileges GRANTed, as for instance, when employees leave the organization, or are no longer engaged in work that brings them into contact with the database. For this purpose, you can use the REVOKE command, as explained below in Section 9.3.6.

Data encryption, an additional security feature of dBASE IV, is explained in Section 9.4.

dBASE IV also provides a locking system to prevent other users from accessing or changing data while you are working on it. See Section 9.5 for information on locking.

The system catalogs, created by dBASE IV SQL whenever a database is CREATEd, maintain a record of all of the contents of the database including privileges GRANTed, tables CREATEd, and information describing every table and view. The catalog tables and the commands you use to maintain them are explained in Section 9.6.

Database integrity is the accuracy and consistency of the information contained in the database. In a system open to many users, the integrity of the database is easily threatened if safeguards are not provided. Many of the security features listed above also provide a measure of insurance against violation of database integrity.

A specific device for insuring integrity is the concept of "transaction processing" and the commands that go with it. This is discussed in Section 9.7 below. In addition, Chapter Eight illustrates a different type of integrity by showing how to check for uniqueness of key columns, and how to prevent duplication of rows in the database.

9.3.1 GRANTing Privileges on SQL Objects

The SQLDBA can grant privileges to other users. These users will have logged on to dBASE IV with their IDs and passwords assigned under the PROTECT system, and only need to be given privileges for working in SQL mode.

No user needs to be GRANTed privileges (other than a valid ID) to CREATE a database, table, or synonym. However, only the creator of a database or table (and the SQLDBA) can DROP it. You have the same privileges for a synonym that you have for the table it represents, and synonyms can be used in place of table names in GRANT and REVOKE statements.

The syntax for GRANTing user privileges in dBASE IV SQL is:

```
GRANT ALL [PRIVILEGES]/<privilege list>
ON [TABLE]<table list>
TO <user(s)>
[WITH GRANT OPTION]
```

where:

ALL [PRIVILEGES]/<privilege list> are your options for the privileges you want to GRANT.

TABLE is an optional keyword that you can include to improve readability.

<table list> is the list of table(s) on which the privileges are being GRANTed.

<user(s)> are the IDs of the personnel to whom you are GRANTing privileges.

[WITH GRANT OPTION] is an optional statement. It means that you are also GRANTing to the grantee the right to pass on his/her privileges to other users. You can GRANT ALL privileges with or without giving the WITH GRANT OPTION right.

The broadest class of database privileges that you can GRANT to a user in SQL mode is ALL. The syntax for doing this is:

```
GRANT ALL
ON <table name>/<synonym>
TO <user list>
[WITH GRANT OPTION]
```

where:

ALL means that you have GRANTed the following privileges:

SELECT
INSERT
DELETE
UPDATE [(column)] You may want to qualify the UPDATE privilege by specifying the columns that you are including in the privilege.

INDEX Cannot be GRANTed on views.

ALTER Cannot be GRANTED on views.

<user list> means that the privilege GRANTed can be to an individual, or to a list of individuals, using the pre-assigned identification name of each.

For example, you can GRANT ALL privileges to the five employees named in the following GRANT statement:

```
GRANT ALL
ON Sales
TO bwhite, jjones, dthomas, lblack, mgray;
```

The persons named in the above GRANT ALL statement have already logged on to the system, and now have ALL privileges with regard to using dBASE IV SQL, except the right to GRANT those privileges to anyone else.

As another example, you can GRANT ALL privileges on the Employee Table to Beth White (using the pre-assigned identification name bwhite) by entering:

```
GRANT ALL
ON Employee
TO bwhite
WITH GRANT OPTION;
```

The above GRANT statement gives Beth White the unqualified privilege to use all appropriate dBASE IV SQL commands on the Employee Table, and to pass those rights on to anyone else she chooses.

9.3.2 Restricting Privileges on Tables and Views

Instead of GRANTing ALL privileges, you can GRANT any one of the privileges listed in Section 9.3.1 above, or any combination of these privileges. In a large organization, this allows you to control access so that each user only accesses the tables necessary for his/her function.

For example, if John Jones handles only the pricing of goods for sale, there is no reason for him to access other parts of the database. You can GRANT him the privilege of UPDATing the Products Table to keep prices current, by entering:

```
GRANT UPDATE (price)
ON  Products
TO  jjones;
```

If you add WITH GRANT OPTION to John Jones' privileges, then the privilege he passes on to someone else can only be the same as that GRANTed to him. In other words, he can pass on only the privilege to UPDATE the price column of the Products Table when he holds the WITH GRANT OPTION privilege shown in the above GRANT command.

9.3.3 GRANTing to the Keyword PUBLIC

There are usually some tables in a database that are referred to by all users. In a large organization, it is simpler for the SQLDBA to use the term PUBLIC for such objects rather than listing the names of all users. To do this, the SQLDBA enters:

```
GRANT <privilege list>
    ON [TABLE]<table list>
    TO PUBLIC;
```

This command gives all users the privileges that you enter in the <privilege list> on the table(s) named in the <table list>.

Although the SQLDBA can give the WITH GRANT OPTION privilege when GRANTing access to an individual user, or to a list of named individual users, he/she cannot give the WITH GRANT OPTION privilege to PUBLIC. (There is no need to, since PUBLIC includes everyone authorized to enter the database, and all such persons already have the GRANTable privileges through the GRANT...TO PUBLIC statement.)

For example, if the SQLDBA wants to give every user the INSERT privilege on a Prospects Table with the tablename Prspects, he can do so by entering:

```
GRANT INSERT
ON  Prspects
TO  PUBLIC;
```

Any or all of the database privileges listed in Section 9.3.1 above can be given to PUBLIC, except the WITH GRANT OPTION privilege.

9.3.4 Using Views as Security Devices

To CREATE a view, you must have SELECT privileges on every table in the view definition. Once you have CREATEd a view, only you and the SQLDBA can access it. You can use the GRANT command to give other users specific privileges for this view.

No one can GRANT ALTER or INDEX privileges on a view, because virtual tables cannot be ALTERed or INDEXed.

One of the most common uses of a view is to set it up as a security device. Since a view provides a look at only a portion of a table, that portion can be made available by the GRANTing process to individuals, while the rest of the table can be kept confidential simply by not GRANTing access to it.

This topic is discussed in detail in Chapter Three, Section 3.3.1. It is one of the easiest security measures to implement.

9.3.5 Using DBDEFINE

The DBDEFINE command moves dBASE .dbf files into SQL so that you can access them with SQL commands. You do not need to be GRANTed this privilege; i.e., any user with a valid ID may use the DBDEFINE command, and that user then becomes the creator of the table in the SQL catalog. However, DBDEFINE will bring into SQL only unencrypted dBASE files. Therefore, to use DBDEFINE with a dBASE-encrypted file, you must SET ENCRYPTION OFF while you are still in dBASE, then use a COPY TO command to create an unencrypted file. (Data encryption is discussed in Section 9.4 below.)

The PROTECT utility assigns levels of privileges with regard to dBASE files to each user. If your PROTECT level does not allow you to use the SET ENCRYPTION OFF and COPY TO commands in connection with the dBASE file you want to bring into SQL, then you cannot use DBDEFINE to convert that file into an SQL table.

9.3.6 REVOKing Privileges

The SQLDBA can remove all SQL privileges given to users by means of the REVOKE command. Other users can also REVOKE privileges that they GRANTed to others. The syntax is:

```
REVOKE  ALL [PRIVILEGES]/<privilege list>
ON  [TABLE] <table list>
FROM <user list>;
```

where:

Each of the terms in the above SQL statement have the same meaning that they had in the privilege GRANTing statement in Section 9.3.1.

You have the option of including the words PRIVILEGES and TABLE in the above REVOKE command to make it readable if you wish.

You cannot remove the WITH GRANT OPTION privilege by adding it into the above command. You can only remove it by REVOKing ALL privileges on a table, then GRANTing the privileges back to that user without the WITH GRANT OPTION. For example, to take away the WITH GRANT OPTION privilege from B. White, enter:

```
REVOKE ALL PRIVILEGES
ON <table list>
FROM bwhite;
```

Then, GRANT back any privileges that you still want her to have.

Grantors and grantees remain linked. This means that when you REVOKE a privilege that a user has passed on to someone else through his WITH GRANT OPTION privilege, your revocation also REVOKEs the privilege(s) that user has passed on to others, no matter how long the chain of GRANTs might be.

Keep in mind that users can be GRANTed access by more than one GRANTor. This means that if you REVOKE a user's privilege that you GRANTed on a table, but someone else who GRANTed that same privilege did not REVOKE it for that user, that user can still access the table.

The WITH GRANT OPTION privilege allows many people other than the DBA to GRANT privileges on tables. For example, the creator of a table may GRANT access to that table to others. The result is that any one person may be GRANTed access by several different grantors. Thus, each of these grantors must REVOKE the privilege(s) they GRANTed.

For example, suppose you are the SQLDBA and you have GRANTed ALL privileges to Beth White on the Employee table, including WITH GRANT OPTION. Suppose also that White GRANTed UPDATE and INSERT privileges on that table to J. Jones, and that L. Fisher, who CREATEd the Employee Table,

GRANTed UPDATE and INSERT privileges on it to J. Jones. Now, because J. Jones is leaving this department, White REVOKES Jones' privileges on the Employee Table, but Fisher (who does not know Jones is leaving) does not.

The result is that Jones will still have UPDATE and INSERT privileges on the Employee Table because of the GRANT by Fisher even though White has REVOKEd her GRANT to Jones.

In other words, it's important that everyone who gave Jones privileges on the table REVOKE those privileges, so that Jones is divested of his privileges of accessing the table. The simplest solution is for the SQLDBA to REVOKE ALL Jones' privileges.

On the other hand, if Beth White should leave the department, and if she is the only one who gave Jones access rights to the Employee Table, then when all of White's privileges to that table are REVOKEd, Jones automatically loses all his rights. In other words, while privileges "cascade down" from one person to the grantees of that person, REVOKEd privileges also cascade, and one revocation can cancel the rights of several users down the line if their rights are all derived from a single grantor.

9.4 DATA ENCRYPTION

Data encryption is one of the security features of the dBASE IV PROTECT utility that protects against unauthorized access to the databases.

When PROTECT has been run, and you CREATE a table, that table is immediately encrypted by dBASE IV and stored on disk in the encrypted code. After that, only authorized users can read it, and only users who have been GRANTed privileges on it can access that table. Also, none of the encrypted tables are accessible outside SQL, even to users authorized to use them within SQL.

To access data from SQL-encrypted tables while you are in dBASE mode, you can use the UNLOAD command inside SQL. This will automatically create a decrypted file.

If you run PROTECT after CREATing tables in an unPROTECTed environment, SQL will treat the system as the creator of the tables; i.e., only the SQLDBA will be able to access them once PROTECT is run. To make the tables available to other users, the SQLDBA must GRANT privileges either to PUBLIC or to individual users to enable them to access the tables for all but DROP commands.

9.5 LOCKING

In a multi-user system, there may sometimes be conflicts between users who are attempting to make changes to the same data at the same time. To avoid such conflicts, dBASE IV SQL provides automatic locking.

You do not have to issue any locking commands, because dBASE IV itself decides whether an entire table should be locked (as for example, when you are doing a multiple update operation), or whether a single record (row) should be locked. However, because of this automatic locking feature, you may occasionally find that you are locked out of a table or row. When this occurs, dBASE IV repeatedly tries to give you access to the table or row. If (over a period of time) dBASE IV is not successful in giving you access, you will receive a message indicating that the operation you are attempting cannot be completed at that time.

To prevent situations where you start a multiple-entry operation and may not be able to finish it, use the dBASE BEGIN and END TRANSACTION commands described under Transaction Processing in Section 9.7 below.

9.6 SYSTEM CATALOG TABLES

Whenever you create a database with the CREATE DATABASE command, dBASE IV SQL creates a set of system catalog tables. dBASE IV SQL also maintains a master catalog table named Sysdbs in the dBASE IV SQLHOME program directory that keeps track of each SQL database. This master catalog table (Sysdbs) contains the name of each database, the DOS path to it, the user ID of the person who CREATEd it, and the date it was CREATEd. To list the databases in the Sysdbs table, use the SQL SHOW DATABASE command.

The name and description of the system catalog tables that dBASE IV SQL sets up for each database you CREATE is shown in Figure 9-1.

Figure 9-1. dBASE IV SQL System Catalog Tables

Table Name	Description
Sysauth	Describes the privileges held by users on tables and views, with one row for every user (includingPUBLIC) holding privileges in the current database.
Syscolau	Describes the privileges held by users to UPDATE columns in a table or view, with one row for each user holding privileges to an individual column in the current database.
Syscols	Describes each column in every table and view, including the catalog tables.
Sysidxs	Describes every index in the database, and the table for which it is defined.
Syskeys	Describes every column (index key) used in each index.
Syssyns	Contains all synonym definitions for each table and view.
Systabls	Contains information describing every table and view in the current database.
Sysvdeps	Describes the relation between views and tables in the current database (so that if tables are dropped, views based on those tables will also be dropped).
Sysviews	Contains the view definitions, and the limitations on use of each view.
Sysdbs	Contains information about all SQL databases.
Systimes	In a multi-user environment, ensures that users' internal copies of catalog tables reflect the most recent catalog updates.

You can use the SELECT command to display information from a system catalog table, just as you would display information from any other table. However, you cannot UPDATE system catalog tables, INDEX them, or DELETE from them (unless you are the SQLDBA).

To show the tables and views in the current database, along with the name of the user who CREATEd each, and the type of each table, enter:

```
SELECT tbname, creator, type
FROM Systabls;
```

To display all of the columns in any of the tables, use the SELECT * command. For example, to show all columns in the Sysauth table, enter:

```
SELECT *
FROM Sysauth;
```

9.6.1 UPDATing the System Catalogs: RUNSTATS

As explained above, you cannot update the system catalogs directly (unless you are the SQLDBA). However, whenever you CREATE or add objects to a database, or add or change table authorization privileges, dBASE IV UPDATEs the system catalogs for you. dBASE IV does not automatically update catalogs after an INSERT or DELETE command.

To accomplish the updating, use the RUNSTATS command. It is important to do so because dBASE IV SQL uses the statistics in the catalog tables to optimize its performance. The syntax for the RUNSTATS command is:

```
RUNSTATS [<table name>];
```

where:

RUNSTATS is a keyword.

[<table name>] is the optional name or synonym of the table for which you want the statistics updated. If a table name is not specified, then RUNSTATS will update statistics for all tables in the active database.

The RUNSTATS command causes dBASE IV SQL to check the catalogs against the actual database objects, and to update the system catalog to take account of changes.

The catalog columns that RUNSTATS will update are shown in Figure 9-2.

Figure 9-2. Catalog Columns UPDATEd by RUNSTATS

Column	Table	Description
Colcard*	Syscols	Number of distinct values in the column
High2key*	Syscols	Statistical entry
Low2key*	Syscols	Statistical entry
Firstkcard	Sysidxs	Number of distinct values in first column of index key
Fullkcard	Sysidxs	Number of distinct values in the full index key
Nleaf	Sysidxs	Number of B-tree leaves in index
Nlevels	Sysidxs	Depth of index B-tree
Updated	Systabls	Last date that ALTER TABLE or RUNSTATS command was run; date of creation for views
Card	Systabls	Cardinality (the number of rows) in table; 0 for views
Npages	Systabls	Number of disk pages a table occupies

* RUNSTATS only updates these columns if the column is of datatype SMALLINT, INTEGER, DECIMAL, NUMERIC or FLOAT.

If RUNSTATS successfully UPDATEs, you get the following message on your screen:

RUNSTATS successful

If RUNSTATS finds inconsistencies in the catalog tables, or between the catalog tables and the actual database and index tags in the database directory, it does not make any updates to the statistics columns. Instead, it will issue error and warning messages, ending with the message:

RUNSTATS completed without catalog updates: errors/warnings found

If the above happens, the following steps will usually correct any inconsistencies that RUNSTATS has found between existing SQL tables and the information in the catalog tables:

1. Leave SQL, and copy database file(s) named in the error message(s) and their production .mdx index files to another directory. (Do not attempt to modify or remove the system catalog files.)

2. Re-enter SQL, and DROP the table(s) from the database. (This removes all entries for that table, its indexes, synonyms, and views based on it from the catalog tables.)

3. Leave SQL again, and copy the database and index files back into the database directory.

4. Re-enter SQL, and run a DBDEFINE <filename> command for each database file to be redefined as an SQL table. (The associated indexes will be redefined as part of the DBDEFINE command.)

How often you use the RUNSTATS command depends on how many and what kind of changes you have made. You should always use RUNSTATS after making changes to a table definition, or after adding or changing more than ten percent of the records in a table.

NOTE: Do not attempt to perform any other database operations while using the RUNSTATS command. Locking errors are likely to ocur if other users are using the database during a RUNSTATS.

You can use RUNSTATS for updating statistics on a single table by naming the table immediately after the command RUNSTATS. It can also be used for all tables in the active database by simply entering the RUNSTATS command with no table name following it.

In a multi-user environment, you may want to stop all other operations on the database while you run RUNSTATS.

9.6.2 UPDATing the System Catalogs: DBCHECK

If SQL tables have been accessed and changed in dBASE mode, then the catalog tables must be brought up to date before you attempt to use these tables in SQL mode. If this is not done, SQL commands used with the changed table will return incorrect results, or in some cases will not operate at all.

To determine whether changes have been made to SQL tables while in dBASE mode, you use the DBCHECK command. This command, which can only be used in interactive mode, checks to see if catalog table entries are consistent with the tables' current structures. DBCHECK will return an error message for every database table and index that does not match the definition in the catalog file.

The syntax for making this check is:

DBCHECK [<tablename>];

If you use the option of specifying a tablename in the above command, DBCHECK verifies the entries for that table only (and for its corresponding indexes). If you do not specify a tablename, DBCHECK verifies the catalog entries for all tables and indexes in the currently active database.

If you receive error messages because of inconsistencies found by DBCHECK, then the following steps will usually correct the inconsistencies:

1. Leave SQL, and copy the database file(s) named in the error message(s) and their index files to another directory. (Do not attempt to modify or remove the system catalog files.)

2. Re-enter SQL, and DROP the tables from the database. This removes all entries for that table, its indexes, synonyms, and any views based on it from the catalog tables.)

3. Again leave SQL, and copy the database file and index file back into the database directory.

4. Re-enter SQL, and run a DBDEFINE <filename> command for each database file to be redefined as an SQL table. Any associated indexes will be redefined as part of the DBDEFINE command (discussed in Section 9.6.3 below).

9.6.3 UPDATing the System Catalogs: DBDEFINE

If there are files CREATEd in dBASE mode that you want to access in SQL mode, you can bring them into the SQL catalog files as tables by using DBDEFINE. This command will CREATE catalog table definitions for the dBASE files and for any index files associated with them.

NOTE: DBDEFINE will not define dBASE UNIQUE indexes.

As with DBCHECK, you can specify a dBASE file to be defined in the SQL catalogs with the DBDEFINE command, or you can update the catalog tables for all the files in a dBASE application by not specifying the file name.

The syntax for DBDEFINE is:

DBDEFINE [<.dbf file>];

where:

[<.dbf file>] is the optional name of the database (.dbf) file to be converted to an SQL table and added to the currently active database.

If you fill in the optional .dbf file name, then only that specific file (with its associated index file) will be UPDATEd. If you omit the optional file name, then all files, and associated indexes in that application, will be UPDATEd and made available for use in SQL mode.

If you are running DBDEFINE in a multi-user environment, you need to stop all other operations on the database.

DBDEFINE issues two lists: one of files successfully defined, the other of files that could not be defined.

If DBDEFINE is successful, and all database and index files have been converted into SQL tables and indexes, DBDEFINE issues the following message:

DBDEFINE successful

If DBDEFINE cannot make a system catalog update for one of the tables being defined, it issues the following message:

DBDEFINE completed; errors/warnings found.

If the above happens, check the following points:

- Rename any .dbf files you want to define, if the files currently have the same name as another object (such as a synonym or view) in the SQL database directory.

- In SQL, all .mdx tags must have distinct names, even if they belong to different .mdx's. If an error occurs during DBDEFINE because a .mdx tag to be defined has the same name as an existing SQL index, you must rename the .mdx tag.

DBDEFINE will enter statistics in the catalog tables when it makes new catalog entries. Use RUNSTATS after DBDEFINE to update these statistics and ensure they are correct.

9.7 TRANSACTION PROCESSING

If you use dBASE IV in conjunction with a number of other users, for example on a local area network (LAN), there may be conflicts when several users attempt to use the same information at the same time. In addition to locking, dBASE IV provides another safeguard that you can use to avoid conflict: the use of the commands BEGIN TRANSACTION and END TRANSACTION.

In this context, a *transaction* is considered to be a piece of work that constitutes a whole entry, regardless of how many or how few SQL commands it contains. For example, recording the shipping of goods to a customer and depleting the inventory by that amount also requires that you enter the amount owed for the goods by that customer. If only one half of this transaction is entered, the database will be out of balance: either inventory will show more than is actually on hand, or accounts receivable will fail to show the customer's indebtedness. The total entries in this type of situation are called a *transaction*.

When you write an SQL statement or series of statements which (if left incomplete) would incorporate incorrect or insufficient data into the database, you should start with the following dBASE command:

BEGIN TRANSACTION [<path name>]

where:

[<path name>] is the optional path to the transaction log file which will be created during the transaction.

After you have completed the series of SQL statements, enter:

END TRANSACTION

If you are interrupted before the end of the series, then use the ROLLBACK command to ensure that the incomplete work done after BEGIN TRANSACTION will be eliminated, and not entered into the database. The ROLLBACK command restores a table or view to its contents prior to execution of the commands within a block specified by BEGIN... END TRANSACTION commands. This will maintain database integrity.

The syntax for ROLLBACK is:

ROLLBACK (<database filename>)

Transaction processing can be used with SQL statements that are embedded in dBASE application programs. This usage is discussed in Chapter Eleven, which illustrates embedded SQL.

For a list of commands *not allowed* during a transaction, see Section 5.3.

9.8 CONCLUSION

All of the above security and integrity features are available in dBASE IV SQL. How many of the security items you put to use in your own system will depend upon the number of users and the need for confidentiality within your organization. It's best to use all possible integrity features, since the reliability of the system depends heavily on how well you maintain the integrity of the database.

10

SQL in dBASE IV

As a query language, SQL is a fourth-generation language, which means that you ask for what you want rather than writing a program to get it. (First-, second-, and third-generation languages required the programmer to know how the information to be found was stored, and required writing code to retrieve from the storage media.)

dBASE IV in SQL mode decides how to get what your query asks for. This makes programming applications much simpler, since you don't have to write complicated code to SELECT, UPDATE, and DELETE records; you simply write SQL commands.

dBASE IV in SQL mode gives you the power of the dBASE programming language combined with the power of SQL. The dBASE commands are provided for controlling and formatting the screen, obtaining input from the user, printing reports, and controlling flow of programs. You can use SQL to interact with the tables in the database, and use dBASE commands to do the rest of the work.

This chapter presents some of the dBASE IV commands that can be used in SQL mode, with attention to those commands which are particularly useful in embedded SQL. A complete list of dBASE IV commands that can be used in SQL mode is given in Appendix B. (Refer to Ashton-Tate's *Language Reference* manual for a complete list of dBASE commands and a complete description of each.)

Chapter Eleven on Embedded SQL uses these dBASE commands to illustrate programming using a combination of SQL and dBASE IV commands.

10.1 PROGRAM FLOW COMMANDS

Program flow commands are commands which control the order in which commands are performed in a program. The flow commands provided by dBASE IV are treated in the following sections.

10.1.1 The DO command

The format for the DO command is:

DO <program file or procedure name> [WITH <parameter list>]

where:

<program file or procedure name> is either the name of a program file or a procedure in a procedure file. SQL program files in dBASE IV have the file extension .prs, while dBASE program files have the file extension .prg.

Both .prs and .prg files are compiled into .dbo files and then executed. If no file extension is specified, and no procedure of the specified name can be found in any active file, DO searches for a .dbo file and executes it. If no .dbo file can be found, DO searches for a .prg file, compiles it, and executes it. If no .prg file is found, DO searches for a .prs file. If both a .prg (.prs) file and a .dbo file are found and SET DEVELOPMENT is OFF, DO will always execute the .dbo file. If SET DEVELOPMENT is ON, DO compares the timestamps of the two files to decide what to do.

If you give a procedure name, the procedure file containing the procedure must previously have been opened by a SET PROCEDURE TO command.

The optional parameter list [WITH <parameter list>] is a set of memory variable names, separated by commas, which are to be passed to the program or procedure.

10.1.2 PARAMETERS

PARAMETERS <parameter list> gives a list of local memory variable names for the variables passed by the DO ... WITH <parameter list> command. In a program file, PARAMETERS must be the first command. In a PROCEDURE file, PARAMETERS must follow the PROCEDURE name.

10.1.3 PROCEDURE

PROCEDURE <procedure name> identifies a *procedure* (subprogram) in a procedure file, and is the beginning of that PROCEDURE. PROCEDURE names can be a maximum of eight characters long. A PROCEDURE is terminated by a RETURN command (see Section 10.1.7).

10.1.4 The IF, ELSE, ENDIF Command

The format for the IF, ELSE, ENDIF command is:

> IF <condition1> [.AND./.OR./.NOT. condition2 .AND./.OR./.NOT.
>   ... .AND. /.OR./.NOT. condition]
> * Lines of code
> [ELSE]
> * Lines of code
> ENDIF
>
> where:
>
> <condition> is any condition which can be evaluated to true or false, such as a logical memory variable, a test that a memory variable has a certain value, such as main = 5, or the constant values .T. or .F. themselves.
>
> [ELSE] is optional, depending on whether or not there is something that needs to be done if the condition after the IF is false.
>
> ENDIF is required to indicate the end of the scope of the IF command.
>
> * Lines of code are the lines of code to be performed under that case of the conditional.

For example, suppose you want to DO prog1 if the user has selected the number 1, and you want to DO prog2 otherwise; and assume the number selected by the user is in the memory variable selection. Then the code to do this is:

```
IF selection = 1
   DO prog1
ELSE
   DO prog2
ENDIF
```

IF's may be nested. For example:

```
IF selection1 = 1
   IF selection2 = 10
      * lines of code
   ENDIF
ENDIF
```

10.1.5 DO WHILE

The format for the DO WHILE command is:

```
DO WHILE <condition>
     * Lines of code
     [EXIT]
     * Lines of code
     [LOOP]
     * Lines of code
     ENDDO
```

where:

<condition> is any condition that can be evaluated to be true or false.

EXIT is optional, and transfers control to the first command following the ENDDO.

LOOP is optional, and returns control to the beginning of the DO WHILE loop where <condition> is reevaluated.

If condition evaluates to true, then all commands following the DO WHILE and before the ENDDO are performed sequentially until an EXIT or LOOP or ENDDO is encountered. Then control is returned to the beginning of the DO WHILE (except in the case of EXIT, which transfers control to the first command after ENDDO). When control is returned to the DO WHILE, the condition is reevaluated. If condition evaluates to false, control is transferred to the first statement after the ENDDO.

CAUTION: Macros can be used with memory variables in the DO WHILE, but will only be evaluated correctly the first time DO WHILE is encountered. Therefore, be extremely cautious in using macros in the condition of a DO WHILE, since—besides causing unexpected results—they may cause an infinite loop.

DO WHILEs may be nested. For example:

```
i1 = 0
DO WHILE i1 < 10
     i1 = i1 + 1
   i2 = 0
   DO WHILE i2 < 5
      i2 = i2 + 1
   ENDDO
ENDDO
```

10.1.6 DO CASE

The format for the DO CASE command is:

```
DO CASE
     CASE <condition>
          * Lines of code
    [CASE <condition>]
          * Lines of code
    ...
    [OTHERWISE]
          * Lines of code
ENDCASE
```

where:

Each case condition is evaluated sequentially until one is found that evaluates to true. Then the lines of code after that case are performed, and DO CASE skips to the first line of code after the ENDCASE. If no case condition evaluates to true, then the lines of code after the OTHERWISE are performed, and then control passes to the first line of code after the ENDCASE.

10.1.7 RETURN

RETURN returns control to the calling program. If you add TO MASTER as in RETURN TO MASTER, control returns to the main program. RETURN also clears any existing error condition.

In dBASE IV, RETURN has been modified to support user-defined functions. The new syntax for RETURN is:

```
RETURN [<expression>] [TO MASTER]
```

where:

the value of the optional <expression> is returned to the calling program. If RETURN appears in a user-defined function without <expression>, the logical value .F. will be returned.

10.1.8 RETRY and ON

RETRY returns control to the prior calling program, and causes the command that called the program to be repeated, thus RETRYing the called program. RETRY is used mainly in error recovery, where a situation which caused an error may have been fixed and you want to try again. For example:

```
* calling program
ON ERROR DO FIX WITH ERROR()
SELECT *
FROM Sales;
......
* End of calling program

* Fix.prg
PARAMETERS Err
IF Err = 1139
   * 1139 is the error number for No database open.
   OPEN DATABASE Sales;
   RETRY
ENDIF
```

RETRY also clears any error condition that exists.

The ON command allows you to tell the program the name of program or PROCEDURE to perform in the event of certain things occurring. There are eight ON commands in dBASE IV:

ON ERROR
ON ESCAPE
ON KEY
ON PAD
ON PAGE
ON READERROR
ON SELECTION PAD
ON SELECTION POPUP.

The format for ON ERROR and ON ESCAPE is:

> ON ERROR/ESCAPE <command>
>
> where:
>
> <command> is a command to be performed. Usually, <command> is a DO where the program called deals with the occurrence of a certain event, as in the above example.

ON ERROR is activated by the occurrence of an error, as in the above example. ON ESCAPE is activated by the operator pressing the Esc key.

10.1.9 RUN

RUN has the following format:

```
RUN <command>
or
! <command>
```

where:

<command> is the name of an executable program which can be either a DOS command, or a program that you have written, or some other program.

10.2 SCREEN CONTROL COMMANDS

Screen control commands are those commands which set up your screen. dBASE IV is amply provided with such commands, as well as with a form generator that you can use to generate the set of commands that you want to set up the screen for your application. Since this book is primarily about SQL, we do not treat the form generator here, but merely describe the commands which you can use to set up the screen any way you want.

10.2.1 @...SAY...GET

The @...SAY...GET command is used to set up screens and to read values typed in by the user. This command has been greatly enhanced in dBASE IV to trap data entry errors, and to display error and help messages. The format for this command is:

```
@ <row,col> [[SAY <exp> [PICTURE <clause>]
        [FUNCTION <function list>]]
    [GET <variable>
        [[OPEN] WINDOW <window name>]
        [PICTURE <clause>]
        [FUNCTION <function list>]
        [RANGE <low>,<high>]
        [[VALID <condition>]
        [ERROR <expC>]]
        [WHEN <condition>]
        [DEFAULT <exp>]
        [MESSAGE <expC>]]]
    [COLOR [<standard>] [<enhanced>]]
```

where:

The <row,col> immediately after the @ indicates the row and column on the screen where the command starts.

The <exp> immediately following the SAY is a character string which is placed at the <row,col> position following the @.

The GET sets up editing of variables depending on the type of variable and the optional PICTURE clause and FUNCTION clause. Values edited with the GET are transferred to memory variables by the READ command. A repeat of the READ command changes pages.

The optional [OPEN] WINDOW clause is used to specify the name of a previously defined window. For more details about windows, see your *dBASE IV Language Reference* manual.

The PICTURE and FUNCTION clauses restrict the type of data that can be typed in by the user. For more details about the picture clause, see the *Language Reference* manual.

RANGE <low>,<high> limits the range of numeric, date, and character variables. In the case of date variables the CTOD() function must be used as follows: RANGE CTOD('12/25/87'),CTOD('01/01/88'), which excludes all dates which are not between December25, 1987 and January 1, 1988.

VALID <condition> is any valid logical expression. This is a condition that must be satisfied before the data is accepted into the GET variable.

ERROR <expC> is a user-defined message that is displayed if the VALID condition is not satisfied.

WHEN <condition> is any valid logical condition that must be satisfied before the user is allowed to edit the GET variable. If the condition is not satisfied, the cursor will skip the variable.

DEFAULT <exp> gives a default value for the GET variable.

MESSAGE <expC> displays a character string on the bottom line of the screen.

COLOR specifies the foreground and background colors of the SAY and GET variables.

10.2.2 @...TO

The expression &...TO creates or clears a box with a double or single line border. The format for @...TO is:

@ <row1>,<col1> [CLEAR] TO <row2>,<col2>
COLOR <color attribute>
[DOUBLE/PANEL/NONE/<border string>]

where:

<row1>,<row2> are the coordinates of the upper left- hand corner of the box, and <row2>,col2> are the coordinates of the lower right-hand corner of the box.

CLEAR is optional and allows you to clear the part of the screen between the two sets of coordinates.

<color attribute> is the screen color code, and follows the same options as the SET COLOR command. (See your *Language Reference* manual.)

DOUBLE makes a box with a double lined border. See your *Language Reference* manual for details of the other options.

10.3 KEYBOARD INPUT

There are several commands in dBASE, besides the @...GET...READ sequence treated in the previous section, for getting input from the user. We discuss them here.

10.3.1 ACCEPT

ACCEPT is used to prompt a user for keyboard input. The format for ACCEPT is:

ACCEPT [<prompt>] TO <memory variable>

where:

<prompt> can be either a character type memory variable or a character string surrounded by single quotes, double quotes, or brackets.

<memory variable> is a character type memory variable name created by ACCEPT.

A maximum of 254 characters may be entered into a memory variable with ACCEPT.

To terminate the entry of the CHARacter string, press **Return**.

10.3.2 INPUT

INPUT has the same format as ACCEPT. However, numbers, logical values, and dates can be entered using INPUT.

10.3.3 WAIT

WAIT causes a pause until the user presses a key. The format for WAIT is:

WAIT [<prompt>] [TO <memory variable>]

where:

<prompt> can be a character string surrounded by single quotes, or a character type memory variable.

If TO <memory variable> is included, a character type memory variable is created which stores the keyboard entry.

10.4 SOME SET COMMANDS

In dBASE IV there are a number of environmental conditions that are like switches which can be turned on and off. These conditions are controlled by the SET commands. The conditions which are particularly important for dBASE IV SQL are:

SET SQL
SET TALK
SET ECHO
SET DEBUG
SET EXACT
SET BELL
SET CONFIRM
SET CONSOLE
SET HISTORY
SET INTENSITY
SET PRECISION
SET PROCEDURE
SET TRAP ON/OFF

These are treated in the sections below. For the rest of the SET commands, refer to your *Language Reference* manual.

Some of the SET commands have the following format:

SET <condition> ON/OFF

where:

<condition> is the environmental condition to be turned ON or OFF.

10.4.1 SET SQL

In interactive mode, SET SQL ON/OFF is used to determine whether or not dBASE IV is operating in SQL mode. In programs, SQL mode is determined by the file extension of the program file. If the file extension is .prs, then dBASE switches to SQL mode. If the file extension is .prg, dBASE switches to dBASE mode.

In order to use SQL interactively, dBASE IV must be in SQL mode. Keep in mind, however, that some dBASE commands are disabled in SQL mode. A list of dBASE IV commands usable in SQL mode is given in Appendix B.

The default setting for SQL is OFF, unless the command SQL = ON is in the config.db file.

10.4.2 SET STEP

SET STEP ON/OFF allows you to have your program perform one command at a time. In the SET STEP ON mode, the result of a command is displayed; then, the following message appears:

Press SPACE to step, S to suspend, or Esc. to cancel...

You then enter your choice.

SET STEP is useful for debugging. SET STEP is usually OFF.

10.4.3 SET TALK

SET TALK ON/OFF determines whether or not the response to certain dBASE commands is displayed. TALK is normally ON during interactive use. SET TALK OFF is used in programs to prevent each result from being displayed to the screen, since that would interfere with the screen display set up by the program.

10.4.4 SET ECHO

When ON, the SET ECHO ON/OFF command prints commands to the screen or printer. This is useful as a debugging tool. ECHO is normally OFF.

10.4.5 SET DEBUG

SET DEBUG ON sends SET ECHO output to the printer. SET DEBUG OFF sends SET ECHO output to the screen.

10.4.6 SET EXACT

SET EXACT ON causes comparisons between character strings to be true only when the two character strings are exactly the same.

SET EXACT OFF causes comparisons between character strings to return true if the two strings match, starting with the first character and ending with the last character in the string to the right of the comparison operator. For example, with SET EXACT OFF the following comparison returns a true value:

'jockey' = 'joc'

The default setting for SET EXACT is off.

10.4.7 SET BELL

The format for SET BELL is:

SET BELL TO [<frequency>,<duration>]

where:

<frequency> is cycles per second, and must be less than 10001 and greater than 18.

<duration> is number of "ticks." A tick is about .0549 seconds.

If [<frequency>,<duration>] is omitted, the BELL is SET to the default of 550 cycles per second and 2 ticks.

The BELL may be SET ON or OFF by the SET BELL ON/OFF command.

The default for SET BELL is OFF. When SET BELL ON has been performed, a warning bell rings if you try to enter an invalid data type in an entry field, or if you reach the end of an input field.

10.4.8 SET CONFIRM

SET CONFIRM OFF causes the cursor to advance from one entry field to the next when the first entry field has been filled.

SET CONFIRM ON causes the cursor to remain at the end of an entry field until you press Return.

The default for SET CONFIRM is OFF.

10.4.9 SET CONSOLE

You use SET CONSOLE OFF to prevent the output of commands from affecting the screen display. For example, if you are printing a report to your printer and you don't want the report to come out on the screen, you SET CONSOLE OFF.

In interactive mode, SET CONSOLE is always ON.

10.4.10 SET ESCAPE

With SET ESCAPE ON, pressing Esc halts the processing of a program, and pressing Ctrl-S halts scrolling. With SET ESCAPE OFF, the Esc and Ctrl-S are disabled.

The default for SET ESCAPE is ON.

10.4.11 SET HISTORY

SET HISTORY ON saves previously executed commands to a history buffer. The commands saved can be viewed by pressing the Up arrow key twice, and then once again to work your way back through the commands in the opposite order to that in which they were performed.

The default for SET HISTORY is ON.

10.4.12 SET INTENSITY

When SET INTENSITY is ON @...GET, fields are displayed in reverse video.

The default for SET INTENSITY is ON.

10.4.13 SET PRECISION

The format for SET PRECISION is:

SET PRECISION TO <expN>

where:

<expN> is an integer between 10 and 20.

The *precision set* is the number of accurate digits in type N data elements. All expressions that produce a type N data result will have the specified precision for the result. The default for the precision is 16.

10.4.14 SET PROCEDURE

The format for SET PROCEDURE is:

SET PROCEDURE TO [<procedure file name>]

where:

<procedure file name> is the name of a file containing procedures to be called from your program. A procedure file usually contains several programs which are to be used repeatedly. SET PROCEDURE opens the procedure file named. Then you can issue a DO command to call one of the procedures in the file.

A procedure file may be closed by the CLOSE PROCEDURE command and SET PROCEDURE TO.

10.4.15 SET TRAP ON/OFF

SET TRAP determines whether or not the debugger is activated when you encounter an error or press the Esc key when a program is running. SET TRAP ON will cause the debugger to be invoked, and SET TRAP OFF will prevent the debugger from being invoked. If SET TRAP is ON, the program will be stopped at the line containing the error, thus making it easy for you to fix the problem. If ON ERROR or ON ESCAPE are in effect, they override SET TRAP. SET TRAP works in both dBASE and SQL modes. For information about the debugger, see Section 10.7 below.

The default for SET TRAP is OFF.

10.5 USER-DEFINED FUNCTIONS

dBASE IV has *user-defined functions,* which means that you can make up your own functions and put them in a procedure file.User-defined functions differ from procedures in that they RETURN a value and are invoked like any function, whereas PROCEDUREs are invoked by the DO command.

User-defined functions in .prg files can be called from dBASE IV. When dBASE IV starts to perform commands in a file with file extension .prg, it switches to dBASE mode.

User-defined functions cannot be embedded in SQL statements or .prs files..

A user-defined function in a PROCEDURE file must begin with:

FUNCTION <function name>

The second line of a user-defined function must be a PARAMETER statement followed by a PARAMETER list.

For a user-defined function, the RETURN command is modified to RETURN an expression or memory variable. For example, the following function would return the area of a rectangle:

```
FUNCTION AREA
PARAMETER Height, Width
Area = Height * Width
RETURN Area
```

If there is a RETURN with no expression or memory variable following it, the function will RETURN the logical value .F. The RETURN can be a RETURN TO MASTER, in which case the expression or memory variable is placed between the RETURN and the TO MASTER as follows:

RETURN [<expression>] TO MASTER

A user-defined function is called in the same way as any dBASE function, by using its name followed by parentheses containing the necessary parameter values. For example, ? AREA(2,3) returns 6.

User-defined functions cannot contain any of the following commands:

APPEND	AVERAGE	BROWSE	CHANGE	CLEAR*
COPY	CREATE	DELETE	DIR	DIRECTORY
DISPLAY	EDIT	EXPORT	HELP	IMPORT
INDEX	INPUT	INSERT	JOIN	LABEL
LIST	LOAD	LOGOUT	MODIFY	PACK
REINDEX	REPORT	SAVE	SORT	SUM
TOTAL	UPDATE	ZAP	READ**	

* CLEAR cannot be referenced if it has any arguments, but can be referenced alone.

** READ cannot be executed if it is using a format file.

10.6 EDITING PROGRAM FILES

You can create and edit program files with either the .prg or interactively. The format for this is:

MODIFY COMMAND <filename>

where:

<filename> is the name of the file you want to edit.

You can put a command line in the Config.db file in order to cause MODIFY COMMAND to call up your favorite editor. The command line is TEDIT=<editor>.

For example, if you want to use Wordstar, you put TEDIT=WS in the Config.db file. When using Wordstar, remember to use the nondocument mode to avoid having Wordstar special characters in your file.

dBASE IV has a very nice, new editor of its own. For more details, see your *Language Reference* manual.

10.7 THE DEBUGGER

The debugger can be enabled in three different ways:

- By the DEBUG command, which has the format:

  DEBUG <program file name> / <procedure name>
  [WITH <parameter list>]

  where:

  <program file name> / <procedure name> is the name of the program file or procedure to be debugged.

  WITH <parameter list> gives an optional set of parameters to be used in debugging a parameter file.

- When SET TRAP is ON, you have pressed the Esc key, and no ON ESCAPE <command> has been previously executed.

- When SET TRAP is ON, an error has occurred, and no ON ERROR <command> has been previously executed.

The debugger uses four different windows: Edit, Display, Breakpoints, and Debug. The *Edit window* occupies the top thirteen rows of the screen. The *Debug window* occupies the five rows above the bottom row of the screen. The *Display* and *Breakpoint windows* appear between the Edit window and the Debug window, with the Display window occupying the first fifty columns, and the Breakpoint window occupying the remaining thirty columns. The F9 key toggles the windows on and off the screen, so you can see what the screen looked like before DEBUG was activated.

The F1 key toggles a help panel on and off the screen. The help panel contains a brief description of which debug commands are on and off.

The Debug window is the active window when the debugger is initially called. The Debug window contains status information, and a line number relative to the beginning of the program or procedure file. You control the debugger by entering commands on the command line of the Debug window. The debug commands you can use are listed in Figure 10-1.

Figure 10-1. Debug Commands

B	Enter the Breakpoint window.
D	Enter the Display window.
E	Enter the Edit window.
[<n>]S	Step through the program n steps at a time. Stop after n steps. If <n> is omitted, step one line at a time.
R	Run the program until either a breakpoint is encountered or an error occurs.
X	Suspend program and go to the dot prompt. RESUME at the dot prompt returns to the debugger.
Q	Quit the debugger and cancel the program.
P	Show program trace information.
L	Go to specified line.
[<n>]N	Execute the next n commands in current or above level. A DO will be taken to be one command.
Enter	Execute a step.

The Display window shows you the changing values of certain expressions as you step through the code. You may enter any valid dBASE IV expression in the left side—for example, empno, or empname. The value of the expression is displayed on the right side of the Display window.

You can exit the Display window by typing **Ctrl-End** or **Esc**.

In the Breakpoint window you can enter up to ten conditions, such as empno > 10. After typing the breakpoint conditions you want, you can return to the debug command line and start the program. The breakpoint conditions will be evaluated after each line of code is executed. If one of them evaluates to true (.T.), the program will be halted and the debugger will be reactivated.

To exit the Breakpoint window, press **Ctrl-End** or **Esc**.

The Edit window displays the program file that is being executed, with the next line to be executed shown in reverse video. In the Edit window, the full power of the dBASE IV editor is available to you. If you make changes to the file, you must save them to avoid losing them.

11

SQL Embedded In dBASE IV

This chapter shows you how to combine SQL, dBASE IV programming commands, dBASE IV memory variables, and dBASE IV functions as a part of a program. The result is called *SQL embedded in dBASE IV*.

In this chapter, we present partial programs or excerpts of programs rather than complete programs. The purpose of this is to present basic concepts and methods which you can fit into your own applications. Concepts and methods are more easily understood when presented alone, without too many application-specific commands which make it difficult to see the main idea. Each excerpt will present a particular embedded SQL programming concept which you can apply to your own programming requirements.

To prepare and edit your programs, use the MODIFY COMMAND command of dBASE IV presented in Section 10.6 of Chapter Ten. Always use the .prs file extension for embedded SQL programs. A program can be started interactively at the dot prompt by typing DO and the name of the file containing the program.

11.1 SQLCODE AND SQLCNT

SQLCODE and SQLCNT are system memory variables for use in dBASE IV SQL.

If an SQL command is successful, SQLCODE is set to zero (0). If an error occurs, SQLCODE is set to -1. If a FETCH occurs when the CURSOR pointer points beyond the last row of the CURSOR, SQLCODE is set to +100. If no rows are retrieved when the cursor is opened, SQLCODE is set to +100, unless an error occurs.

SQLCNT is always set to the number of rows touched by an SQL command. For example, if a SELECT SELECTs forty rows, then SQLCNT is set to 40. If an UPDATE UPDATEs 10 rows, then SQLCNT is set to 10.

11.2 EMBEDDED SQL WITHOUT CURSORS

If you have a sequence of SQL commands that you regularly type in interactively, it will be more efficient (and save lots of typing) to write a program containing all the commands.

All of your SQL commands can be embedded in programs. You can CREATE tables, views, indexes, or synonyms, and then DROP them later in the program. You can INSERT data into tables and SELECT information from tables to display result tables as well as INTO variables. You can UPDATE rows in tables or DELETE rows from tables. You can use memory variables that have been computed in the program, or entered by the user, in WHERE clauses or as UPDATE values in tables.

For example, suppose you regularly INSERT records into a Sales Table having columns id_no, item_sld, and no_sld, standing for salesman's identification number, item sold, and number sold, respectively. If you do this interactively, you have to look up the salesman's ID number, then type the following SQL command:

INSERT INTO Sales
VALUES (id_no, item, number sold);

Your typing task will be simplified by using the following brief program:

```
STORE SPACE(15) TO m_name
STORE SPACE(10) TO m_item
STORE 0 TO m_no
STORE SPACE(4) TO m_id
@ 0,0 CLEAR
*Clears the screen starting at row 0 column 0.
@ 4,5 SAY "Salesman's name: " GET m_name
@ 6,5 SAY "Item sold: " GET m_item
@ 8,5 SAY "Number sold: " GET m_no
READ
SELECT id_no
INTO m_id
FROM Salesman
WHERE name = m_name;
INSERT INTO Sales
VALUES (m_id,m_item,m_no);
@ 10,5 SAY "Sale inserted into Sales table."
WAIT
*WAIT displays the message, Press any key to continue...,
*and causes all processing to pause until a key is pressed.
@ 0,0 CLEAR
*Clears the screen starting at row 0, column 0.
```

If you have a lot of sales to record, you can use a DO WHILE loop as follows:

```
STORE SPACE(4) TO m_name
STORE SPACE(10) TO m_item
STORE 0 TO m_no
STORE SPACE(1) TO m_answer
STORE .T. TO m_more
@ 0,0 CLEAR
DO WHILE m_more
    @ 4,5 SAY "Salesman's name: " GET m_name
    @ 6,5 SAY "Item sold: " GET m_item
    @ 8,5 SAY "Number sold" GET m_no
    READ
    SELECT id_no
    INTO m_id
    FROM Salesman
    WHERE name = m_name;
    IF SQLCNT = 1
        INSERT INTO Sales
        VALUES (m_id,m_item,m_no);
        @ 10,5 SAY "Sale inserted into Sales table."
    ELSE
        @ 10,5 SAY "There is no salesman with that name."
    ENDIF
    WAIT
    @ 12,5 SAY "Insert another? (Y/N) " GET m_answer
    READ
    IF .NOT. UPPER(m_answer) = "Y"
        EXIT
    ENDIF
    @ 0,0 CLEAR
ENDDO
@ 0,0 CLEAR
```

You can add PICTURE clauses to the @ SAY ... GET commands, and modify the program to suit your own application.

The SELECT ... INTO form of the SELECT command used in the above program has the format:

SELECT <target list>
INTO <memory variable list>
FROM <table name>
[WHERE <condition>];

where:

<target list> is a list of columns to be SELECTed.

<memory variable list> is a list of memory variables, one for each member of the target list.

<condition> must be a condition or set of conditions that is satisfied by exactly one row of the table named by <table name>. If it is satisfied by more than one row, the first one will be SELECTed INTO.

The result of the SELECT ... INTO command is that the values SELECTed are transferred into the memory variables for further use.

For example, suppose we have a table, Emp, of employees, containing the names of employees and their Social Security numbers. We want a short program to obtain the Social Security number of an employee, given his name. A program excerpt for doing that is:

```
ACCEPT "Enter employee's name:" TO m_emp
SELECT ss_no
INTO m_ss_no
FROM Emp
WHERE UPPER(name) = UPPER(m_emp);
@ 10,5 SAY m_ss_no
WAIT
*WAIT displays the message, Press any key to continue...,
*and causes all processing to pause until a key is pressed.
```

If you misspell the employee's name, or there is more than one employee with the same name, an error condition will occur, and the above program excerpt will not work.

The variables SQLCODE and SQLCNT referred to in Section 11.1 above can be used to check for such an error condition. Instead of the @ ... SAY command right after the WHERE clause, you can use the following excerpt:

```
IF SQLCODE = 0
    IF SQLCNT < 1
        @ 10,5 SAY "There is no employee with that name."
        WAIT
        *WAIT displays the message, Press any key to
        *continue..., and causes all processing to pause
        *until a key is pressed.
    ENDIF
```

```
    IF SQLCNT = 1
        @ 10,5 SAY m_ss_no
        WAIT
    ENDIF
    IF SQLCNT > 1
        @ 10,5 SAY "There is more than one employee with
          that name"
        WAIT
    ENDIF
ENDIF
```

You could also use the DO CASE command:

```
IF SQLCODE = 0
    DO CASE
        CASE SQLCNT < 1
            @ 10,5 SAY "There is no employee with that
              name."
            WAIT
        CASE SQLCNT = 1
            @ 10,5 SAY m_ss_no
            WAIT
        OTHERWISE
    @ 10,5 SAY "There is more than one employee with that
      name"
            WAIT
    ENDCASE
ENDIF
```

11.3 CURSORS

Cursors are useful for writing user programs to access the rows of a result table. A CURSOR is like a file containing the rows of a result table created by an SQL SELECT statement.

Like a file, a CURSOR may be opened and rows can be read out of it. Like a file, a CURSOR has a row pointer which points to the next row to be read. When the CURSOR is OPENed, the CURSOR pointer points before the first row of the result table.

When a FETCH command is performed the first time, the CURSOR pointer is advanced to the first row of the result table, and the values in the fields in the first row are FETCHed into memory variables. Subsequent FETCHs advance the CURSOR pointer one row, and FETCH the values in the fields of the row pointed to into memory variables. (Further details on FETCH can be found in Section 11.3.2.)

The row pointed to by the CURSOR pointer can be UPDATEd or DELETEd. The first FETCH beyond the last row sets SQLCODE to +100 but produces no error message. In software, CURSOR is not CLOSEd until the user CLOSEs it or until encountering a RETURN from the highest level .prs. When a CURSOR is CLOSEd, it can be (re)OPENed.

For example, suppose salesmen are to be given a special bonus, with the amount depending on the items sold, and with items sold and bonuses kept in different tables. The table of items sold and who sold them can be FETCHed one row at a time by means of a CURSOR in a program. Then, depending on the item found, the program can update the table containing bonuses.

You can have ten CURSORs OPEN at a time. However, to determine the maximum number of CURSORs, you must subtract the number of files in use, since there cannot be more CURSORs OPEN than there are available work areas.

The number of work areas necessary to perform an SQL operation can be roughly estimated as follows:

- Allow one work area for each file left open in dBASE.
- Allow one work area for each table referenced.
- Allow one or more work areas for each open CURSOR, depending on the CURSOR definition.
- Allow one or more work areas for each subquery or self-join, depending on the nature of the subquery or self-join.
- Allow one work area for system catalogs.
- Allow one work area for each GROUP BY or ORDER BY clause.
- Allow one work area for each temporary table created with the SAVE TO TEMP clause.

The result of a query is a *result table*. There are many and varied uses of an application program that can access the rows of such a table. Some of the most common uses are:

- To prepare a report. Here are the different ways of doing this:
  - You can use the SAVE TO TEMP clause with the KEEP option to create a table for use with the dBASE report writer. For example, see Section 11.3.10.

- Another way to prepare a report is to CREATE in advance an empty table whose rows are to be filled in with current data to be used in a report.

- Still another way to prepare a report is to obtain the needed data for the report, one line at a time, within a program, and send it to the printer. However, this method will not allow you to use the formatting capabilities of the dBASE report writer. For an example of this method, see Section 11.3.9.

- To UPDATE or DELETE rows in a table where the UPDATing or DELETion depends on the contents of the fields in the row being UPDATEd or DELETEd. For an example, see Section 11.3.4.

- To make UPDATEs or DELETions in one table based, on the contents of a row in another table. For example, see Sections 11.3.3, 11.3.6, and 11.3.8.

- To check integrity constraints.

  For example, you might want to check for duplicate occurrences of a key value and make corrections if any duplications are found. See Section 11.3.10.

  Another possibility is that duplicate rows may have occurred in one of your tables. This can happen when two different people are INSERTing data in your tables. For an example of a program to help remove duplicate rows, see Section 11.3.11.

- To move some of the information in a table to a table somewhere else in a distributed database.

  For example, in a distributed database, on a local area network (LAN), you may decide to move data on one disk storage system to another disk storage system for more efficient retrieval, or for security. You can use a program at the initial site to remove the data and send it over the LAN to the second site where another program will store it in the database at that site.

11.3.1 The DECLARE CURSOR and OPEN Commands

A CURSOR name is associated with an SQL SELECT statement by the following command:

DECLARE <cursor name> CURSOR FOR <SQL SELECT statement>
[FOR UPDATE OF <column list> | <ORDER BY clause>];

where:

<cursor name> can be up to ten characters long, may consist of letters, numbers, and underscores, and must begin with a letter. A CURSOR remains declared, and is associated with the same SQL SELECT statement, from the time it is DECLAREd until a SET SQL OFF command is performed.

FOR UPDATE OF is generally optional, but is required if any rows of the base table are to be UPDATEd while using the CURSOR.

<column list> is a list of names of columns to be UPDATEd, separated by commas.

Note that the ORDER BY clause and the FOR UPDATE OF clause are mutually exclusive.

The semicolon on the end is a terminator.

A program opens a CURSOR by the following command:

OPEN <cursor name>;

11.3.2 FETCH and CLOSE

After the OPEN command, the CURSOR pointer points before the first row. The command that advances the CURSOR pointer to the first row or the next row of the result table, and reads the row into memory variables, is:

FETCH <cursor name> INTO <list of variables (one for each column name being SELECTed)>;

where:

<list of variables> is a set of memory variables. The column values SELECTed in the SELECT statement in the DECLARE CURSOR command will be read into the list of variables.

For example, if you SELECT no_items and name from a certain table, and your list of variables is no and nam, then the values for no_items and name in the row pointed at by the CURSOR pointer will be transferred into the memory variables no and nam, respectively, by the FETCH statement.

The FETCH command changes the CURSOR pointer to point at the next row. If you try to FETCH when the CURSOR pointer is already pointing at the last row, the CURSOR pointer is moved to point after the last row, the memory variable SQLCODE is set to +100, and the CURSORS's work area is released.

If all of the FETCHs have been completed, it is a good idea to close the CURSOR in the same way you would close a file. To do this, use the following command:

```
CLOSE <cursor name>;
```

If the program tries to FETCH beyond the last row of the CURSOR, the system will release the CURSOR work area, and set SQLCODE to +100. Thus, a program can either keep count of the number of rows FETCHed and CLOSE the CURSOR, or keep fetching until SQLCODE equals +100 and the CURSOR work area is released by the system. If this happens, you still must use a CLOSE statement before attempting to reOPEN the cursor.

Once the CURSOR has been CLOSEd, the program may reOPEN it. CLOSing and reOPENing may be repeated any number of times. A CURSOR cannot be reOPENed until it has been CLOSEd.

A reason for repeated OPENings is to use different sets of values in the CURSOR SELECT statement. The program can do this by using memory variables in the DECLARE CURSOR SELECT statement. An example of this is given in Section 11.3.6 below.

A CLOSE must occur between every pair of OPEN statements, or you will get a compiler error. For example, if you have an OPEN Salestab; on lines 10 and 13 of your code, line 11 or line 12 must be CLOSE Salestab;.

Usually the FETCH statement will be inside of a DO WHILE command loop whereby each row is FETCHed sequentially. If you don't know how many rows are in the result table created by your CURSOR's SELECT statement, it will be necessary to test SQLCODE after each FETCH. However, a program can get the number of rows in the CURSOR's SELECT statement, since the memory variable

SQLCNT will contain this number immediately after the CURSOR is opened. You can use the value in SQLCNT to control how many times you repeat the DO WHILE loop.

For example:

```
DECLARE Dummy CURSOR FOR
SELECT Dummy1, Dummy2
FROM Dumtab
WHERE Dummy3 < 100;
OPEN Dummy;
IF SQLCODE = 0
   m_count = SQLCNT
   DO WHILE m_count > 0
         FETCH Dummy INTO m_1, m_2;
         m_count = m_count - 1
         * lines of code
   ENDDO
ENDIF
CLOSE Dummy;
```

11.3.3 A Simple Program Using a CURSOR

Assume we have two tables, Salesman and Sales, CREATEd as follows:

CREATE TABLE Salesman

(name	CHAR(20),
address	CHAR(30),
hired	DATE,
age	SMALLINT,
sman_id_no	SMALLINT,
sales_todt	NUMERIC(9,2),
salary	NUMERIC(9,2),
bonus	NUMERIC(9,2));

where:

sman_id_no is a unique number identifying each salesman.

sales_todt is the amount of sales for that salesman during the current fiscal period.

CREATE TABLE Sales

(sman_id_no	SMALLINT,
item_desc	CHAR(20),
item_price	NUMERIC(9,2),
no_units	SMALLINT);

Suppose you want to give each salesman who sold $10,000 worth of widgets a $500 bonus. The code to do this is:

```
STORE 0 TO Sid
STORE SPACE(20) TO Id
STORE 0.00 TO Ip
STORE 0 TO Nu
DECLARE Salestab CURSOR FOR
SELECT sman_id_no, item_desc, item_price, no_units
FROM Sales;
OPEN Salestab;
IF SQLCODE = 0
    STORE SQLCNT TO No_rows
    *The value set in the memory variable No_rows
    *is for the DO WHILE which follows next.
    DO WHILE No_rows > 0
        FETCH Salestab INTO Sid,Id,Ip,Nu;
        STORE No_rows - 1 TO No_rows
        *This STORE keeps count of the number of rows
        *remaining.
        IF Id = "widget" .AND. Ip * Nu >= 10000
            UPDATE Salesman
            SET bonus = bonus + 500.00
            WHERE Sman_Id_no = Sid;
        ENDIF
    ENDDO
ENDIF
CLOSE Salestab;
```

You can make the above code more efficient by putting the criterion for the bonus into the DECLARE CURSOR SELECT statement, as follows:

```
STORE 0 TO Sid
DECLARE Salestab CURSOR FOR
SELECT sman_id_no
FROM Sales
WHERE item_desc = 'widget'
AND item_price * no_units >= 10000;
OPEN Salestab;
IF SQLCODE = 0
    STORE SQLCNT TO No_rows
    DO WHILE No_rows > 0
        FETCH Salestab INTO Sid;
        STORE No_rows - 1 TO No_rows
        UPDATE Salesman
        SET bonus = bonus + 500.00
        WHERE Sman_Id_no = Sid;
    ENDDO
ENDIF
CLOSE Salestab;
```

As mentioned above, it is possible to let the FETCH command close release the CURSOR work area by trying to FETCH beyond the last row. Modifying the code above to do this, we get:

```
STORE 0 TO Sid
DECLARE Salestab CURSOR FOR
SELECT sman_id_no
FROM Sales
WHERE item_desc = 'widget'
AND item_price * no_units >= 10000;
OPEN Salestab;
    DO WHILE .T.
        FETCH Salestab INTO Sid;
        IF SQLCODE = 100
            EXIT
        ENDIF
        UPDATE Salesman
        SET bonus = bonus + 500.00
        WHERE Sman_Id_no = Sid;
    ENDDO
CLOSE Salestab;
```

The CLOSE statement at the end of the above code is included because it is necessary in order to actually CLOSE the CURSOR. It's a good idea to always include a CLOSE statement to explicitly CLOSE the CURSOR, even though you have FETCHed beyond the last row.

11.3.4 DECLARE CURSOR FOR UPDATE and UPDATE WHERE CURRENT OF

The format for DECLARE CURSOR FOR UPDATE is:

DECLARE <cursor name> CURSOR
FOR <SELECT statement>
FOR UPDATE of <column list>;

where:

<column list> is a list of columns to be UPDATed.

The format for UPDATE WHERE CURRENT OF is:

UPDATE <table name>
SET <column name> = <expression>
[,<column name> = <expression> ...]
WHERE CURRENT OF <Cursor name>;

You cannot UPDATE WHERE CURRENT OF if the DECLARE CURSOR SELECT statement includes ORDER BY or GROUP BY.

When doing UPDATE ... WHERE CURRENT OF, FETCH is still used to advance the CURSOR pointer, and to read the current row into variables.

For example, using the Salesman Table of Section 11.3.3, suppose you want to increase by five percent the salaries of those salesmen who are over forty years of age. Code to do this is:

```
DECLARE Salestab CURSOR
FOR SELECT name, hired, age, sales_todt, salary, bonus
FROM Salesman
WHERE age > 40
FOR UPDATE of salary;
OPEN Salestab;
IF SQLCODE = 0
    DO WHILE .T.
        FETCH Salestab INTO nam, hir, ag, st, sal, bon;
        IF SQLCODE = 100
```

```
            EXIT
        ENDIF
        @ 0, 0 CLEAR
        @ 1, 0 SAY "Name:"
        @ 1, 10 SAY nam
        @ 3, 0 SAY "Hired:"
        @ 3, 10 SAY hir
        @ 5, 0 SAY "Age:"
        @ 5, 10 SAY ag
        @ 7, 0 SAY "Sales:"
        @ 7, 10 SAY st
        @ 9, 0 SAY "Salary:"
        @ 9. 1- SAY sal
        @ 11, 0 SAY "Bonus:"
        @ 11, 10 SAY bon
        @ 13, 0 SAY " "
        WAIT "Increase this salesman's salary? (Y/N) " TO yn
        IF UPPER(yn) = "Y"
            UPDATE Salesman
            SET salary = salary * 1.05
            WHERE CURRENT OF Salestab;
        ENDIF
    ENDDO
ENDIF
CLOSE Salestab;
```

11.3.5 DELETE WHERE CURRENT OF

DELETE WHERE CURRENT OF is similar to UPDATE WHERE CURRENT OF, except that you need not include the clause, FOR UPDATE OF, in the DECLARE CURSOR command. DELETE WHERE CURRENT OF DELETEs the record pointed at by the CURSOR pointer. The format for DELETE WHERE CURRENT OF is:

DELETE FROM <table or view name>
WHERE CURRENT OF <CURSOR name>;

where:

<table or view name> must be a table or view referenced in the DECLARE <CURSOR name> CURSOR ELECT clause. If <table or view name> is a view name, it must be an updatable view.

<CURSOR name> is the name of the CURSOR DECLAREd in the DECLARE CURSOR command.

You cannot DELETE WHERE CURRENT OF if the DECLARE CURSOR SELECT statement includes ORDER BY or GROUP BY.

An example of DELETE FROM WHERE CURRENT OF occurs in the program excerpt in the next section.

11.3.6 Using Memory Variables in the DECLARE CURSOR SELECT

You can use memory variables in your DECLARE CURSOR SELECT statement to limit the rows that are selected.

Assume that, in addition to the tables Sales and Salesman given in Section 11.3.3 above, there is a table named Stock to describe stock on hand, CREATEd as follows:

```
CREATE TABLE Stock

(item_type      CHAR(15),
item_desc       CHAR(20),
item_price      NUMERIC(9,2),
no_on_hand      SMALLINT,
no_sold         SMALLINT,
man_bonus       NUMERIC(9,2));
```

Assume further that there is a temporary table named Unrecded, that gives unrecorded sales for each salesman, CREATEd as follows:

```
CREATE TABLE Unrecded

(sman_id_no     SMALLINT,
item_desc       CHAR(20),
no_units        SMALLINT);
```

Assume that you want to UPDATE the Sales Table using this table, and then to DELETE the entries in this table after UPDATing the Sales Table.

```
DECLARE Unrec CURSOR FOR
SELECT *
FROM Unrecded;
DECLARE Salesmn CURSOR FOR
SELECT sales_todt
FROM Salesman
WHERE sman_id_no = Smin
*Smin is a memory variable which can be used to control
*which rows are SELECTed.
```

```
FOR UPDATE OF sales_todt;
DECLARE Stk CURSOR
FOR SELECT item_price, no_on_hand, no_sold
FROM Stock
WHERE item_desc = Itds
*Itds is a memory variable which will control the rows
*SELECTed.
FOR UPDATE OF no_on_hand, no_sold;
OPEN Unrec;
IF SQLCODE = 0
    *We open Unrec first so we can use it to UPDATE the
    *other tables.
    STORE SQLCNT TO Unrec_cnt
    DO WHILE Unrec_cnt > 0
        FETCH Unrec
        INTO Smid, Itds, Nounits;
        STORE Unrec_cnt - 1 TO Unrec_cnt
        ON ERROR DO Err_hand
        *So that, in the event of an error, a ROLLBACK can
        *be executed.
        *Sample code for the Err_hand procedure is in
        *Section 11.3.7.
        BEGIN TRANSACTION
        *Start a TRANSACTION so that the record FETCHed
        *from will not be deleted unless all of the UPDATEs
        *are successful.
        OPEN Stk;
        IF SQLCODE = 0
            FETCH Stk INTO Itempr, No_onhand, m_sold;
            *Now INSERT a record into the Sales table to
            *reflect the unrecorded sale.
            INSERT INTO Sales
            VALUE   S (Smid,Itds,Itempr,Nounits);
            *Now UPDATE Stock to reflect the change in the
            *number of units on hand.
            UPDATE Stock
            SET No_on_hand = No_on_hand - Nounits,
            No_sold = No_sold + Nounits
            WHERE CURRENT OF Stk;
        ENDIF
        CLOSE Stk;
        *Now UPDATE the salesman's sales to date.
        OPEN Salesmn;
        IF SQLCODE = 0
            FETCH Salesmn INTO Sals;
```

```
            STORE Itempr * Nounits TO Itempr
            UPDATE Salesman
            SET sales_todt = sales_todt + Itempr
            WHERE CURRENT OF Salesmn;
        ENDIF
        CLOSE Salesmn;
        *Now delete the record in Unrecded since it has
        *been recorded.
        DELETE FROM Unrecded
        WHERE CURRENT OF Unrec;
        END TRANSACTION
        *You can END the TRANSACTION here because all of
        *the UPDATEs and DELETion of the record FETCHed
        *have been successfully carried out.
        ON ERROR
        *This command, without a condition, removes the
        *ON ERROR set before BEGIN TRANSACTION.
    ENDDO
ENDIF
CLOSE Unrec;
```

11.3.7 Error Handling

The error handler program in Err_hand.prs must check to see if a TRANSACTION has been begun and not completed. If that is the case, a *ROLLBACK* must be performed, and the program must wait for confirmation that the ROLLBACK has been successfully completed before RETURNing TO MASTER.

(The ROLLBACK function is discussed in Chapter Nine, Section 9.7.) The code can be as follows:

```
IF .NOT. COMPLETED()
    *A TRANSACTION has not been completed. An error has
    *occurred and your program has arrived here.
    @ 3,10 SAY MESSAGE()
    WAIT
    *Put the error message on the screen and ROLLBACK any
    *changes.
    ROLLBACK;
    *You might prefer to do a RETRY before ROLLBACK, but
    *this code is simplest.
    DO WHILE .NOT. ROLLBACK()
        @ 5,10 SAY 'ROLLBACK not completed.'
    ENDDO
    @ 5,10 SAY 'ROLLBACK completed.'
```

```
    WAIT
    RETURN TO MASTER
    *There are, of course, many other ways to terminate
    *depending on the needs of your application.
ENDIF
```

11.3.8 A Case Where More Than One CURSOR Is Useful

In the example in Section 11.3.5, the CURSORs for Salesman and Stock were unnecessary since the UPDATEs performed could have been performed by single SQL statements. It is not necessary to open more than one CURSOR unless, in the course of FETCHing the rows in one CURSOR, you have reason to examine or UPDATE more than one row in some other table; and, even then, it is not necessary to OPEN more than one CURSOR unless each of the rows in the second table requires individual inspection.

Suppose you want to keep a list of items for which prices are to be increased and then, when you have enough items, run a program to increase the prices. For this purpose you have a table called Increase, which has just one column called item_desc with data type CHAR(15). You can enter the items in this table as you think of them. Then, when you are ready, you can run a program to perform the increase.

Assume that the increase depends on the manufacturer's bonus. If the manufacturer's bonus is less than $100, the price increase is $10. If the manufacturer's bonus is between $100 and $200, the price increase is $15. And, if the manufacturer's bonus is between $200 and $300, the price increase is $30. Then, the following code will UPDATE prices on the item types in Increase:

```
DECLARE Inc CURSOR FOR
SELECT * FROM Increase;
DECLARE Stk CURSOR FOR
SELECT item_price, man_bonus FROM Stock
WHERE item_desc = m_desc
FOR UPDATE OF item_price;
OPEN Inc;
IF SQLCODE = 0
    STORE SQLCNT TO Cnt_inc
    DO WHILE Cnt_inc > 0
        ON ERROR DO Err_hand
        BEGIN TRANSACTION
        FETCH Inc INTO m_desc;
        STORE Cnt_inc - 1 TO Cnt_inc
        OPEN Stk;
        IF SQLCODE = 0
            STORE SQLCNT TO Cnt_stk
```

```
            DO WHILE Cnt_stk > 0
                FETCH Stk INTO price, m_bonus;
                STORE Cnt_stk - 1 TO Cnt_stk
                *Now test for the three conditions and
                *UPDATE accordingly.
                IF m_bonus < 100.00
                    UPDATE Stock
                    SET item_price = item_price + 10.00
                    WHERE CURRENT OF Stk;
                ENDIF
                IF m_bonus >= 100.00 .AND. m_bonus < 200.00
                    UPDATE Stock
                    SET item_price = item_price + 15.00
                    WHERE CURRENT OF Stk;
                ENDIF
                IF m_bonus >= 200.00 .AND. m_bonus < 300.00
                    UPDATE Stock
                    SET item_price = item_price + 30.00
                    WHERE CURRENT OF Stk;
                ENDIF
            ENDDO
            *Now, CLOSE Stk so it can be opened again on the
            *next loop.
        ENDIF
        CLOSE Stk;
        *DELETE this row from Increase. We are through with
        *it.
            DELETE FROM Increase WHERE CURRENT OF Inc;
            END TRANSACTION
            ON ERROR
    ENDDO
    *Now CLOSE Inc, since we have used all the rows.
    CLOSE Inc;
ENDIF
```

Instead of the IF statements above, the values for the UPDATEs could have been taken from a table. For example, assume a table giving the amount of the price increase has been CREATEd as:

CREATE TABLE Amt_inc

*Amt_inc stands for the amount of the price increase.

(Low_bnd NUMERIC(9,2),

Up_bnd NUMERIC(9,2),

Increase NUMERIC(9,2));

To use the Amt_inc table and include transaction processing, the code above would be modified as follows:

```
DECLARE Inc CURSOR FOR
SELECT * FROM Increase;
DECLARE Stk CURSOR FOR
SELECT item_price, man_bonus FROM Stock
WHERE item_desc = m_desc
FOR UPDATE OF item_price;
OPEN Inc;
IF SQLCODE = 0
    STORE SQLCNT TO Cnt_inc
    DO WHILE Cnt_inc > 0
        FETCH Inc INTO m_desc;
        ON ERROR DO Err_hand
        *Err_hand is the program to ROLLBACK any changes
        *made in the event that something goes wrong during
        *the following transaction. The code for Err_hand
        *is in Section 11.3.7, above.

        BEGIN TRANSACTION
        *There are two steps in the following UPDATE:
        *1. Change the item prices.
        *2. DELETE the current row from the table Increase.
        *If only one of them occurs, the database will be
        *inconsistent. By enclosing them in a transaction,
        *you can make sure that either both or neither
        *occur. If one of them fails, the other one will be
        *rolled back by the Err_hand procedure.
        STORE Cnt_inc - 1 TO Cnt_inc
        OPEN Stk;
        IF SQLCODE = 0
            STORE SQLCNT TO Cnt_stk
            DO WHILE Cnt_stk > 0
                FETCH Stk INTO price,m_bonus;
                STORE Cnt_stk - 1 TO Cnt_stk
                *Now get the amount of the increase from
                *Amt_inc.
                SELECT Increase
                INTO m_inc
                FROM Amt_inc
                WHERE m_bonus > Low_bnd AND m_bonus <
                  Up_bnd;
```

```
                *m_inc is a memory variable where we store
                *the amount for use in the following
                *UPDATE.
                UPDATE Stock
                SET item_price = price + m_inc
                WHERE CURRENT OF Stk;
            ENDDO
            CLOSE Stk;
            *Now DELETE this type from Increase.
            DELETE FROM Increase WHERE CURRENT OF Inc;
        ENDIF
        *Now you have increased all of the prices for this
        *item, so, the transaction can be ended.
        END TRANSACTION
        *Now the following ON ERROR turns off the possible
        *call to Err_hand in the event of an error.
        ON ERROR
    ENDDO
    CLOSE Inc;
ENDIF
```

Another way to UPDATE prices would be to define a FUNCTION, INCRS, to RETURN the increase in item_price as follows:

```
FUNCTION INCRS
PARAMETER bonus
IF bonus < 100.00
    RETURN 10.00
ENDIF

IF bonus >= 100.00 .AND. bonus < 200.00
    RETURN 15.00
ENDIF

IF bonus >= 200.00 .AND. bonus < 300.00
    RETURN 30.00
ENDIF
```

When you are setting up a user-defined FUNCTION in a .prs file, you must be careful to only include dBASE functions and commands which are allowed in SQL mode. Furthermore, user-defined FUNCTIONs cannot be embedded in SQL statements.

If INCRS is in the file proc1.prs then you can use the following code:

```
SET PROCEDURE TO proc1.prs

DECLARE Inc CURSOR FOR
SELECT * FROM Increase;
DECLARE Stk CURSOR FOR
SELECT item_price,bonus FROM Stock
WHERE item_desc = m_desc
FOR UPDATE OF item_price;
OPEN Inc;
IF SQLCODE = 0
    STORE SQLCNT TO Cnt_inc
    DO WHILE Cnt_inc > 0
        ON ERROR DO Err_hand
        BEGIN TRANSACTION
        FETCH Inc INTO m_desc;
        STORE Cnt_inc - 1 TO Cnt_inc
        OPEN Stk;
        IF SQLCODE = 0
            STORE SQLCNT TO Cnt_stk
            DO WHILE Cnt_stk > 0
                FETCH Stk INTO price,m_bonus;
                STORE Cnt_stk - 1 TO Cnt_stk
                STORE INCRS(m_bonus) TO m_inc
                UPDATE Stock
                SET item_price = price + m_inc
                WHERE CURRENT OF Stk;
            ENDDO
            *Now, CLOSE Stk so it can be opened again on the
            *next loop.
        ENDIF
        CLOSE Stk;
        *DELETE this row from Increase. We are through
        *with it.
        DELETE FROM Increase WHERE CURRENT OF Inc;
        END TRANSACTION
        ON ERROR
    ENDDO
    *Now CLOSE Inc, since we have used all the rows.
    CLOSE Inc;
ENDIF
```

11.3.9 Using the ORDER BY Clause in a CURSOR

Suppose we want a report on salesmen, where the salesman with the highest sales total is at the top. The way to do this is:

```
DECLARE Salesmn CURSOR FOR
SELECT * FROM Salesman
ORDER BY sales_todt DESC;
*The DESC will cause the first row FETCHED to be that of
*the salesman with the largest $ volume of sales, to be
*followed by those salesmen with $ volume of sales in
*descending order.

OPEN Salesmn;
IF SQLCODE = 0
    STORE SQLCNT TO Cnt_salesm
    STORE 0 TO Count
    DO WHILE Count < Cnt_salesm
        FETCH Salesmn INTO m1,m2,m3,m4,m5,m6,m7,m8;
        STORE Count + 1 TO Count
        DO NEXTLINE
        *Where NEXTLINE is a program to print out the next
        *line of the report.
    ENDDO
    CLOSE Salesmn;
ENDIF
```

11.3.10 Integrity Checking with Cursors

An integrity violation occurs whenever you have a duplicate row or key. The most important case is a key for a table which should be unique, but by mistake a duplicate value for the key has been INSERTed. For example, in the Salesman Table with columns id_no, name, address, and phone, there may be two salesmen with the same Sman_id_no. This would cause a lot of trouble, since it would then be impossible to decide from the Sales Table (where salesmen are referenced only by id_no) which salesman had made a certain sale.

Here is an application program to find instances of more than one salesman with the same Sman_id_no.

First, CREATE a table to store the results. Then, when the program is finished, you will be able to consider the rows one by one and decide what needs to be done to restore the integrity of the database. Name the table Sales_tg.

```
CREATE TABLE Sales_tg
(Id_no Smallint,
```

```
Name Char(20));
*Cursor Intg is to fetch every tuple of the table Salesman
DECLARE Intg CURSOR FOR
SELECT Sman_id_no, Name
FROM Salesman
ORDER BY Sman_id_no;
*Open the cursor
OPEN Intg;
*Every tuple of Salesman will be fetched one by one until
*the last tuple. The DO WHILE loop will terminate when
*there is no tuple to be fetched (when SQLCODE = 100)
DO WHILE .T.
    FETCH Intg INTO m_id, m_name;
    IF SQLCODE = 100      && Last operation touches no rows;
      exit DO WHILE loop.
        EXIT
    ELSE
        *SELECT COUNT(*) is to check how many tuples in
        *Salesman have the same key (Sman_id_no).
        SELECT COUNT(*)
        FROM Salesman
        WHERE Sman_id_no = m_id;
        *If SQLCNT (or COUNT (*)) is larger than 1, tuples
        *with the same key must exist in Salesman. Then,
        *the program inserts these tuples into the new
        *table Sales_tg.
        IF SQLCNT > 1
            INSERT INTO Sales_tg
            SELECT Sman_id_no, Name
            FROM Salesman
            WHERE Sman_id_no = m_id
        ENDIF
    ENDIF
ENDDO
*CLOSE the cursor
CLOSE Intg;
*End of the program
```

You can find instances of more than one salesman having the same id_no without a CURSOR by means of the following SELECT statement:

```
SELECT S1.Sman_id_no, S1.Name
FROM Salesman S1
WHERE EXISTS
    (SELECT S2.Sman_id_no
```

```
    FROM Salesman S2
    WHERE S1.Sman_id_no = S2.Sman_id_no AND S1.Name !=
      S2.Name)
SAVE TO TEMP Sales_tg KEEP;
```

The subquery above is an example of a *correlated subquery* which is evaluated once for each of the rows in the table. Since the subquery must also check each of the rows in the table, the entire query involves checking the square of the number of the rows in the table which, for a table of just 1,000 rows, could involve checking 1,000,000 rows, depending on certain other factors such as what indexes are in use. Therefore, if the table has many rows, the SELECT above may be much slower than the CURSOR program. The CURSOR program also has the advantage that it will capture duplicate rows. If, on the other hand, the table is small, then the simplicity of the SELECT statement recommends it for use over the CURSOR program.

The SAVE TO TEMP clause in the above SELECT statement saves the result of the query in the temporary table Sales_tg. The keyword KEEP insures that the table will not be deleted if you leave SQL. You can print a report using Sales_tg, and make the necessary corrections to the salesmen's ID numbers at your leisure.

11.3.11 A CURSOR Program to Eliminate Duplicate Rows

One of the most difficult things to do in SQL is to eliminate duplicate rows, since there is no way to separate one from the other in a WHERE clause. One way to do this in dBASE IV is to leave SQL and use record numbers. However, it is more convenient to remain in SQL and use one of the two techniques illustrated in the following examples.

The following CURSOR program eliminates duplicate records from the Salesman Table having columns id_no, name, address, phone.

```
DECLARE m_id[2],m_name[2],m_address[2],m_phone[2]
SET EXACT ON

*SET EXACT ON so comparisons will be exact

DECLARE Salesmn CURSOR
FOR SELECT *
FROM Salesman
ORDER BY id_no, name, address, phone;
OPEN Salesmn;
*Open the cursor
Open Salesman
```

```
*Every tuple of a Salesman fetched one by one until the
*last tuple. The DO WHILE loop will terminate when there
*is no tuple to be fetched (when SQLCODE = 100).
DO WHILE .T.
    FETCH Salesman
    INTO m_id,m_name,m_address,m_)phone;
    IF SQLCODE = 100
        EXIT
    ELSE
        *SELECT COUNT (*) is to check how many tuples in
        *Salesman have the same data.
        SELECT COUNT (*)
        FROM Salesman
        WHERE id_no = m_id
        AND name = m_name
        AND address = m_address
        AND phone = m_phone;
        *If SQLCNT (or COUNT (*)) is larger than 1, tuples
        *must exist in Salesman. Delete all duplicates,
        *then INSERT one row with these values.
        IF SQLCNT > 1
            DELETE FROM Salesman
            WHERE id_no = m_id
            AND name = m_name
            AND address = m_address
            AND phone = m_phone;
            INSERT INTO Salesman
            VALUES
            (m_id,m_name,m_address,m_phone);
        ENDIF
ENDDO
CLOSE Salesmn;
```

If there happened to be a large number of repetitions of the same row in the table, the program above would be very inefficient. The following program excerpt is more efficient, especially if there are not too many different rows which have duplicates.

```
DECLARE m_id[2],m_name[2],m_address[2],m_phone[2]
*To check duplicate as in the previous example.
DECLARE m_repeat[100,4]
*To hold duplicated records. One copy of each.
m_arr_cnt = 0
*To index m_repeat
Too_many = .F.
```

```
*To be used in the event that there are more than 100
*different duplicated rows.
SET EXACT ON
*SET EXACT ON so comparisons will be exact
DECLARE Salesmn CURSOR
FOR SELECT *
FROM Salesman
ORDER BY id_no, name, address, phone;
OPEN Salesman;
IF SQLCODE = 0 .AND. SQLCNT != 0
    m_count = SQLCNT
    DO WHILE m_count > 0
        FETCH Salesmn
        INTO m_id[2],m_name[2],m_address[2],m_phone[2];
        m_count = m_count - 1
        IF m_id[1] = m_id[2] .AND. m_name[1] = m_name[2];
        .AND.m_address[1] = m_address[2];
        .AND. m_phone[1] = m_phone[2]
            IF m_arr_cnt = 100
                Too_many = .T.
                EXIT
                *If the ARRAY is full, exit the DO WHILE
                *loop.
            ENDIF
            new = .F.
            IF m_arr_cnt = 0
                m_arr_cnt = 1
                new = .T.
                *To indicate new duplicate.
            ELSE
                IF m_id[1] != m_repeat[m_arr_cnt,1];
                .OR. m_name[1] != m_repeat[m_arr_cnt,2];
                .OR. m_address[1] != m_repeat[m_arr_cnt,3];
                .OR. m_phone[1] != m_repeat[m_arr_cnt,4]
                    m_arr_cnt = m_arr_cnt + 1
                    new = .T.
                ENDIF
            ENDIF
            IF new
                m_repeat[m_arr_cnt,1] = m_id[1]
                m_repeat[m_arr_cnt,2] = m_name[1]
                m_repeat[m_arr_cnt,3] = m_address[1]
                m_repeat[m_arr_cnt,4] = m_phone[1]
            ENDIF
        ENDIF
```

```
          *Now move the values FETCHed into the memory
          *variables used for comparison.
          m_id[1] = m_id[2]
          m_name[1] = m_name[2]
          m_address[1] = m_address[2]
          m_phone[1] = m_phone[2]
     ENDDO
     CLOSE Salesmn
     *Now clear out the duplicates in the same way as in the
     *previous program.
     m_ct = 1
     DO WHILE m_ct <= m_arr_cnt
          ON ERROR DO Err_hand
          BEGIN TRANSACTION
          *To make certain the following DELETE will be rolled
          *back if something goes wrong with the INSERT that
          *follows it. See Err_hand above.
          DELETE FROM Salesman
          WHERE id_no = m_repeat[m_ct,1]
          AND name = m_repeat[m_ct,2]
          AND address = m_repeat[m_ct,3]
          AND phone = m_repeat[m_ct,4];
          INSERT INTO Salesman
          VALUES (m_repeat[m_ct,1],m_repeat[m_ct,2],
          m_repeat[m_ct,3],m_repeat[m_ct,4]);
          END TRANSACTION
          ON ERROR
          m_ct = m_ct + 1
     ENDDO
     IF Too_many
          @ 10,5 SAY 'There are still duplicate records.'
          @ 12,5 SAY 'About to make another pass.'
          WAIT 'Do you want to continue? (Y/N) ' TO cont
          IF UPPER(cont) != 'Y'
               RETURN
          ENDIF
     ENDIF
ENDIF
```

If the above program is in rem_dup.prs, the memory variable, Too_many, can be checked by the calling program, and the above program can be repeated until all duplicate records have been removed, as follows:

```
PUBLIC Too_many
Too_many = .T.
DO WHILE Too_many
    DO rem_dup.prs
ENDDO
@ 10,5 SAY 'All duplicate records have been removed.'
WAIT
*WAIT displays the message, "Press any key to continue...",
*and causes all processing to pause until a key is pressed.
```

12

Keys and Normalization

In this Chapter we discuss some of the theory behind relational databases, since this will assist you in designing your database, and in understanding how to form queries. To illustrate relational theory and the design of queries, we will make use of simple databases.

For example, you can have a database to keep track of your checks. Such a database has in it check number, amount, date, payee, and, usually, some notation regarding the purpose of the payment.

The information in your check database can be arranged in a tabular format as, for example, the table shown in Figure 12-1.

Figure 12-1. Check Table

check_no	amount	date	payee	purpose
100	25.38	Feb 27, 1987	Bell Telephone	Feb bill
101	900.64	Mar 1, 1987	Federal loan Co.	Mtgge payment
102	35.00	Mar 2, 1987	AA Plumbing Co.	repair faucet

Your Check Table contains rows and columns. The columns all have names, in this case: check_no, amount, date, payee, and purpose. The rows have information about individual checks, and the information in a given row is all related to one check. The check_no column is called a *key*, because it designates a unique check.

The Check Table by itself is an example of a very simple database. Usually databases are much more complicated, containing multiple tables of related information.

One of the advantages of relational databases is that an extensive theory exists concerning the best way to break up your information into tables. The theory is so extensive that it could easily fill a book or two. Here, we confine ourselves to very fundamental aspects of the theory.

Once you have normalized your database by breaking your information up into several tables, you should consider how to get the information you need out of your database. Frequently, you will want to bring parts of several different tables together. Thus, you will be designing queries which combine tables, using comparison operators, also known as *relational operators*. (See Chapter Four, Section 4.2.)

Functional dependencies, keys, foreign keys, and normal forms are discussed in Section 12.1. Section 12.2 discusses the desirability of the normal forms. Section 12.3 discusses how to achieve normal forms.

12.1 KEYS AND NORMALIZATION

Suppose you are an employer and you have a database containing information about your salesmen. You want to keep information such as each salesman's name, Social Security number, address, and home phone number. In addition, you want to keep information about each salesman's sales, such as item sold, date sold, quantity sold, and dollar value of sale.

You could have one table where the column names are the items listed above. However, this would have the disadvantage that every time a salesman made a sale, you would have to repeat the salesman's name and Social Security number in the row corresponding to that sale. These items would be repeated in many rows with the same values, creating redundancy and wasting a lot of space.

You could save space by using two tables, one for the salesman's personal data, and another for the details of the individual sales. To relate the two tables, it would be convenient to give each salesman an identification number, which would then appear as a column in both tables. In the table containing the salesman's personal data, the identification number would be related to the salesman. In the sales table, there would be a column for the identification number so that the sale would be credited to a specific salesman, and each salesman would have a different identification number. The salesman's identification number is an example of a *key* in the salesman's personal data table.

To define the term key, we begin by defining superkey. A *superkey* in a table is a column (or collection of columns) which uniquely determine rows. A *key* is a column (or a *minimal* collection of columns) which uniquely determine rows. Every key is a superkey, and every collection of columns containing the columns of a key is a superkey. Examples of keys are:

- The check number in the Check Table.
- The salesman's identification number in the Salesman Table.

The salesman's identification number is not a key in the Sales Table, because the same identification number will be repeated in more than one row. It is called a foreign key. A *foreign key* is a column (or group of columns) in a table which is a key in some other table. Thus, the salesman's identification number is a foreign key in the Sales Table because it is a key in the Salesman Table. Unless there are duplicate rows, a table always has at least one key, because the collection of all columns is a superkey, and either the collection of all columns is a key, or some subset of the columns is a key.

Occasionally, an error in data entry will result in duplicate rows. Duplicate rows should be eliminated because they waste space, cause confusion, and destroy the integrity of the database. (See Chapter Eleven, Section 11.3.11 for a program to eliminate duplicate rows.)

Examples of a Salesman Table and a Sales Table in Figures 12-2 and 12-3 below, will be used in later examples in this Chapter.

Figure 12-2. Salesman Table

id_no	name	address	phone
1000	Joe James	1201 Adams St.	832 4509
1001	Bill Cray	1011 Marion St.	486 2100
1002	John Smith	1812 Kearney St.	211 9875

Figure 12-3. Sales Table

id_no	item	no_sold
1001	Furnace	50
1000	Radio	10
1000	Stove	5
1001	Stove	6

We split the information for the sales database into two tables in order to avoid repeating information about the salesman every time a sale was entered. In a relational database, unnecessary repetition of information is called a *redundancy anomaly*.

Another problem that is avoided by breaking the salesman database into two tables is the problem of having to update many rows when a change in information about the salesman occurs. With the Salesman Table, we only need to update one row for any change in information about the salesman. If the information about a salesman were repeated in many rows, then we would have to update all the rows for that salesman, and we might miss one. This problem is called the *update anomaly*.

Breaking tables into one or more new tables is one way of achieving a *normalized database*, that is, a database which is in one of the normal forms of the theory of relational databases.

In the sections to follow, we treat four normal forms that relational database tables can satisfy. The *normal forms* are designed to eliminate anomalies, and to adhere to the principles laid down by the founders of relational database theory. In each case, a database is said to be in that normal form if and only if each of the tables in the database are in that normal form.

12.1.1 First Normal Form

A table is said to be in *first normal form* if and only if no row has multiple entries in any column. Some authors do not even consider a table to be relational unless the first normal form criterion is satisfied; see, for example, the article by Codd referenced at the end of this chapter.

For example, if you have reason to keep a record of the salesmen's children, and you have a column labeled Children in the Salesman Table, you are violating the criteria for first normal form, since some salesmen may have more than one child, and you will have to list them all in the row for that salesman—which means that you will have more than one entry in that row under the Children column.

The best way to correct the problem of having more than one child in a row is to create a table called Children with two columns: salesmen's id number (abbreviated in some way) and child. Then list the children in separate rows, with the child's name in the second column and the salesman's id number in the first column. The salesmen's id number will be a foreign key in the Children Table. To obtain a list of James Brown's children, you can use the following query:

```
SELECT name,child

FROM Salesmen,Children

WHERE name = 'James Brown'

AND Salesmen.id_no = Children.id_no;
```

12.1.2 Functional Dependency

The other normal forms that we will consider here all involve the concept of *functional dependency*. For example, a column B is said to be *functionally dependent* upon a column A if, whenever column B has different values in two rows, Column A must also have different values in those two rows. In other words, Column B is functionally dependent on Column A if column A is a key in the table obtained by projecting on columns A and B.

For example, in our Salesman Table above, every column is functionally dependent on the salesman's identification number because there can be only one salesman with a given identification number. However, none of the columns of the sales table are functionally dependent on the salesman's identification number, because every column in the Sales Table can have distinct values while the salesman's identification number remains the same.

Functional dependencies are sometimes called *integrity constraints*; and when they are violated—as would be the case in the Salesman Table if two different salesmen had the same salesman's id number—it is said that "the integrity of the database has been violated". (Database integrity is also discussed in Section 9.11 of Chapter Nine, and Section 11.3.10 of Chapter Eleven.)

It's a good idea to have some application programs to check for violation of integrity constraints. (You might want to run these at night, or on weekends, since they are time-consuming, and might interfere with other users of the database.) Even on small databases, such programs are useful. For example, if, in the salesman's table, you were to accidentally assign the same salesman's identification number to two different salesmen, this could cause a lot of trouble.

The concept of functional dependency also holds for sets of columns. Thus, if both B and A in the above definition are sets of columns, B is said to be functionally dependent on A if the values in the columns of A, taken all together, determine the values in the columns in B.

The concept of functional dependency gives another way to define a key, namely: a *key* for a table is a minimal set of columns, such that every column in the table is functionally dependent on that set of columns.

The notation for functional dependency is:

column1column2column3... -> column4column5column6...

which means columns 4, 5, 6, and so on are functionally dependent on columns 1, 2, 3, and so on, taken all together. For example, in the Salesman Table above we can write:

id_no -> name address phone

It is important to realize that the notation A->B doesn't mean just that the database does not have a table with two rows in which the value under the column A is the same, and the values under the column B are different. A->B is stronger than that. It means that the database can never have a table in which two rows have the same value in column A, and different values in column B.

Therefore, it is not possible to discover the functional dependencies by inspecting the tables of the database as they stand at any given time. Such an inspection would usually give a false impression of functional dependencies, because there would be columns which would appear to depend on other sets of columns, such that the addition of one acceptable row would show that the dependency did not hold.

For example, inspection of the Sales Table in Figure 12-3 above would lead you to the false functional dependency no_sold ->id_no. However, if you update by inserting the following row:

id_no	item	no_sold
1001	radio	5

the results will show that the functional dependency no_sold ->id_no does not hold for the Sales Table, because there would be two rows, one in which id_no equals 1000 and the other in which id_no equals 1001, both of which have no_sold equal to 5. In other words, the functional dependencies must be decided upon by you ahead of time, and maintained that way, based upon your knowledge of the information you keep in your database.

In the following sections, it will be assumed that a complete list of the functional dependencies is known. Given the set of functional dependencies, a key is only a key with respect to that set. The same thing holds with respect to each of the concepts in the following sections.

12.1.3 Prime Attribute, Full Dependency, Second Normal Form

An attribute (column) is said to be a *prime attribute* in some table if it is one of a collection of columns which is a key for that table.

A column is said to be *fully dependent* on a set of columns if it is functionally dependent on the set of columns, and is not functionally dependent on any subset of the set of columns.

A table is said to be in *second normal form* if:

- It is in first normal form
- Every nonprime attribute is fully dependent on every key for the table.

A database is said to be in *second normal form* if every table in it is in second normal form.

For example, consider the Taxicab Table shown in Figure12-4.

Figure 12-4. Taxicab Table

taxi_no	day	driver	start
12	8 Oct	Smith	Airport
14	9 Oct	Jones	Holiday Inn
16	10 Oct	Bailey	Radisson Hotel

The functional dependencies in this table are taxi_no day -> driver start,taxi_no -> start. taxi_no and day together are a key. start is not in any key, and is nonprime. Also start is not fully dependent on the key taxi_no day. Therefore, the Taxicab Table is not in second normal form.

You can "decompose" the Taxicab Table into two tables that are both in second normal form by removing start from the Taxicab Table and putting it in a separate table with taxi_no. Then your two tables are as shown in Figures 12-5 and 12-6.

Figure 12-5. Projection of Taxicab Table on taxi_no, day, and driver

taxi_no	day	driver
12	8 Oct	Smith
14	9 Oct	Jones
16	10 Oct	Bailey

Figure 12-6. Projection of Taxicab Table on taxi_no and start

taxi_no	start
12	Airport
14	Holiday Inn
16	Radisson Hotel

12.1.4 Transitive Dependency, Third Normal Form

An attribute A (column) of a table is said to be *transitively dependent* upon a subset X of the columns of the table if there exists a subset Y of the columns of the table, such that:

- All of the columns in the subset Y are functionally dependent on the subset X
- Not all of the columns in the subset X are functionally dependent on the set of columns in Y
- A is functionally dependent on the set of columns in Y
- A is not in either of the subsets X or Y

A table is said to be in *third normal form* if:

- It is in first normal form
- No nonprime attribute is transitively dependent upon a key of the table

It is easy to see that if a nonprime attribute is not fully dependent on a key, then it is transitively dependent on that key.Thus, a table which is in third normal form is in second normal form.

A database is said to be in *third normal form* if every table in it is in third normal form.

For example, consider the Modified Taxicab Table shown in Figure 12-7.

Figure 12-7. Modified Taxicab Table

taxi_no	day	driver_id	driver_name
22	5 May	1000	Smith
24	6 May	1001	Jones
26	7 May	1002	Hess

The functional dependencies are taxi_no day -> driver_idname, driver_id -> name, name -> driver_id. taxi_no and day is a key. driver_name is not in any key, and is therefore nonprime.The key taxi_no day is not functionally dependent on driver_id. However, driver_name is transitively dependent on the key taxi_no day by way of driver_id. Therefore, the table is not in third normal form.

You can decompose the Modified Taxicab Table into two tables so that they are both in third normal form by making a new table with driver_id and driver_name in it, and removing driver_name from the first table, to get the two tables shown in Figures 12-8 and 12-9.

Figure 12-8. Projection of Modified Taxicab Table on taxi_no, day, and driver_id

taxi_no	day	driver_id
22	5 May	1000
24	6 May	1001
26	7 May	1002

Figure 12-9. Projection of Modified Taxicab Table on driver_id and driver_name

driver_id	driver_name
1000	Smith
1001	Jones
1002	Hess

12.1.5 Boyce-Codd Normal Form

A table is said to be in *Boyce-Codd normal form* if it meets the following criteria:

- It is in first normal form
- No attribute of the table is transitively dependent on a key of the table

Notice that the only difference between Boyce-Codd normal form and third normal form is that the attribute which is transitively dependent in the second criteria above can be prime. It is easy to see that, if a table is in Boyce-Codd normal form, then it is in third normal form. For a simple proof, see Section12.1.6 below.

For example, assume a table with columns named manufacturer, corporation, and department, such that the manufacturer who manufactures products for the corporation always sends his products to the department of the corporation listed in the database. Then, the functional dependencies are department -> corporation, and manufacturer and corporation -> department. Thus, both manufacturer and corporation, and manufacturer and department are keys for the table. Since all of the columns are in one of these two keys, the table is in third normal form because all columns are prime. However, corporation is dependent on the key, manufacturer and department—but not fully dependent, since it is dependent on the department alone. Thus, there is a transitive dependency of corporation on the key, manufacturer and department. So, the table is not in Boyce-Codd normal form.

A database is said to be in Boyce-Codd normal form if every table in the database is in Boyce-Codd normal form.

12.1.6 A Convenient Way to Remember Normal Forms

A convenient way to remember the second, third, and Boyce-Codd normal forms is to remember the following transitive dependency diagram:

X->Y->A

If an instance of this diagram occurs in a table (in first normal form) where:

- X is a subset of the columns, and is a key for the table
- Y is a subset of the columns of the table
- X is not functionally dependent on Y
- A is a column of the table which is functionally dependent on Y, but is not in either X or Y

then all of the following are true:

- If Y is a subset of X, and A is a nonprime attribute, thetable is *not* in second normal form.
- If A is a nonprime attribute, the table is *not* in third normal form.
- The table is *not* in Boyce-Codd normal form (whether or not A is a prime attribute).

It is easy to see that a.) implies b.), and b.) implies c.). By negation, Boyce-Codd normal form implies third normal form, and third normal form implies second normal form.

There are several other normal forms, such as *fourth normal form* and *project join normal form*. They are based upon dependencies other than functional dependencies. Those dependencies, and the normal forms based upon them, are beyond the scope of this short section. The interested reader should consult Maier (2), referenced at the end of this chapter, or one of the many other books on relational database theory.

12.2 DESIRABILITY OF THE NORMAL FORMS

Transitive dependencies are always undesirable, since they produce redundancy. To see this, notice that X -> Y -> A where it is not true that Y -> X, leaves open the possibility that the values in the combined columns of Y and A will be repeated for many different values in the columns of X. Redundancy always leads to the possibility of update problems, since repeated values in many different rows may have to be updated simultaneously; if one of the rows is missed, then the table will contain false data.

Clearly, tables in second normal form have fewer transitive dependencies that those which are not in second normal form; tables in third normal form have fewer transitive dependencies than tables which are only in second normal form; and only tables in Boyce-Codd normal form will be completely free of transitive dependencies on keys. Therefore, you might conclude that all of your tables should be in Boyce-Codd normal form. This is not necessarily so, as we shall see.

12.3 ACHIEVING NORMAL FORMS

Given a table with a transitive dependency, X -> Y -> A, you can decompose it into two tables which no longer have the transitive dependency, as follows:

1. Project on the columns in the subsets X and Y plus there maining columns other than A to obtain one table.

2. Project on the columns in Y plus column A to obtain a second table.

The columns of Y will contain a key for the second table which will be a foreign key in the first table; so that your two tables will be related by a key and a foreign key; thus, you can perform a join on them if you wish to see the rows of the original table. Furthermore, the transitive dependency will not occur in either of the resulting tables. If there are still transitive dependencies in the resulting tables, the process may be repeated. Eventually all transitive dependencies will have been removed. However, if there are many transitive dependencies, the order in which you do this can lead to differing results.Some of the outcomes may be better than others. What constitutes a "better" outcome is explained below.

One criterion for the outcome is to have as few tables as possible, such that the transitive dependencies have been removed. Another criterion is characterization of the functional dependencies by the resulting tables: a functional dependency X- >Y is said to be *embodied* by a table if X is a key for the table, and all the columns of Y are columns in the table.

A collection of tables *completely characterizes* a set of functional dependencies if and only if all functional dependencies are implied by the functional dependencies embodied in the tables.

It is desirable to have the functional dependencies completely characterized by the set of tables in the database because, then, the functional dependencies can be *enforced* by creating a unique index on each of the keys in the tables. If the functional dependencies are not enforced, updating of tables can accidentally lead to violation of some of the functional dependencies, which may mean that your data is unreliable.

It is not always possible to have a set of tables which completely characterizes the functional dependencies, and which is in Boyce-Codd normal form.

However, it is possible to have a set of tables satisfying the following:

a.) The tables completely characterize the set of functional dependencies.

b.) Every table is in third normal form.

c.) No set of tables having a smaller number of tables in it satisfies a.) and b.) above.

A set of tables satisfying a.), b.), and c.) is said to be a *complete database scheme for the set of functional dependencies.*

A complete database scheme can be achieved by an algorithm known as *synthesis*. The synthesis algorithm is beyond the scope of this book, and can be found in Maier (2). The most we can do here is to suggest that you very carefully decompose your tables, removing transitive dependencies while maintaining complete characterizability.

For example, suppose that you have a table with columns, salesman_id_no, name, address, phone, invoice_no, item, and no_sold. Suppose that the functional dependencies you wish to enforce are: salesman_id_no-> name, address, phone, and invoice_no-> salesman_id_no, item, no_sold. If you put all these columns in one table, then you will have several transitive dependencies like invoice_no -> salesman_id_no -> name.

However, you can decompose the one table into two tables:

1. The Salesman Table, with columns salesman_id_no, name, address, phone, and key, salesman_id_no.

2. The Sales Table, with columns invoice_no, salesman_id_no, item, no_sold, and key, invoice_no.

Thus, neither table will have any transitive dependencies, and the set of functional dependencies will be completely characterized by the two tables. Furthermore, you will be able to enforce the functional dependencies by creating unique indexes: one in the Salesman Table on salesman_id_no, and one in the Sales Table on invoice_no.

For complicated databases, there are many other considerations than just removal of transitive dependencies. The theory of database design is constantly evolving, with different points of view appearing in the literature. One recent point of view involving much of the relational theory is presented in Beeri and Kifer (3), referenced at the end of this chapter.

In summary, a relational database is a collection of tables related by keys and foreign keys. However, the collection can be hard to update and wasteful of space if it is not well-designed.

References:

Beeri, Catriel and Kifer, Michael. "An Integrated Approach to Logical Design of Relational Database Schemes". *ACM Transactions on Database Systems*, Vol 11, No 2, June 1986, pp. 134-158.

Codd, E. F. "A Relational Model of Data for Large Shared Data Banks". *Communications of the ACM 13*, No. 6 (June 1970). Reprinted in *Communications of the ACM 26*, No. 1 (January 1983).

Maier, David. *The Theory of Relational Databases*. Rockville, MD: Computer Science Press. 1983.

SQL Error Messages

This Appendix lists SQL Syntax Error Messages, followed by SQL Runtime Error Messages, each in alphabetical order.

Error message numbers appear in parentheses after each message.

SQL SYNTAX ERROR MESSAGES

*** allowed for COUNT function only (1082).** An asterisk has been used as the argument to a function other than COUNT. The argument for functions AVG, MAX, MIN, and SUM must be a column name.

ADD clause expected in ALTER TABLE (1036). ADD clause missing, misspelled, or misplaced in ALTER TABLE command.

Aggregate function not allowed in WHERE clause (1103). THE SQL aggregate functions AVG, COUNT, MAX, MIN, and SUM are not allowed in a WHERE clause (except as part of the SELECT clause in a subselect). Use two commands: first use a new SELECT command to find the value that would be returned by the function, then use that value as a constant in the WHERE clause of the original SELECT command.

Alias name already exists (1083). You have already applied this alias name to another table at some earlier point in the statement. Use a different alias name.

All SELECT columns must be inside an aggregate function (1164). When HAVING is used without GROUP BY, all SELECT columns must either be constants, or be inside a SQL aggregate function. Place all column names inside an aggregate function, or remove them from the SELECT clause.

All SELECT items must be GROUP BY columns or aggregate functions(1100). A SELECT clause includes both aggregate functions (AVG, COUNT, MAX, MIN and SUM) and column names not included in functions. All columns not included in functions must be included in GROUP BY clause. Add a GROUP BY clause to the command. If the GROUP BY clause is already part of the command, add the missing SELECT clause column names to it.

Ambiguous column name (1077). A column with the same name appears in two tables, both referenced in the current statement. Prefix ambiguous columns with their table name and a period, as in <table name>.<column name>.

An illegal table is referenced in a subSELECT FROM clause (1115). The table upon which the INSERT UPDATE or DELETE command is carried out cannot also be referenced in the FROM clause of a subSELECT.

Argument too long in CREATE INDEX, GROUP BY, ORDER BY, or SELECT DISTINCT (1185). An index expression of more than 100 chars has caused an error on a CREATE INDEX command, or on a SELECT command including clauses (such as GROUP BY or ORDER BY) which use indexes. Specify a shorter index key for a CREATE INDEX command. If this error occurred on a SELECT command, it is an internal error. Remove GROUP BY or ORDER BY clause or DISTINCT keyword.

Badly formed subquery (1172). Local predicate of an outer query is placed within a nested query. Re-formulate query without using a subquery (i.e., use outer predicate to restrict rows retrieved).

BY clause is not supported and will be ignored. This is a *warning*, not an error. dBASE IV SQL does not support a BY clause in the GRANT and REVOKE statements. No action needed.

Can't create subdirectory for new database (1155). A SQL table or a non-SQL file or subdirectory has the same name as that used in the CREATE DATABASE statement. Use a different name for the SQL database, or erase and remove the non-SQL file or directory before CREATing the DATABASE.

Cannot ALTER views (1151). Only base tables and their synonyms may be used in an ALTER TABLE statement. You can DROP a view, then redefine it to include additional columns.

Cannot CREATE INDEX/GROUP BY/ORDER BY/SELECT DISTINCT on a LOGICAL column (1182). Index cannot be built on a column of LOGICAL data type, and all these operations involve either user-defined or internal SQL indexes. Remove the LOGICAL type column.

Cannot DROP open database (1141). You tried to DROP the active database. STOP DATABASE, then use the DROP DATABASE command.

Cannot GRANT or REVOKE a privilege to yourself (1201). A GRANT or REVOKE command specifies your own user ID in the TO or FROM clause. You may only GRANT and REVOKE privileges of other users. Check the user ID list, and make sure it does not contain your own user ID. Make sure you logged in with your own user ID.

Cannot LOAD or UNLOAD DATA for views (1143). LOAD and UNLOAD DATA commands must be used with SQL base tables or their synonyms. You may use a SELECT * statement with SAVE TO TEMP clause on the view, and then UNLOAD from the temporary table.

Cannot mix ASC and DESC options in index key (1183). If the keyword DESC is specified, it must be specified for all keys in the index.

Catalog table Sysdbs does not exist (1229). The Sysdbs table must be in the SQL Home directory. Make sure that the SQLHOME directive in Config.db is correct. If it has been changed from its Install setting, make sure the complete set of SQL system tables, including Sysdbs, has been transferred to the new SQL Home directory.

Catalog tables are read-only (1161). Direct modification of the catalog tables is not allowed. Only the SQLDBA can directly update the system catalogs.

Catalog tables locked by another user (1140). Locks on the SQL catalog tables prevent completion of an operation. Wait and retry operation. If this message appears often, set SET REPROCESS to a higher number of retries.

Character string too long (1145). A character string exceeds the dBASE maximum length for character strings. Shorten the string.

CHECK OPTION cannot be used with current view (1107). The WITH CHECK OPTION clause cannot be used with a view that cannot be updated. See the UPDATE command entry in Chapter Five for rules on updating views.

Column is not updatable (1109). A column specified in the SELECT clause cannot be updated. See the UPDATE command entry in Chapter Five for rules on updating columns.

Column name already exists (1081). A command that names new columns has repeated the same name twice, or has attempted to use a name that already exists for some column in the table. Use a different column name.

Column name missing in AVG, MAX, MIN or SUM function (1130). The SQL aggregate functions AVG, MAX, MIN, and SUM require a column name as their argument. Make sure SQL functions take the form <aggregate function> (<column name>).

Column name or number expected in ORDER BY (1020). Only column names or integers can appear in the ORDER BY list. After the keywords ORDER BY, either give the column(s) by which you want the result table ordered, or substitute integers indicating the columns according to their place in the SELECT clause.

Column/field names must be specified in SAVE TO TEMP clause (1149). The SELECT returns column derived from functions or constants, so SAVE TO TEMP column/field names must be specified. Add a list of column/field names enclosed in parentheses after the filename in the SAVE TO TEMP clause.

Comma or right parenthesis expected (1052). A list has been specified incorrectly. Check for commas between the items, and for a right parenthesis at end of list.

Command cannot be executed within a transaction (1167). SQL data definition statements and utility commands cannot be used within transactions. Run the command outside of the transaction.

Comparison operator or keyword expected (1134). A comparison operator or keyword must follow the first column name or constant in a WHERE clause. The comparison operators are: =, >, <, <>, !=, <=, >=, !<, and !>. The comparison keywords are LIKE, IN, and BETWEEN.

Correlated subquery not allowed in HAVING clause (1160). A subselect in a HAVING clause cannot reference the same table as the outer query. Restructure query into two or more simpler queries, using SAVE TO TEMP clauses if necessary.

Cursor already open (1125). An OPEN command in a .prs program specifies a cursor that has already been OPENed. Precede the OPEN command with a CLOSE command.

Cursor declaration does not include the FOR UPDATE OF clause (1123). An error has occurred during execution of an UPDATE WHERE CURRENT OF statement because the DECLARE CURSOR command that defined the cursor used for the UPDATE did not include a FOR UPDATE OF clause. Include the FOR UPDATE OF clause in the DECLARE CURSOR statement of the cursor used for the UPDATE. Note that the ORDER BY clause cannot be used when the FOR UPDATE OF clause is included.

Cursor name previously declared (1133). A DECLARE CURSOR statement contains a cursor name that has already been used in another DECLARE CURSOR statement in the same .prs program. Choose a new name for the cursor.

Cursor not declared (1121). No DECLARE CURSOR statement defines this cursor. Include a DECLARE CURSOR statement in .prs program. Make sure the DECLARE CURSOR statement precedes the first statement which references the cursor.

Cursor not open (1124). A FETCH or CLOSE cursor command in a .prs program cannot be executed, because the specified cursor has not been OPENed. Precede the FETCH or CLOSE command with an OPEN command.

Cursor not updatable (1120). The DECLARE CURSOR statement that defined the cursor included a SELECT DISTINCT, a UNION, aggregate functions, or included more than one table, or a non-updatable view. Use the cursor only in SELECTs. DECLARE another cursor for use in DELETE/UPDATE WHERE CURRENT OF and INSERT statements.

Data type keyword expected (1033). In a CREATE TABLE or ALTER TABLE command, the data type of a column must be specified after the column name. The SQL data types are: SMALLINT, INTEGER, DECIMAL, NUMERIC, FLOAT, CHAR, LOGICAL, and DATE. If data type is already specified, check for misspelling or misplacement of keyword.

Data type mismatch of corresponding columns in UNION operation (1093). The corresponding columns of SELECT statements joined by the UNION keyword are not of matching data types. Check the data types of corresponding columns: SMALLINT, INTEGER, DECIMAL, NUMERIC, and FLOAT types are considered matching for UNION operations. Other data types must match exactly.

Database name already exists (1136). The database name used in a CREATE DATABASE command already exists as a SQL database. Use a different name for the new database.

DBCHECK and RUNSTATS must be used with base tables (1225). A DBCHECK or RUNSTATS command specified a view name or a non-.dbf filename instead of a base table name. Use a different name for the new database.

Delimiter must be one character long or keyword BLANK (1048). After the keywords DELIMITED WITH in a LOAD or UNLOAD utility, you must specify BLANK or a single character as delimiter.

Different table name is specified in cursor declaration (1126). The table specified in the DECLARE CURSOR statement is not the same as the table specified by the UPDATE/DELETE WHERE CURRENT OF statement using that cursor. Check table and cursor names to make sure both are identified correctly in both the DECLARE CURSOR and UPDATE/DELETE WHERE CURRENT OF statements.

DISTINCT must be followed by a column name (1097). When the keyword DISTINCT is used with the SQL aggregate functions, it must be followed by a column name.

Duplicate userid (1202). The GRANT or REVOKE command user ID list contains duplicate user IDs. Remove duplicate user IDs.

Equals sign expected (1022). Equals sign missing or misplaced after the keyword SET in an UPDATE statement.

Expression not allowed in GROUP BY/ORDER BY (1186). Only column names are allowed in GROUP BY lists. Only column names or integers are allowed in ORDER BY lists. Remove all expressions from the clause.

File encryption error (1282). Check file encryption. You can SET ENCRYPTION OFF and use a SQL UNLOAD or dBASE COPY TO command to create an unencrypted copy of a file.

File has invalid SQL encryption (1228). DBCHECK or RUNSTATS has encountered a file that has an invalid SQL encryption. Try to copy an unencrypted version of the file by using SET ENCRYPTION OFF and the SQL UNLOAD command. If this is successful, erase the encrypted version, use DBDEFINE <filename>, and then re-execute the DBCHECK or RUNSTATS command. If UNLOAD is not successful, the table must be DROPped in SQL before DBCHECK or RUNSTATS will execute successfully.

File is encrypted (1226). DBDEFINE cannot be used with an encrypted file. If the file is dBASE encrypted, SET SQL OFF, SET ENCRYPTION OFF, and use the dBASE COPY TO command to create an unencrypted copy of the file. Erase the encrypted version before re-executing DBDEFINE. If file is SQL encrypted, SET ENCRYPTION OFF and use the SQL UNLOAD command to create an unencrypted copy of the file. Erase the encrypted version before re-executing DBDEFINE.

File is not legal dBASE/SQL : <filename> (1230). An error has occurred on DBCHECK, DBDEFINE, or RUNSTATS because the header of a file indicates that it is not a dBASE or SQL file. Or, a system table has been corrupted and is no longer read-only. Make sure you have not copied a non-dBASE/SQL file with a

.dbf extension. Remove the bad file from the SQL database before re-executing the utility command. If file is a system table, database is corrupt. Copy data tables to a new database and DROP the old one.

File is not SQL encrypted (1227). DBCHECK or RUNSTATS has encountered a file that is encrypted, but not under the SQL encryption key. File must be decrypted and/or removed before re-executing the command.

File not found in the current database (1231). An error occurred on a DBCHECK, DBDEFINE, or RUNSTATS command because the filename following the command keyword does not name a file in the active database directory. Check that you have not misspelled a filename. Check the contents of the active database directory to make sure the .dbf in question is located there.

File open error : <filename> (1280). File open error.

File read error : <filename> (1277). File read error.

File seek error : <filename> (1276). File seek error.

File write error : <filename> (1278). File write error.

Filename is same as existing synonym (1217). Error occurs on DBDEFINE when the .dbf file specified in the command has the same name as an existing SQL synonym. Rename the .dbf before re-executing DBDEFINE <filename>.

First argument of LIKE clause must be a CHAR column (1090). The column name preceding the keyword LIKE in a WHERE clause does not identify a CHARACTER type column. Do not use LIKE with a non-CHARACTER type column.

Float value out of range (1146). A float value greater than 10 to the 38th power, or smaller than 10 to the minus 38th power, cannot be entered.

GRANT OPTION ignored for UPDATE with column list specified. This is a *warning*, not an error. The grantee will not be able to GRANT the UPDATE privilege to others because the UPDATE privilege was GRANTed only for certain columns. No action is needed. If the UPDATE privilege is GRANTed without a column list, then the WITH GRANT OPTION will become effective.

GRANT OPTION ignored when GRANT is TO PUBLIC. This is a *warning*, not an error. The GRANT OPTION is ignored because the privileges are being GRANTed to PUBLIC and so no further GRANTs will be necessary. No action needed.

GROUP BY clause needed (1129). The SELECT clause includes both SQL aggregate functions (AVG, COUNT, MAX, MIN, or SUM) and column names. All column names that are not part of the aggregate functions must be included in a GROUP BY clause.

GROUP BY column(s) not specified in the SELECT clause (1094). A column has been specified in the GROUP BY clause that is not included in the SELECT clause. Include the GROUP BY column(s) in the SELECT clause. All non-GROUP BY columns in the SELECT clause must be columns derived from aggregate functions.

GROUP BY or HAVING clause not allowed with INTO clause (1128). A SELECT statement in a .prs program includes both the INTO clause and GROUP BY or HAVING clauses. A SELECT with INTO clause should return only one row and cannot include GROUP BY or HAVING clauses.

HAVING clause must include aggregate functions (1116). The HAVING clause is used after a GROUP BY clause to specify a search condition. Since rows are already aggregated by the GROUP BY clause, the HAVING condition must also be based on aggregated data. Use the aggregate function(s) AVG, COUNT, MAX, MIN, or SUM in the HAVING clause.

Host variable count in INTO clause is not equal to number of SELECT items (1119). A SELECT statement in a .prs program contains an INTO clause with a number of variables that does not match the number of columns in the SELECT clause.

In UNION, ORDER BY column(s) must be specified by integers (1096). You may use an ORDER BY clause to order the result table of two SELECTs joined by a UNION, but you must use integers instead of column names since column names may differ in the two SELECT clauses. Replace column names with integers (for example, to ORDER BY the first column, use 1; to ORDER BY the second column, use 2, and so on).

Incompatible data types in comparison (1132). The data types of columns, constants, or expressions in a comparison do not match. Check the data types of columns used. Check for missing quotes on string constants.

Incompatible data types in expression (1131). Columns or constants with incompatible data types have been used in an expression. CHAR., LOGICAL and DATE types cannot be mixed with the data types that hold numeric values, or with each other. Check the data types of columns used in the expression to make sure they are compatible with other columns, constants, or functions used in it.

Incomplete SQL statement (1034). A name, keyword, operator, comma, or semicolon is missing or misspelled. Check the correct syntax of the command. Check for a missing semicolon at end of the SQL command.

Incorrect data type for arguments in dBASE function (1112). Refers to a dBASE function used in a SQL statement. Check the dBASE manual for the correct data types in the dBASE function.

Incorrect number of arguments in dBASE function (1113). Refers to a dBASE function used in a SQL statement. For example, this error might occur when the CTOD() function is used with an invalid value for the date, as in CTOD (99/99/99). Check the dBASE manual for correct syntax and usage of the dBASE function.

Incorrect number of INSERT items (1078). The number of values from the VALUES clause or the subselect doesn't match the number of columns specified in the column list (or in the table if no column list was given). Check that the column list includes the exact columns for which data is to be INSERTed. Check the VALUES list or subselect SELECT clause to make sure the correct number of values are provided.

Index name already exists (1102). The index name used in a CREATE INDEX command already exists as a SQL index. Use a different index name for the new index.

Insufficient memory (1275). Insufficient memory available for allocation. Simplify queries by breaking long statements into several.

Insufficient privilege (1204). You do not have the privilege to perform the requested operation on the table or view specified. Have the creator of the table/view GRANT you privileges on it. Anyone who received the privileges WITH GRANT OPTION may also GRANT them to you.

Insufficient privilege to CREATE VIEW (1205). To CREATE a view, you must have SELECT privileges for every table on which the view is based. DELETE the table for which you lack SELECT privileges from the view definition. Or, have someone GRANT you SELECT privileges on the table.

Integer expected (1032). A non-integer value was encountered. Replace with an integer value.

Internal SQL error #1 (1261). Undefined nodename.

Internal SQL error #2 (1262). String table overflow. Simplify your query.

Internal SQL error #3 (1263). Illegal SQL statement.

Internal SQL error #4 (1264). Internal relation table overflows. Simplify your query.

Internal SQL error #5 (1265). Error in parse tree. Simplify your query.

Internal SQL error #6 (1266). A unique index has been used, and more than ten unique indexes all use the same column as part of their unique key. Drop some unique indexes.

Internal SQL error #7 (1267). Internal file open error.

Internal SQL error #8 (1268). Internal relation table overflow. Simplify your query.

Internal SQL error #9 (1269). Too many columns created in temporary relations. Simplify your query.

Internal SQL error #10 (1270). Optimizer join class error. Simplify your query.

Internal SQL error #11 (1271). Temporary Systabl overflows in optimizer. Simplify your query.

Internal SQL error #12 (1272). Temporary SYSCOLUMNS overflows in optimizer. Simplify your query.

Internal SQL error #13 (1273). Error in temporary system catalogs in optimizer. Simplify your query.

Internal SQL error #14 (1274). Invalid pointer to free allocated memory.

Internal SQL error #15 (1275). Insufficient memory available for allocation. Simplify queries by breaking long statements into several shorter ones.

Internal SQL error #16 (1276). File seek error.

Internal SQL error #17 (1277). File read error.

Internal SQL error #18 (1278). File write error.

Internal SQL error #19 (1279). Internal hash table for system catalogs overflow. Simplify your query.

Internal SQL error #21 (1281). Systimes error.

Internal SQL error #22 (1282). File encryption error. Check file encryption. You can SET ENCRYPTION OFF, and use an SQL UNLOAD or dBASE COPY TO command to create an unencrypted copy of a file.

Internal SQL error #24 (1284). Query array overflow.

Internal SQL error #29 (1245). The emitted dBASE source line is longer than 1024 bytes. Check for an * in a SELECT clause that stands for many columns. Check for a complex WHERE predicate, especially in IN, ANY and ALL predicates. Reformulate query.

Internal SQL utility error #1 (1218). Error in dBASE routine that returns information to DBCHECK, DBDEFINE, or RUNSTATS.

Internal SQL utility error #2 (1219). Bad file pointer encountered during execution of DBCHECK, DBDEFINE, or RUNSTATS.

Internal SQL utility error #3 (1220). Bad structure pointer encountered during execution of DBCHECK, DBDEFINE, or RUNSTATS.

Internal SQL utility error #4 (1221). Bad index pointer encountered during execution of DBCHECK, DBDEFINE, or RUNSTATS.

Internal SQL utility error #5 (1222). Bad column pointer encountered during execution of DBCHECK, DBDEFINE, or RUNSTATS.

INTO clause not allowed in cursor declaration (1127). The SELECT in a DECLARE CURSOR statement cannot include the INTO clause. Delete the INTO clause.

Invalid argument for aggregate function (1099). You have used an asterisk (*) or a column of a disallowed data type column in the AVG, MAX, MIN, or SUM function. Columns of data type Logical cannot be used in SQL functions. The argument of SUM and AVG functions must be a column or expression that yields a numeric value.

Invalid arithmetic expression (1135). An arithmetic expression was expected. Check expression for syntax errors.

Invalid character (1002). Only letters, digits, and underscores are allowed in object and column names. Numbers may contain only digits and decimal points. Delete any disallowed characters.

Invalid column number in ORDER BY clause (1084). Column number is not an integer, or is greater than the number of columns returned by the SELECT clause.

Make sure the column number corresponds to column's placement in the SELECT clause, that is, the first column is designated by the number 1, the second by 2, and so on.

Invalid constant (1011). An SQL statement is expecting a constant, but no value is specified. Check for empty parentheses in values lists.

Invalid COUNT argument (1037). COUNT argument must be (*) or (DISTINCT/ALL <column name>).

Invalid decimal length (1159). CREATE TABLE command specifies the length of a Numeric or Decimal type column incorrectly. The width and scale of Numeric and Decimal type columns is specified as (x,y) where y is not greater than x-2 for Numerics, or x-1 for Decimals. For both types, y may not exceed 15.

Invalid file type specified (1050). In the LOAD and UNLOAD statements, file type may be specified as SDF, DIF, WKS, SYLK, DELIMITED, FW2, RPD, or dBASE II. Check file type. If the file LOADed from, or UNLOADed to is a dBASE .dfb file, type need not be specified.

Invalid filename (1049). An invalid filename appears in the LOAD or UNLOAD statement. Check that the filename (and path) are correctly specified. When the file is a dBASE .dbf, the extension need not be specified.

Invalid INSERT item (1152). Items in the value list following the keyword VALUES cannot be column names or compound expressions involving arithmetic operators. Check the value list to make sure it contains only the following items: constants, dBASE functions, memory variables, or USER.

Invalid logical predicate (1168). Comparison operators or keywords other than equal (=) or not equal (<>, #, or !=) cannot be used with columns of datatype LOGICAL in a WHERE predicate. Do not use <,>, <=, or >= operators, or BETWEEN, LIKE, or IN keywords.

Invalid password : <userid> (1283). Invalid password in file header.

Invalid SQL statement (1059). In the stand-alone version, the first word in a statement is not recognized as an SQL keyword. This message will probably be superseded by the PI parser, which will check all non-dBASE first tokens against a table of legal SQL first tokens.

Invalid string operator (1150). Operators other than plus (+) and minus (-) cannot be used with strings. Remove disallowed operator. Also check that you have not mistakenly identified something as a string by inadvertently starting a name with a quotation mark.

Invalid SYSTIME.MEM (1285). The SYSTIME.MEM time stamp in the active database directory is invalid. Make sure you have not accidentally overwritten SYSTIME.MEM. Try copying it from a backup of the database.

Invalid unary operator (1157). A plus (+) or minus (-) operator has been inappropriately applied to a non-numeric value. Check for + or - operators in front of CHAR, LOGICAL or DATA columns, constants, or dBASE functions.

Keyword AND expected (1018). Keyword AND is expected after first argument in BETWEEN clause. Check that keyword AND is not missing, misspelled, or misplaced.

Keyword AS expected (1028). Keyword AS is missing, misspelled, or misplaced in CREATE VIEW command. AS follows the view name (and optional column list), and precedes the subselect.

Keyword ASC or DESC, comma or right parenthesis expected (1057). The CREATE INDEX command is incomplete. Add ASC or DESC option (if desired) after the column name(s) in the column list (use commas to separate items in the list), and be sure a right parenthesis ends the column list.

Keyword ASC or DESC, comma, or semicolon expected (1058). An ORDER BY clause is incomplete. ASCending, or DESCending order may be specified after the column name(s) in the ORDER BY clause. ASC is the default. The statement must be terminated with a semicolon (;).

Keyword BY expected (1016). The keyword ORDER must be followed by the keyword BY. Check that BY is not missing, misspelled, or misplaced.

Keyword CHECK expected (1038). Keyword CHECK missing, misspelled or misplaced in the WITH CHECK OPTION clause of the CREATE VIEW command.

Keyword CURSOR expected (1041). The keyword CURSOR is missing, or misspelled in the DECLARE CURSOR statement in a .prs program.

Keyword DATA expected (1040). Missing keyword DATA in LOAD or UNLOAD statement. Check that the word DATA is placed directly after the word LOAD or UNLOAD, and that it is spelled correctly.

Keyword DATABASE expected (1051). Keyword DATABASE missing, misplaced, or misspelled in the START, STOP, or SHOW DATABASE command.

Keyword DATABASE, TABLE, INDEX, SYNONYM, or VIEW expected (1031). Keyword missing or misspelled after DROP keyword. Use DATABASE, TABLE, INDEX, SYNONYM, or VIEW, depending on the kind of object to be DROPped.

Keyword DATABASE, TABLE, INDEX, SYNONYM or VIEW expected (1027). Keyword missing, misplaced, or misspelled in a CREATE statement.

Keyword FOR expected (1030). The keyword FOR is missing, misplaced, or misspelled in the CREATE SYNONYM or DECLARE CURSOR command.

Keyword FROM expected (1015). Keyword FROM missing, misplaced, or misspelled in LOAD, UNLOAD, SELECT, REVOKE, or DELETE command.

Keyword GRANT expected (1054). Keyword GRANT missing, misplaced, or misspelled in the WITH GRANT OPTION clause of a GRANT statement.

Keyword INDEX expected (1017). The keywords CREATE UNIQUE must be followed by the word INDEX. Check that the keyword INDEX is not missing, misspelled, or misplaced.

Keyword INTO expected (1023). Keyword INTO missing, misplaced, or misspelled in the FETCH, INSERT, or LOAD DATA statement.

Keyword not allowed in interactive mode (1118). A keyword used during an interactive SQL session can only be used in .prs programs. All keywords related to the use of SQL cursors are used only in programs. Replace the keyword with an interactive SQL command.

Keyword OF expected (1043). Keyword OF missing, misplaced, or misspelled in the FOR UPDATE OF or WHERE CURRENT OF clause.

Keyword ON expected (1026). Keyword ON missing, misspelled, or misplaced in the CREATE INDEX, GRANT or REVOKE command.

Keyword OPTION expected (1039). Keyword OPTION missing, misspelled, or misplaced in the WITH GRANT OPTION clause of a GRANT command.

Keyword SELECT expected (1029). The keyword SELECT is missing, misplaced, or misspelled after the keyword UNION, or in a CREATE VIEW command after the keyword AS. The missing SELECT keyword is the first word of the required subselect used in these statements.

Keyword SELECT missing in DECLARE CURSOR statement (1046). Keyword SELECT missing, misplaced, or misspelled in the DECLARE CURSOR statement. A SELECT statement must follow the keyword FOR.

Keyword SET expected (1021). Keyword SET missing, misplaced, or misspelled in the UPDATE statement.

Keyword TABLE expected (1035). Keyword TABLE missing, misspelled, or misplaced in the ALTER TABLE, LOAD, or UNLOAD command.

Keyword TEMP expected (1053). Keyword TEMP missing, misplaced, or misspelled in the SAVE TO TEMP clause of a SELECT statement.

Keyword TO expected (1025). Keyword TO missing, misspelled, or misplaced in the GRANT or UNLOAD command, or the SAVE TO TEMP clause of a SELECT command.

Keyword UPDATE expected (1042). Keyword UPDATE missing, misspelled or misplaced in the FOR UPDATE OF clause in the DECLARE CURSOR statement.

Keyword VALUES or SELECT expected (1024). The INSERT statement must include either a VALUES clause or a subselect. Check that one of the keywords is included and that it is not misspelled or misplaced.

Keyword WITH expected (1047). Keyword WITH missing, misplaced, or misspelled in the LOAD or UNLOAD utility where delimiters are specified. When data is LOADed to or UNLOADed from dBASE files, the TYPE and WIDTH clauses need not be specified.

Keywords BETWEEN, LIKE, or IN expected (1019). A WHERE clause is incorrectly specified. Check correct syntax of the desired form of the WHERE clause.

Left parenthesis missing (1013). A left parenthesis is missing before the beginning of a list. Check syntax of command for required parenthesis.

Memory variable and dBASE fct. not allowed in SELECT with UNION (1163). All SELECT columns must be named columns or constants when UNION is used. Remove memory variables, dBASE functions, and array references from SELECT clauses.

Missing end quotes for string (1003). Strings must be enclosed in quotes. Add missing quote ('). Check to make sure that you mean to be specifying a string, and that you have not inadvertently used a quote which has been interpreted as a begin string marker.

Name already exists (1080). The name used in a CREATE TABLE, CREATE SYNONYM, or CREATE VIEW command already names an existing SQL table, synonym, or view. Use a different name for the new table, synonym, or view.

Name, constant, or expression expected (1010). A scalar value was expected. Check that a column name, constant, or expression has not been omitted from the statement.

Name expected (1012). An object name is missing, misplaced, or misspelled. Check that database, table, view, synonym, or column names are correctly specified.

Name longer than 20 characters (1001). All SQL names must contain 20 or fewer characters. (Database and table names must contain 8 or fewer.) They must begin with a letter and contain only letters, digits, and underscores. Check for column names that are too long.

Name longer than 8 characters not allowed (1156). The name for a database or table exceeds 8 characters in length. Use a name of eight characters or less (beginning with a letter and containing only letters, digits, and underscores).

Nested function not allowed (1098). An aggregate function contains another function nested within it. Remove the nested function.

No alias defined for self-join (1142). When a self-join form of the WHERE clause is used, an alias must be defined in the FROM clause. The table name cannot be referenced twice, nor can a synonym name be used in place of an alias. Use a FROM clause of the form: FROM <table name> <alias name>. Then prefix column names in the SELECT and WHERE clauses as necessary.

No ALTER or INDEX privileges for views (1203). These privileges cannot be GRANTed or REVOKEd because views cannot be ALTERed or INDEXed. You cannot GRANT ALL PRIVILEGES on views because ALL includes the ALTER and INDEX privileges. Do not use the keyword ALL. Do specify a privilege list which may contain the following privileges: DELETE, INSERT, SELECT, or UPDATE.

No current row available for UPDATE or DELETE (1154). This error occurs only in .prs programs where UPDATEs and DELETEs are being performed under SQL cursor control. Make sure a FETCH has been executed before the UPDATE or DELETE is attempted.

No database open (1139). The command requested can only be executed when a database is open. If you have entered SQL with all databases closed, or if you used the STOP DATABASE command, the current command cannot be executed. Use a START DATABASE command before retrieving information.

No .dfb file in the current database (1224). No .dbf files (other than the SQL catalog tables) were found during execution of a DBDEFINE command. Make sure that the copied into the current database directory before executing the DBDEFINE command.

No GROUP BY or HAVING in subquery (1167). The GROUP BY and HAVING clauses are not allowed in subqueries of a basic WHERE predicate. Remove the GROUP BY or HAVING, or change the form of the predicate.

Non-numeric array subscript (1162). All array subscripts must evalute to integers. If columns or functions are used, check that the data type of the expression is numeric.

Number of columns must be the same in UNION operation (1092). The SELECT statements joined by the UNION keyword do not generate the same number of columns. Change the SELECT clauses of the SELECT statements so that they return the same number of columns. Columns must also be of matching data type and length.

Number of SAVE TO TEMP columns does not match number of SELECT columns (1148). The SAVE TO TEMP column list must contain the same number of columns as the SELECT statement results being saved. If all the columns in the result table are named columns (not derived from functions, constants, and so on), then no column list need be specified in the SAVE TO TEMP clause.

Number of view columns does not match number of SELECT columns (1104). In a CREATE VIEW command, the number of columns specified in the view column list is not the same as the number of columns generated in the SELECT clause. If all the columns in the view are named columns (not the result of aggregate functions, expressions, and so on), then the column list may be omitted, and the view column will inherit SELECT column names.

Numeric value too large (1144). A value exceeds dBASE limits on numeric values.

Numeric value too small (1153). A value is smaller than the smallest allowable dBASE numeric value.

Only one DISTINCT allowed in any SELECT clause (1114). The keyword DISTINCT has appeared more than once in a SELECT clause.

Only one column may be SELECTed in a subquery (1101). A subselect in a WHERE clause returns multiple values. Change the form of the WHERE clause. Use the keyword IN, or ANY, or ALL if multiple values will be returned by a subselect. Or change the SELECT clause of the subselect to return only one column.

ORDER BY clause not allowed in CREATE VIEW (1056). An ORDER BY clause was included as part of the AS SELECT in a CREATE VIEW statement. The ORDER BY clause may only be used in a full SELECT, with UNION, and in the DECLARE CURSOR statement. Remove the ORDER BY clause. You may use an ORDER BY clause when you SELECT from the view.

ORDER BY column(s) not specified in the SELECT clause (1095). A column has been specified in the ORDER BY clause that is not included in the SELECT clause. Include the ORDER BY column(s) in the SELECT clause.

Path too long (1044). A path name may not exceed 64 characters.

Right bracket missing (1060). A left bracket appears without a matching right bracket. Check array references to make sure brackets match. Square brackets are not used elsewhere in SQL.

Right parenthesis missing (1014). A left parenthesis is present without a matching right parenthesis. Check for missing right parenthesis in subselects, aggregate functions, and so on.

SAVE TO TEMP clause not allowed (1147). SAVE TO TEMP clause not allowed as part of a DECLARE CURSOR statement, or when an INTO clause is used in a SELECT statement. Re-execute the statement as a SELECT without an INTO clause.

Second argument of LIKE clause must be a character string (1091). A column name or other non-character string item follows the keyword LIKE in a WHERE clause. LIKE must be followed by a character string. Replace dis-allowed item with a character string. Check that you have not inadvertently forgotten the beginning quote of the character string.

SELECT cannot include both FOR UPDATE OF and ORDER BY clauses (1045). A SELECT or DECLARE CURSOR statement includes both the FOR UPDATE OF and ORDER BY clauses. If a cursor defined in a DECLARE CURSOR statement is to be used in an UPDATE WHERE CURRENT OF statement, then the FOR UPDATE OF clause must be chosen. Otherwise, drop FOR UPDATE OF and keep the ORDER BY clause.

SELECT column names must be in aggregate functions (1163). When HAVING is used without GROUP BY, all column names in the SELECT clause must be in SQL aggregate functions. Add a GROUP BY clause with all SELECT clause column names included in it, or use aggregate function in SELECT clause.

Systimes error (1281). Systems error. No remedy.

Table already exists (1216). The filename following the DBDEFINE keyword already exists as an SQL table. No new entries can be made in the SQL catalog tables for this file. If you need to redefine this table (because of DBCHECK errors, or for any other reason), you must copy the .dbf to another directory, DROP it in SQL, copy the .dbf back, then use DBDEFINE <filename>.

Table not found in the SQL catalog tables (1223). Table name specified in DBCHECK or RUNSTATS command does not exist in the SQL catalog tables. Verify correct table name with a SELECT from Systabls catalog table.

Table not included in current statement (1075). A column prefixed with the table name from which it comes is referenced, but its table is not included in a FROM clause. Add the missing table name to the FROM clause.

Too many indexes for a table (1170). Table already has 47 indexes. An SQL table cannot have more than 47 indexes (i.e., no more than 47 .ndx tags in its production .mdx).

Too many columns in a table (1166). A CREATE TABLE or ALTER TABLE command would result in a table of more than 255 columns. Use the following query to see how many columns a table already has: SELECT Colcount FROM Systable WHERE TBname = "<table name>";.

Too many unique indexes (1266). A unique index has been used, and more than ten unique indexes all use the same column as part of their unique key. Drop some unique indexes.

Too many values specified in INSERT (1085). A column list was specified which contained more columns than exist in the table. Check the column list for duplicate column names, and remove extra columns.

Too many work areas open (1184). Either more than ten tables are referenced in one SQL statement, or the user left some work areas open before issuing the SET SQL ON command, and the total number of work areas open is greater than ten. Reference fewer tables in the FROM clause, or return to dBASE and close work areas.

Undefined column name (1076). The column name which caused the error is not a column of any of the tables referenced in the command. Either you have referenced the wrong table, or you have forgotten to include a table in the FROM clause; or, you have misspelled the column name, or used a column name which doesn't exist.

Undefined database name (1137). There is no entry in the SQL system catalog table Sysdbs.dbf for this database. Check that you have not given an incorrect database name, or use a CREATE DATABASE statement to create the database. If you already have a non-SQL sub-directory with the same name, you must first erase and remove this directory outside of SQL.

Undefined index name (1088). The index named in a DROP INDEX command does not exist as an SQL index. (The index name is not entered in the SQL catalog table SYSIDXS.) Do a SELECT from the system catalog table Sysidxs to verify the correct name of the index.

Undefined privilege in GRANT or REVOKE statement (1055). You may GRANT and REVOKE the following privileges: SELECT, INSERT, DELETE, UPDATE, INDEX, ALTER. Check for misspellings, or for keywords such as CREATE that cannot be GRANTed.

Undefined symbol (1004). An unrecognized or inappropriate symbol has been accidentally included in the statement. Check for and delete any symbols such as $ or &, or for arithmetic comparison or operator symbols accidentally included in names or keywords.

Undefined synonym name (1089). The synonym named in a DROP SYNONYM command does not exist as an SQL synonym. (The synonym name is not entered in the catalog table Syssyns.) Check that you have not given a table or view name by mistake. Use a SELECT from the catalog table Syssyns to get a listing of all existing synonym names.

Undefined table name (1086). The table, synonym, or view requested is not entered in the relevant SQL catalog table. Either the name is misspelled, or a CREATE (or DBDEFINE) command was never used. Check that you have not put a column name or other item where a table name was expected. Do a SELECT from the appropriate catalog table (Systabls, Syssyns, or Sysviews) to list correct names.

Undefined view name (1087). The view named in a DROP VIEW command is not an SQL view. (The view name is not entered in the catalog table Sysviews). Do a SELECT from the catalog table Sysviews to verify existing view names.

UNION is not allowed in a view definition (1106). The UNION keyword has been included in a CREATE VIEW command. You may SELECT columns from more than one table to CREATE a single view, but the UNION operation is not allowed.

UPDATE column list is ignored in REVOKE statement. This is a *warning*, not an error. The REVOKE of an UPDATE privilege applies to all columns in a table. After REVOKing the UPDATE privilege, GRANT it again, specifying the columns to which it applies.

UPDATE column(s) not defined in cursor declaration (1122). The UPDATE WHERE CURRENT OF statement in a .prs program UPDATEs columns that were not included in the column list of the FOR UPDATE OF clause of the associated DECLARE CURSOR statement. Add all columns to be UPDATEd to the column list in the FOR UPDATE OF clause of the DECLARE CURSOR statement.

Value exceeds column length (1158). A value is longer than the column into which it is to be entered. SELECT FROM Syscols to determine the length of the column into which you are entering values.

Value must match column data type (1079). An UPDATE or INSERT value doesn't match the data type of the column into which it is to be placed. Check the data type of the column. Be sure dates are correctly entered in the form CTOD('dd/mm/yy'). Check for missing beginning quotes on character strings.

View column names must be specified (1105). The SELECT clause of the CREATE VIEW statement includes columns derived from aggregate functions or from two different tables, and view column names cannot simply be inherited from the SELECT. Add a list of column names enclosed in parentheses after the keywords CREATE VIEW.

View defined with GROUP BY cannot be used in a join (1110). A view referenced in the FROM clause of a statement joining views (and tables) has a GROUP BY clause as part of its definition. This view cannot be used in a join.

View defined with GROUP BY cannot be used in a query including a GROUP BY clause (1111). A SELECT statement including a GROUP BY clause references a view that has a GROUP BY clause as part of its definition. Remove the GROUP BY clause in the current SELECT, or do not use this view in this query.

View is not updatable (1108). A DELETE, INSERT, or UPDATE was attempted on a view which cannot be UPDATEd. Views with definitions referencing more than one table, or including GROUP BY, SELECT DISTINCT, or aggregate functions, are not UPDATable.

Views cannot be INDEXed (1117). A CREATE INDEX command included a view name instead of a table or synonym name. Views cannot be INDEXed.

SQL RUN-TIME ERROR MESSAGES

Run-time error messages are in alphabetical order.

Database does not exist (2002). A database no longer exists, or does not exist on this machine. A database may have been DROPped since the program was compiled.

DBDEFINE completed without catalog updates; errors/warnings found (2010). DBDEFINE was not successful because of errors in the command or inconsistencies in the database. Check the error messages that preceded this message. Follow suggested remedies and rerun DBDEFINE.

Duplicated value in unique index - aborted (2000). UPDATE or INSERT not performed because it would have duplicated a value in an index key that belongs to a unique index. Change the new value so that it is distinct from all current values. You can also DROP the index, but consider carefully before doing so, since unique indexes are used to insure database integrity.

Keys not unique, index not created (2006). A CREATE INDEX command specified the UNIQUE option but the column(s) on which the index was to be built contain duplicate values. Add another column to the index key, or DELETE rows containing duplicate index key values before re-executing the CREATE INDEX with UNIQUE option.

Memory variable or column name undefined or memory variable of invalid type (2007). A name has been found that is not a column name, and has not been defined as a memory variable. Check that a column name or memvar name has not been misspelled. Check that columns belong to referenced table; make sure values have been STOREd to memvars.

Row violates view definition - INSERT/UPDATE row rejected (2005). A row cannot be UPDATEd or INSERTed in a view because the view was created WITH CHECK OPTION, and the inserted or updated row violates the view's definition. You can read the view's definition by SELECTing the SQLtext column from the catalog table Sysviews. You can also INSERT into or UPDATE the underlying base table, but such rows will not appear in the view.

RUNSTATS completed without catalog updates; error/warnings found (2009). RUNSTATS was not successful because of errors in the command or inconsistencies in the database. Note that no updates are made even for tables for which no error/warning appeared. Check the error messages that preceded this message; follow suggested remedies, and rerun RUNSTATS.

Subquery did not return any value (2011). The subquery in a WHERE or HAVING clause did not return any values. (Only the WHERE EXISTS predicate may include a subquery that returns no values.) Modify the search condition subquery by running it separately until correct values are returned.

Subquery did not return exactly one value (2003). A subquery following an arithmetic comparison operator in a WHERE clause must return only one value. An error occurred because multiple values were returned. Either precede the subquery with the keyword ANY or ALL, or rewrite the WHERE clause using the keyword IN instead of an operator.

System table entry missing for table (2004). Catalog table Systabls does not contain an entry for this table; it has been DROPped, or does not exist on this machine. Too many work areas open (2008). The SQL operation requires additional work areas, but the ten available areas are all in use. Return to dBASE and close any open files. Reduce complexity of SQL query. If error occurred in transaction, remove operations from transaction.

Too many work areas open (2008). The SQL operation requires additional work areas, but the ten available areas are all in use. Return to dBASE and close any open files. Reduce complexity of SQL query. If error occurred in transaction, remove operations from transaction.

B

dBASE IV Commands Allowed in dBASE IV SQL

dBASE Command	Allowed	Description in SQL
! or RUN	Yes	Runs a DOS-level system command
? ... STYLE	Yes	Print expression
??	Yes	Continue printing
???	Yes	Print expression list
&&	Yes	Embedded comment. Not allowed in SQL statements
*	Yes	Comment indicator in programs
@...CLEAR...	Yes	Draws and erases boxes and lines
@...DOUBLE/PANEL/NONE...	Yes	Draws boxes
@...FILL TO...	Yes	Fills an area with a color
@...SAY...GET	Yes	Displays/gets user data

dBASE Command	Allowed	Description in SQL
ACCEPT	Yes	Enters a character string into a memory variable
ACTIVATE MENU	Yes	Activates/locates a menu into memory
ACTIVATE POPUP	Yes	Activates/locates a popup into memory
ACTIVATE SCREEN	Yes	Activates/locates a screen in memory
ACTIVATE WINDOW	Yes	Activates one or all defined windows
APPEND [BLANK]	No	Appends records
APPEND FROM	No	Appends/imports records from other files
APPEND MEMO	No	Appends a memo field from an existing field
ASSIST	No	Invokes the menu system
AVERAGE	No	Computes the average of field values
BEGIN TRANSACTION	Yes	Opens a log file for transaction processing
BROWSE	No	Invokes Browse system
CALCULATE	No	Calculates financial and statistical functions
CALL	Yes	Executes a binary program module
CANCEL	Yes	Stops program execution
CHANGE	No	Changes specified fields and records

dBASE Command	Allowed	Description in SQL
CLEAR	Yes	Clears specified parameters from memory (all allowed except ALL and FIELDS)
CLOSE	Yes	Closes specified files (all allowed except ALL, DATABASES, and INDEX)
COMPILE	Yes	Generates dBASE object code for dBASE programs
CONTINUE	No	Continues to next located record
CONVERT TO	No	Adds timestamp column to database
COPY FILE	Yes	Duplicates a file
COPY INDEXES/TAG	No	Creates .mdx file tags from existing .mdx file tags or from .ndx files
COPY MEMO	No	Copies specified memo to field
COPY STRUCTURE	No	Duplicates a structure in a new file
COPY TO ARRAY	No	Copies records to an array
COPY TO	No	Copies/exports records to a new file
COUNT	No	Counts records in a file
CREATE FROM	No	Creates a new file from a file created with COPY STRUCTURE EXTENDED
CREATE/MODIFY	No	Creates or modifies a database file
CREATE/MODIFY APPLICATION	No	Creates an Applications Generator application
CREATE/MODIFY LABEL/?	No	Creates or modifies a label form file

dBASE Command	Allowed	Description in SQL
CREATE/MODIFY QUERY/?	No	Creates or edits a view file
CREATE/MODIFY REPORT/?	No	Creates or modifies a report file
CREATE/MODIFY SCREEN/?	No	Creates or modifies a screen form file
CREATE/MODIFY VIEW/?	No	Creates a vue file
DBLINK	No	Links .dbo's
DEACTIVATE MENU	Yes	Removes an active menu from memory
DEACTIVATE POPUP	Yes	Removes an active popup from memory
DEACTIVATE WINDOW	Yes	Removes windows from memory
DEBUG	Yes	Calls the debugger program
DECLARE	Yes	Declares an array
DEFINE BAR	Yes	Defines a menu bar
DEFINE BOX	Yes	Defines screen box
DEFINE MENU	Yes	Defines a menu
DEFINE PAD	Yes	Defines a menu pad in defined menu
DEFINE POPUP	Yes	Defines a popup window
DEFINE WINDOW	Yes	Defines a window
DELETE	No	Deletes records from a file
DELETE FILE	Yes	Deletes a file
DELETE TAG	No	Deletes an index tag
DIR/DIRECTORY	Yes	Displays a drive directory

dBASE Command	Allowed	Description in SQL
DISPLAY FILES	Yes	Displays/prints files
DISPLAY HISTORY	Yes	Displays/prints previously executed commands from history
DISPLAY MEMORY	Yes	Displays/prints current memory variables
DISPLAY STATUS	Yes	Displays/prints system status
DISPLAY STRUCTURE	No	Displays/prints current file structure
DISPLAY USERS	Yes	Displays user name list on a network
DISPLAY	No	Displays/prints selected fields and records
DO	Yes	Executes a program
DO CASE	Yes	Starts block of CASE statements
DO WHILE	Yes	Executes conditional loop in a program
EDIT	No	Displays records one at a time
EJECT	Yes	Sends a form feed to a printer
END PRINTJOB	Yes	Defines end of print job
END TRANSACTION	Yes	Closes a transaction processing log file
ERASE	Yes	Deletes a specified file
EXIT	Yes	Exits program execution
EXPORT TO	No	Converts/exports a .dbf file
FIND	No	Finds a record

dBASE Command	Allowed	Description in SQL
FUNCTION	Yes	Declares a user-defined function
GO/GOTO	No	Positions the record pointer in a file
[GOTO] <exp>	No	Positions the record pointer in a file
HELP	Yes	Displays context-sensitive help
IF...ELSE...ENDIF	Yes	Provides conditional branching in program execution
IMPORT FROM	No	Imports a file
INDEX	No	Creates an index file (.ndx or .mdx)
INPUT	Yes	Enters an expression into a memory variable
INSERT	No	Inserts a record into a file
JOIN	No	Combines records from two database files
LABEL FORM	No	Prints labels
LIST FILES	Yes	Lists/prints matching files
LIST HISTORY	Yes	Lists/prints commands in history (in chronological order)
LIST MEMORY	Yes	Lists/prints memory variables
LIST STATUS	Yes	Lists/prints system status and parameters
LIST STRUCTURE	No	Lists/prints a database file structure
LIST USERS	Yes	Lists/prints network user names
LIST	No	Lists/prints specified fields and records
LOAD	Yes	Loads a binary program module

dBASE Command	Allowed	Description in SQL
LOCATE	No	Locates a record and positions the record pointer
LOGOUT	Yes	Logs a user out of dBASE IV on a LAN
LOOP	Yes	Returns execution to the beginning of a DO WHILE loop
MODIFY COMMAND/FILE	Yes	Starts text editor for editing program files
MODIFY STRUCTURE	No	Changes a database file structure
MOVE WINDOW	Yes	Moves a window
NOTE	Yes	Indicates comments in a program file
ON ERROR	Yes	Executes specified command on error
ON ESCAPE	Yes	Executes specified command on Esc key
ON KEY	Yes	Executes specified command on key press
ON PAD	Yes	Activates an associated menu pad popup
ON PAGE	Yes	Executes command at page break
ON READERROR	Yes	Executes specified command on incorrect entry
ON SELECTION PAD	Yes	Specifies the execution of a command for selection of a menu pad
ON SELECTION POPUP	Yes	Specifies the execution of a command for selection of a popup menu

dBASE Command	Allowed	Description in SQL
PACK	No	Removes records marked for deletion
PARAMETERS	Yes	Specifies memory variables used with DO command
PLAY MACRO	Yes	Plays back a macro
PRINTJOB	Yes	Defines start of print job
PRIVATE	Yes	Defines memory variables as private
PROCEDURE	Yes	Identifies the beginning of a procedure file
PROTECT	Yes	Menu-driven command that assigns user log-in names and access privileges
PUBLIC	Yes	Defines memory variables as public
QUIT	Yes	Closes all files and exits to DOS
READ [SAVE]	Yes	Reads current GET fields
RECALL	No	Unmarks records marked for deletion
REINDEX	No	Rebuilds open index files
RELEASE	Yes	Erases memory variables from RAM (all options supported except RELEASE ALL)
RELEASE MENUS	Yes	Erases menus from the screen and RAM
RELEASE MODULE	Yes	Erases a program module loaded in RAM
RELEASE POPUPS	Yes	Erases popup menus from the screen and RAM

dBASE Command	Allowed	Description in SQL
RELEASE WINDOWS	Yes	Erases windows from the screen and RAM
RENAME	Yes	Assigns a new name to an existing file
REPLACE	No	Changes the contents of fields in a record
REPORT FORM	No	Displays/prints tabular reports of data
RESET	No	Resets tag of transaction in log file
RESTORE	Yes	Restores named memory variables to RAM
RESTORE MACROS	Yes	Restores macros to RAM from disk file
RESTORE WINDOW	Yes	Restores windows from a disk file
RESUME	Yes	Resumes execution of a suspended program
RETRY	Yes	Retries a command after its previous execution from a program
RETURN	Yes	Returns to a point from which a program call was made
ROLLBACK	No	Restores a file to a pre-transaction status
RUN	Yes	Runs a DOS-level file from within dBASE IV
SAVE MACROS	Yes	Saves macros to a disk file
SAVE TO	Yes	Copies memory variables to a disk file
SAVE WINDOW	Yes	Saves windows to a disk file

dBASE Command	Allowed	Description in SQL
SCAN	No	Finds the next record of a search
SEEK	No	Positions the record pointer to the first record with an index key matching a_/ expression
SELECT	No	Activates the specified work area
SET	No	Full screen SET command
SET ALTERNATE ON/OFF	Yes	Controls recording of dBASE commands and output in a text file
SET ALTERNATE TO	Yes	Sends screen output to a text file
SET AUTOSAVE ON/OFF	Yes	Controls automatic storage of open files
SET BELL ON/OFF	Yes	Sets the audible prompt on or off
SET BELL TO	Yes	Sets the tone and duration of the audible prompt
SET BLOCKSIZE	No	Sets memo field size
SET BORDER	Yes	Sets menu, window, or popup border
SET CARRY ON/OFF	No	Sets carryover of fields to next record
SET CARRY TO	No	Specifies fields updated with carry
SET CATALOG ON/OFF	No	Controls addition of open files to catalog
SET CATALOG TO	No	Opens a catalog file
SET CENTURY ON/OFF	Yes	Controls display of century in a date field
SET CLOCK ON/OF	Yes	Controls the display of the system clock

dBASE Command	Allowed	Description in SQL
SET CLOCK TO	Yes	Controls position of the clock display
SET COLOR OF	Yes	Sets color of special screen areas
SET COLOR ON/OFF	Yes	Specifies monochrome or color display
SET COLOR TO	Yes	Sets overall color
SET CONFIRM ON/OFF	Yes	Controls advance of cursor from field to field
SET CONSOLE ON/OFF	Yes	Controls output of display to screen
SET CURRENCY LEFT/RIGHT	Yes	Controls display of currency symbols
SET CURRENCY TO	Yes	Specifies the currency symbol used
SET DATE TO	Yes	Sets date format
SET DEBUG ON/OFF	Yes	Controls the output of SET ECHO ON to the printer
SET DECIMALS TO	Yes	Specifies the number of decimal places displayed with SET FIXED off
SET DEFAULT TO	Yes	Specifies the default drive
SET DELETED ON/OFF	Yes	Controls use of records marked for deletion
SET DELIMITERS ON/OFF	Yes	Controls the use of entry form delimiters
SET DELIMITERS TO	Yes	Specifies delimiters for field and variable displays
SET DESIGN ON/OFF	No	Restricts transfers to design mode

dBASE Command	Allowed	Description in SQL
SET DEVICE TO	Yes	Controls output of the @...SAY command to the screen, a printer, or a file
SET DISPLAY TO	Yes	Sets display mode of monochrome or color displays
SET DOHISTORY ON/OFF	Yes	Controls saving of commands executed in a program file to history
SET ECHO ON/OF	Yes	Controls output of executed commands to screen or printer
SET ENCRYPTION ON/OFF	Yes	Controls encryption of protected files
SET ESCAPE ON/OFF	Yes	Controls interruption of program with Esc key
SET EXACT ON/OFF	Yes	Controls exactness of matches in character string comparisons
SET EXCLUSIVE ON/OFF	Yes	Controls whether files are accessed exclusively on a network
SET FIELDS ON/OFF	No	Controls use of fields list
SET FIELDS TO	No	Specifies a fields list (SET FIELDS settings are NOT restored when SQL is SET OFF.)
SET FILTER TO	No	Specifies select conditions that fields in records must meet
SET FIXED ON/OFF	Yes	Controls whether a fixed number of decimal places is displayed in calculations
SET FORMAT TO	Yes	Opens a format file for data entry
SET FULLPATH	Yes	Shows full path for MDX() and NDX()

dBASE Command	Allowed	Description in SQL
SET FUNCTION	Yes	Sets operation of function keys
SET HEADING ON/OFF	Yes	Controls display of headings over the display of fields in LIST or DISPLAY
SET HELP ON/OFF	Yes	Controls the display of help prompts
SET HISTORY ON/OFF	Yes	Controls whether commands are saved in the history buffer
SET HISTORY TO	Yes	Specifies the number of commands saved in the history buffer
SET HOURS TO	Yes	Specifies a 12- or 24-hour clock
SET INDEX TO	No	Opens index files
SET INSTRUCT ON/OFF	No	Controls display of instruction boxes in menus
SET INTENSITY ON/OFF	Yes	Controls whether screens include enhanced display
SET LOCK ON/OFF	Yes	Controls use of automatic record locking
SET MARGIN TO	Yes	Controls setting of left printer margin
SET MARK TO	Yes	Specifies the date separator character
SET MEMOWIDTH TO	No	Specifies setting of memo field columns
SET MENUS ON/OFF	Yes	Controls whether memo fields are displayed in full-screen displays
SET MESSAGE TO	Yes	Specifies messages displayed at the bottom of the screen

dBASE Command	Allowed	Description in SQL
SET NEAR ON/OFF	No	Specifies whether a seek is satisfied by near-match
SET ODOMETER TO	No	Controls the update interval for the record interval
SET ORDER TO	No	Specifies a controlling index
SET PATH TO	Yes	Specifies a directory path for file searches
SET PAUSE ON/OFF	Yes	Controls scrolling of SQL results
SET POINT TO	Yes	Specifies the character used for decimal point displays
SET PRECISION TO	Yes	Specifies the precision of fixed point arithmetic
SET PRINTER ON/OFF	Yes	Controls output sent to a printer
SET PRINTER TO	Yes	Redirects print output
SET PROCEDURE TO	Yes	Opens a procedure file
SET REFRESH TO	Yes	Sets time to check for record change
SET RELATION TO	No	Links specified database files
SET REPROCESS TO	Yes	Sets command retry count
SET SAFETY ON/OFF	Yes	Prompts for confirmation before overwriting file
SET SCOREBOARD ON/OFF	Yes	Enables message line display on line 0
SET SEPARATOR TO	Yes	Specifies a numeric value separator
SET SKIP TO	No	Specifies a file in a relation

dBASE Command	Allowed	Description in SQL
SET SPACE TO	Yes	Causes an extra space to print between fields when ? and ?? commands are used
SET SQL ON/OFF	Yes	Starts/stops SQL mode in interactive mode
SET STATUS ON/OFF	Yes	Enables display of status bar
SET STEP ON/OFF	Yes	Specifies whether commands are executed one at a time in a program
SET TALK ON/OFF	Yes	Enables display of command execution on the screen
SET TITLE ON/OFF	No	Specifies whether files are titled when added to a dBASE catalog
SET TRAP ON/OFF	Yes	Invokes Debugger on Error
SET TYPEAHEAD TO	Yes	Specifies the size of the type-ahead buffer
SET UNIQUE ON/OFF	No	Determines if only unique records are displayed
SET VIEW TO	No	Activates a dBASE view
SET WINDOW OF MENU	No	Sets the default window for editing a memo field with BROWSE or EDIT commands
SHOW MENU	Yes	Displays a menu without activating it
SHOW POPUP	Yes	Displays a popup without activating it
SKIP	No	Moves the record pointer forward or backward

dBASE Command	Allowed	Description in SQL
SORT	No	Creates a new copy of a database file arranging the records in specified order
STORE	Yes	Stores an expression to a memory variable
SUM	No	Computes an arithmetic sum
SUSPEND	Yes	Interrupts program execution without terminating
TEXT...ENDTEXT	Yes	Displays a block of text from a program file
TOTAL ON	No	Creates a summary database of numeric totals
TYPE	Yes	Displays contents of a file to the screen or printer
UNLOCK	No	Unlocks files or records in a specified work area
UPDATE	No	Makes batch changes to a database file
USE	No	Activates a database file
WAIT	Yes	Pauses program execution and waits for user response
ZAP	No	Removes all records from an active database file

C

dBASE IV Functions Allowed in dBASE IV SQL

Function	Description	Allowed in SQL Mode	Allowed in SQL Statement
&	Performs macro substitution	Yes	No
ABS()	Returns absolute value	Yes	Yes
ACCESS()	Returns access level of current user	No	No
ACOS()	Returns angle in radians from cosine	Yes	Yes
ALIAS()	Returns alias name of unselected work area	No	No
ASC()	Does character to ASCII conversion	Yes	Yes
ASIN()	Returns arcsine	Yes	Yes
AT()	Does substring search in character or memo field	Yes	Yes

Function	Description	In Mode	In Statement
ATAN()	Returns angle in radians from tangent	Yes	Yes
ATN2()	Returns angle in radians from cosine and sine	Yes	Yes
BAR()	Returns bar name of last selected prompt bar	Yes	No
BOF()	Indicates beginning of file	No	No
CALL()	Returns result of bin file execution	Yes	No
CDOW()	Returns day of week	Yes	Yes
CEILING()	Returns ceiling of an expression	Yes	Yes
CHANGE()	Returns if record has changed	No	No
CHR()	Does ASCII decimal to char conversion	Yes	Yes
CMONTH()	Returns name of month from a date	Yes	Yes
COL()	Returns cursor column position on screen	Yes	No
COMPLETED()	Indicates whether a transaction is completed	Yes	Yes
COS()	Returns cosine from angle in radians	Yes	Yes
CTOD()	Does char to date conversion	Yes	Yes
DATE()	Returns system date	Yes	Yes
DAY()	Returns number of day of month	Yes	Yes
DBF()	Returns name of database file in use	No	No

Function	Description	In Mode	In Statement
DELETED()	Determines whether record is marked for deletion	No	No
DIFFERENCE()	Indicates difference betweeen two SOUNDEX() codes	Yes	Yes
DISKSPACE()	Returns number of free bytes on default drive	Yes	No
DMY()	Does date format conversion to DD/Mon/YY	Yes	Yes
DOW()	Returns number of the day of week	Yes	Yes
DTOC()	Converts date to char string	Yes	Yes
DTOR()	Converts degrees to radians	Yes	Yes
DTOS()	Returns the ANSI date	Yes	Yes
EOF()	Indicates end of file	No	No
ERROR()	Returns error number causing ON ERROR condition	Yes	No
EXP()	Determines number from its natural log	Yes	Yes
FIELD()	Determines names of fields from their numbers	No	No
FILE()	Verifies the existence of a file	Yes	No
FIXED()	Does floating point to fixed decimal Number conversion	Yes	Yes
FKLABEL()	Determines name of function key from its number	Yes	No
FKMAX(	Indicates maximum number of programmable function keys	Yes	No
FLOAT()	Converts Numeric to Float	Yes	Yes

Function	Description	In Mode	In Statement
FLOCK()	Locks all records in a database file	No	No
FLOOR()	Returns floor of expression	Yes	Yes
FOUND()	Indicates if record found	No	No
FV()*	Future value of investment	No	No
GETENV()	Returns DOS SET environment parameters	Yes	No
IIF(	Performs immediate if operation	Yes	No
INKEY()	Returns decimal ASCII value of the last key pressed	Yes	No
INT()	Does conversion to integer by truncating decimals	Yes	No
ISALPHA()	Determines if first character is alpha	Yes	No
ISCOLOR()	Determines if color graphics board is installed	Yes	No
ISLOWER()	Determines if first character is lower case	Yes	No
ISMARKED()	Indicates if changes exist in current database file	No	No
ISUPPER()	Determines if first character is uppercase	Yes	No
KEY()	Key expression of index file or MDX tag	No	No
LASTKEY()	Returns ASCII code of key pressed to exit full-screen command	Yes	No
LEFT()	Returns a speacified number of characters counting from left of string	Yes	Yes

Function	Description	In Mode	In Statement
LEN()	Returns number of characters in a string or a memo field	Yes	Yes
LIKE()	QBE function that compares strings using wild cards	Yes	No
LINENO()	Line number in program about to be executed	Yes	Yes
LKSYS()	Returns info on lock owner	No	No
LOCK()	Used in networking to lock a database record;will remain in effect until UNLOCK is issued	No	No
LOG()	Returns natural logarithm to base	Yes	Yes
LOG10()	Returns logarithm to base 10	Yes	Yes
LOOKUP()	Looks up record from another database file	No	No
LOWER()	Indicates whether letter is upper or lower case	Yes	Yes
LTRIM()	Removes leading blanks from field	Yes	Yes
LUPDATE()	Returns last file update date	No	No
MAX()	Maximum of two numbers	Yes	No
MDX()	Returns active mdx name	No	No
MDY()	Converts date to format Mon DD YY	Yes	Yes
MEMLINES()	Returns number of word-wrapped lines in memo field	No	No
MEMORY()	Returns RAM in K bytes	Yes	No
MENU()	Returns name of active menu	Yes	No

Function	Description	In Mode	In Statement
MESSAGE()	Returns the error message string of last error causing ON ERROR condition	Yes	No
MIN()	Minimum of two values	Yes	No
MLINE()	Indicates line of memo field	No	No
MOD()	Does modulus arithmetic (remainder of a division)	Yes	Yes
MONTH()	Returns number of month in a date	Yes	Yes
NDX()	Returns name of an index file	No	No
NETWORK()	.T. if system on a network	Yes	No
ORDER()	Name of primary order index file	No	No
OS()	Operating system	Yes	No
PAD()	Prompt pad name of active menu	Yes	No
PAYMENT()*	Amount of periodic payment on loan	No	No
PCOL()	Printer column position	Yes	No
PI()	Returns the constant pi No	Yes	Yes
PRINTSTATUS()	Printer status	Yes	No
PROGRAM()	Current executing program	Yes	No
PROMPT()	Prompt of last selected option	Yes	No
PROW()	Printer row	Yes	No
PV()*	Present value of payments	No	No
RAND()	Provides random number between 0 and 1	Yes	Yes

Function	Description	In Mode	In Statement
READKEY()	Integer value of key pressed	Yes	No
READVAR()	Name of field or memory variable being edited	Yes	No
RECCOUNT()	Number of records in current database	No	No
RECNO()	Current record number	No	No
RECSIZE()	Size of record	No	No
REPLICATE()	Repeats a char expression a given number of times	Yes	Yes
RIGHT()	Returns specified number of chars from the right of string	Yes	Yes
RLOCK()	Locks a file	No	No
ROLLBACK()	Determines if rollback is successful	Yes	No
ROUND()	Rounds off numbers to specified number of decimals	Yes	Yes
ROW()	Row number of screen cursor	Yes	No
RTOD()	Converts radians to degrees	Yes	Yes
RTRIM()	Removes trailing blanks	Yes	Yes
SEEK()	Determines if index key found	No	No
SELECT()	Returns number representing an unused work area	No	No
SET()	Returns parameters of SET commands	Yes	No
SIGN()	Returns parameters set with the SET...TO, SET...ON commands	Yes	No

Function	Description	In Mode	In Statement
SIGN()	Returns mathematical sign of number	Yes	Yes
SIN()	Returns sine value from an angle in radians	Yes	Yes
SOUNDEX()	Returns SOUNDEX codes	Yes	Yes
SPACE()	Provides char string made of blank spaces	Yes	Yes
SQRT()	Calculates square root of a number	Yes	Yes
STR()	Converts number to char string	Yes	Yes
STUFF()	Replaces part of a string with another	Yes	Yes
SUBSTR()	Extracts specified number of chars from a string or a memo field	Yes	Yes
TAG()	Name of specified tag	No	No
TAN()	Returns tangent value from an angle in radians	Yes	Yes
TIME()	Provides system clock value	Yes	Yes
TRANSFORM()	Performs PICTURE formatting without @...SAY of character or number	Yes	No
TRIM()	Removes trailing blanks	Yes	Yes
TYPE()	Data type of an expression	Yes	No
UPPER()	Converts to upper case	Yes	Yes
USER()	Returns login user name	Yes	Yes
VAL()	Converts character to number	Yes	Yes

Function	Description	In Mode	In Statement
VARREAD()	Returns name of field or memory variable being edited	Yes	No
VERSION()	dBASE IV version number	Yes	No
YEAR()	Returns year from date expression	Yes	Yes

* **NOTE**: FV, PAYMENT, and PV are all arguments to the CALCULATE command, which is not allowed in SQL mode.

G

Glossary

aggregate function — A *group function*. A function operating on the values in one column of a table and producing a single value as its result. Same as "built-in" function. The aggregate functions in dBASE IV are: AVG, COUNT, MAX, MIN, and SUM.

argument — An expression inside the parentheses of a function, supplying a value for the function to operate on.

ASCII — A standard for using digital data to represent characters. An acronym for American Standard Code for Information Exchange.

attribute — A column in a table.

base table — Any "real" table in the database, as opposed to a virtual table.

candidate row — A row selected by a *main query*, the field values of which are used in the execution of a correlated subquery.

Cartesian product — An *equijoin* where the set of conditions is empty.

case sensitivity — Ability of a program to distinguish between upper and lower case letters.

catalog A set of system-controlled tables maintained by SQL for statistical and data definition purposes.

CHAR A *datatype* that stores character strings.

character string A sequence of characters.

Commit Make permanent changes to the database. Before INSERTs, UPDATEs, and DELETEs entered as part of a transaction are stored, both old and new data exist, so changes can be stored or data can be restored to its previous state. When data are committed, all new data that is part of the transaction are made permanent, thereby replacing the old data in the database. In dBASE IV, a commit is activated by the END TRANSACTION command.

concatenated index An *index* created on more than one column of a table. If the UNIQUE keyword is used in the CREATE INDEX statement, the index can be used to guarantee that those columns are unique for every row in the table.

DBA See *database administrator*.

DCL See *Data Control Language.*

DDL See *Data Definition Language.*

DML See *Data Manipulation Language*

database administrator The SQLDBA. A user authorized to grant and revoke other users' access to the system, modify options affecting all users, and perform other administrative functions.

Data Control Language (DCL) One category of SQL statements. These statements control access to the data and to the database. Examples: GRANT, GRANT SELECT, REVOKE.

Data Definition Language (DDL)	One category of SQL statements.These statements define (CREATE) or delete (DROP) database objects. Examples: CREATE VIEW, CREATE TABLE, CREATE INDEX, DROP TABLE.
data dictionary	A comprehensive set of tables and views containing information about users, privileges, tables, columns, and views. It is a source of information for the database itself, as well as for all users.
Data Manipulation Language (DML)	One category of SQL statements. These statements query and update the actual data. Examples: SELECT, INSERT, DELETE, UPDATE.
datatype	Any one of the forms of data stored and manipulated. Datatypes supported by dBASE IV SQL are: CHAR, DATE, LOGICAL, NUMERIC, FLOAT, SMALLINT, INTEGER, and DECIMAL.
date field	A *field* whose value is a date. Sometimes applied to a field whose value is a number representing a date.
datum	a single unit of data.
deadlock	A situation where two users are each vying for resources locked by the other, and therefore neither user can obtain the necessary resource to complete the work.
default	The value of any option which is built into the system, and which will be used by the system if the user fails to specify a value for that option.
dummy table	A table containing fictitious or temporary data. Useful as the object of a SELECT command intended to copy the value of one *field* to another field.

embedded SQL
Commands that can be used in programs.

equijoin
A *join* condition specifying the relationship "equals" (=).

export
To transfer database files into some other storage area.

expression
A combination of constants, variables, and operators producing a result of a single datatype, usually used as the arguments to commands.

field
A part of a table that holds one piece of data. The intersection of a row and a column.

foreign key
A column (or combination of columns) in one table which is not a *key* in that table, but is a key elsewhere (e.g., in another table). Used for relating data in multiple tables using *joins*.

formfeed
A control character which causes the printer to skip to the top of a new sheet of paper.

function
An operation which may be performed by placing the function's name in an expression. Most functions take one or more arguments within the parentheses, and use the value(s) of the argument(s) in the operation.

functional dependency
A relationship between columns, whereby the values in one set of columns completely determines the values in a second set of columns.

group function
A *function* operating on a column or expression in all of the rows selected by a *query*, and computing a single value from them. Example: AVG, which computes an average. Same as *aggregate function* and "built-in" function.

index — A data structure used primarily to speed searching for data. In the case of a table, an index provides faster access than doing a full table scan. Also, UNIQUE indexes can be used to enforce integrity constraints.

initialization — The initial preparing of a database; always done when installing a database system for the first time.

inner query — A subquery.

interactive SQL — An operating environment in which SQL commands can be executed one at a time. Commands are entered at the SQL dot prompt (similar to the environment provided at the dBASE dot prompt), with results immediately displayed.

join — An operation on two or more tables, resulting in a single table, depending on test conditions between some of the columns in the tables.

Julian date — A means of converting date data, so that every date can be expressed as a unique integer.

key — The column(s) in one table that can be used to uniquely identify a row. Column(s) forming a key are usually indexed.

macro — In dBASE IV, a macro is a substitution method whereby a value is substituted for a *memory variable* or a function key. This value can then be used as a command or part of a command.

main query — The outermost query in a *query* containing a *subquery*. The query containing the first SELECT command in a series of SELECT commands. Also called the *outer query*—as opposed to a *subquery*, which is called the *inner query*.

memory variable
A dBASE variable that allows you to specify a value in expressions, search conditions, and with SQL predicates such as IN or LIKE. Also can be used in commands to transfer data to columns in tables with the INSERT command. When used with the FETCH command, a memory variable will return values from columns.

natural join
An *equijoin* taken on the common column(s) of two or more tables, with the duplicate(s) of the common column(s) removed.

nested SELECT
See *subquery*.

nesting
An arrangement in which one statement is used as part of an expression within another statement.

non-equijoin
A *join* condition specifying a relationship other than "equals", e.g. <, >, <=, >=. A *theta join*.

NUMERIC
A *datatype* .

object
Something stored in a database. Examples: tables, views, synonyms, indexes, columns, reports, stored procedures, stored programs.

outer join
The rows that do not match the *join* condition.

outer query
See *main query*.

parameter
A *memory variable* whose value is passed to a subprogram.

precedence
The order in which the system performs operations on an *expression*.

predicate clause
A clause based on one of the operators (=, !=, >, >=, <, <=, LIKE, IN, EXISTS) and containing no AND, OR, or NOT.

propagation
The process of copying a value from one *field* to another logically related field, or computing a value to be stored in a related field. For example: when an employee's Social Security number is entered in a block of a salary record form, it may be propagated to a block of a withholding tax form.

query
An instruction to SQL that will retrieve information from one or more tables or views.

read consistency
Feature whereby an SQL query always sees a *snapshot view* of a table as it existed at the start of query execution, even while other users may be modifying the table.

record
One row of a table.

recursive definition
A definition where the rule may be repeated an arbitrary number of times.

relational algebra
A set of operations on relations, each of which produces other relations.

relational database
A database that appears to the user to be just a collection of tables.

reserved word
A word that has with a special meaning in dBASE IV SQL mode, and therefore is not available for naming tables, views or columns.

ROLLBACK
To undo incomplete changes made to the database during a transaction or logical unit of work, using the ROLLBACK command.

RUNSTATS
A command that updates database statistics (such as number of rows, high and low data values in columns, distribution of data) in the SQL system catalog tables in the current database. It can only be run in *interactive SQL* mode.

self-join
A *join* operationin which rows of the same table are joined to each other.

Set operators
In relational algebra, these are *Union* (the set of all tuples that are in either one of two relations), *Intersect* (the set of all tuples that are in both of two relations) and *Difference* (the set of all tuples that are in one but not the other).

SQL
Structured Query Language.

SQLDBA
See *database administrator*.

Structured Query Language (SQL)
A particular formal language for storing and retrieving information in a database.

subquery
A *query* used as a clause in an SQL command. Also called an *inner query*, as opposed to the *main query*, which is called the *outer query*, or a *nested SELECT* or a *subSELECT*. The result of a subquery is to provide information needed for completion of the main query.

syntax
The structure of a command; the linear order of words or symbols in a programming language.

target list
The list of columns appearing directly after the SELECT in a *query* or *subquery*.

temporary tables
Frequently required to order data, and to execute SQL statements including DISTINCT, ORDER BY, GROUP BY, or SAVE TO TEMP clauses.

theta join A generalization of equijoin using not equal (!=), less than (<), and greater than (>) comparison operators as well as equal(=).

transaction A logical unit of work as defined by the user. In dBASE IV, a transaction is the set of tasks to be performed by the commands between a BEGIN TRANSACTION command and an END TRANSACTION command.

transaction processing The processing of logical units of work, rather than individual entries, in order to keep the database consistent.

unique index An *index* that imposes uniqueness on each value it indexes. May be a single column or concatenated columns.

UNION The union operator of traditional set theory. Example: A UNION B (where A and B are sets) is the set of all objects x, such that x is a member of A or x is a member of B, or both.

unit of work A logical unit of work is equivalent to a *transaction*. Includes all SQL statements since the time you logged on, last committed, or last rolled back your work. A transaction can encompass one SQL statement or many SQL statements.

view A special type of SQL table that does not physically exist as such in storage, but looks to the user as though it does. A part of a table that does exist in the database, a *virtual table*.

virtual column A column in a query result, the value of which was calculated from the value(s) of other column(s).

virtual table
A table that does not actually exist in the database, but looks to the user as though it does. Contrast with *base table*. See *view*.

wrapping
Moving the end of a heading or *field* to a new line when it is too long to fit on one line.

List of Figures

INDEX

Q

R

S

Framework III: An Introduction

By Bill Harrison

Tap into the power of Framework III™ with this revision of Ashton-Tate's most successful book for Framework®. Harrison, the author of two previous editions of this book, takes you on a guided tour of each of the six functional areas of Framework III: word processing, outlining, spreadsheets, database management, graphs, and communications. New Framework III features such as mouse support, integrated thesaurus with 40,000 root words and 470,000 synonym responses, footnoting, built-in electronic mail support, and local area networking are examined. You'll also find numerous detailed examples showing you how to combine various Framework III capabilities into complete business applications like a loan amortization schedule, client database, timekeeper system and an automated stock profolio analyzer. *Framework III: An Introduction* quickly acquaints you with the latest version of this acclaimed integrated decision support software package.

$24.95 • Softcover
447 pages • 7 3/8" x 9 1/4" • ISBN: 1-55519-062-6

FullWrite Professional: A User's Guide

By Keith Thompson and Theodore Peterson

This thorough introduction to using FullWrite Professional™ for business applications will have you producing persuasive documents with tremendous visual impact in no time flat. Thompson and Peterson provide you with instructions for customizing FullWrite Professional; creating and editing documents; chapter, page, and paragraph formatting techniques; printing techniques; and producing and using graphics with FullWrite Professional. At the heart of this book are useful applications for creating templates for form documents, printing form letters and envelopes, desktop publishing, preparing FullWrite Professional documents for electronic transmission, and creating and editing tables. Let *FullWrite Professional: A User's Guide* help you become a FullWrite Professional power user.

$24.95 • Softcover
350 pages • 7 3/8" x 9 1/4" • ISBN: 1-55519-070-7

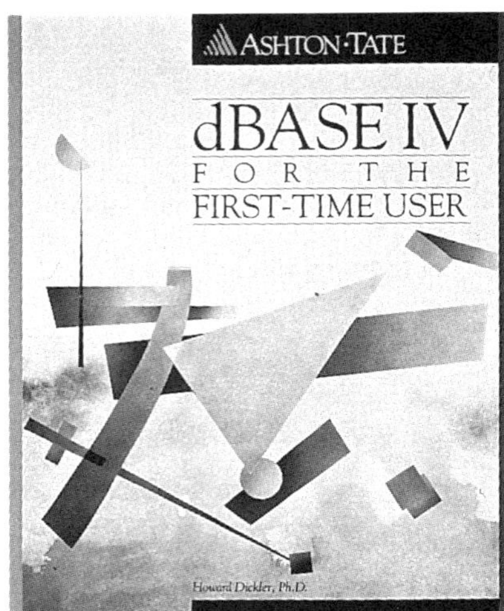

dBASE IV For The First-Time User

By Howard Dickler, Ph.D.
Illustrated by Catherine Ledbetter

For a highly illustrated, hands-on introduction to dBASE IV™ reach for *dBASE IV For The First-Time User.* Written for the novice dBASE IV user, this book provides a systematic approach to learning dBASE IV commands and features through the Control Center, the new dBASE IV user interface. Readers are guided through the process of developing a small model system with dBASE IV, during which they will learn to create reports, mailing labels, personalized form letters and more. In addition, instruction is given on how to employ the new dBASE IV Applications Generator. Its clear, concise presentation also makes *dBASE IV For The First-Time User* the perfect text for an introductory dBASE IV class.

$19.95 • Softcover
450 pages • 7 3/8" x 9 1/4" • ISBN: 1-55519-068-5
Winter `88

Everyman's Database Primer Featuring dBASE IV

Robert A. Byers and Cary N. Prague

The best-selling introductory guide for dBASE® software is now updated for dBASE IV. *Everyman's Database Primer Featuring dBASE IV* is filled with valuable information for novice dBASE IV users, as well as experienced dBASE users who need to learn about the dBASE IV software. The book begins with an introduction to database management concepts and proceeds to an examination of the new dBASE IV user interface, the Control Center. From the chapters on the dBASE IV Control Center it's a quick transition into planning, building, modifying, and sorting a database; working with multiple databases; creating reports, labels, and custom screens; importing and exporting data and more. In addition, there's a discussion on developing applications with the dBASE IV Applications Generator. Fully illustrated with dBASE IV screens, *Everyman's Database Primer Featuring dBASE IV* is an easy-to-understand, straightforward primer for all dBASE IV users.

$19.95 • Softcover
450 pages • 7 3/8" x 9 1/4" • ISBN: 1-55519-056-1
Fall `88

Other titles of interest

dBASE IV/SQL Advanced Applications Development
Rick Trutna & Fred Crownover

Written for the intermediate/advanced dBASE IV/SQL programmer, this development guide includes valuable information about using SQL commands.

$24.95 1-55519-026-X Available August '89

dBASE Systems Handbook
By Boston Systems Group

A comprehensive methodology for corporate systems development, using dBASE IV. An essential reference guide for project managers and programmers.

$49.95 1-55519-050-2 Available July '89

Currently Available

Title	Price	Part Number
Advanced Programmer's Guide* dBASE II/dBASE III/dBASE III PLUS	$28.95	912677-058
Better Business Presentations	$24.95	555190-081
dBASE IV For The First-Time User	$21.95	555190-685
dBASE IV SQL User's Guide	$24.95	555190-529
dBASE III PLUS for Every Business	$19.95	912677-864
dBASE III PLUS Programming Tips & Techniques	$19.95	912677-910
dBASE III PLUS Trail Guide	$29.95	912677-848
dBASE Mac in Business	$19.95	912677-902
dBASE Power: Building & Using Programming Tools*	$29.95	555190-219
dBASE Programmer's Field Guide*	$14.95	555190-277
Everyman's Database Primer/dBASE III PLUS	$19.95	912677-856
Everyman's Database Primer/dBASE IV	$19.95	555190-561
Framework III: An Introduction	$24.95	555190-626
FullWrite Professional: A User's Guide	$24.95	555190-707
MultiMate Advantage II Tips and Techniques	$19.95	555190-057
RapidFile Business Applications	$19.95	555190-006
Secrets of dBASE*	$16.95	555190-243

**Not for dBASE IV*

Prices and titles are subject to change without prior notice.
To buy these books, see your favorite book or computer store. Or, use the order form on the next page.

ORDER FORM

Thank you for purchasing this Ashton-Tate book. To order a book, or to receive a FREE copy of a Tate Publishing catalog, listing our complete line of microcomputer books, software add-ons and utilities, complete the form below. Or call 1-800-437-4329.

Name ____
(Please Print)

Address ____

City ______________________ State __________ Zip __________

Are you interested in technical sessions on Ashton-Tate products?

☐ YES ☐ NO

Are you an application developer (i.e. VAR, consultant, system integrator, develop applications for internal use or for resale)?

☐ YES ☐ NO

QTY	ITEM #	DESCRIPTION	PRICE EACH	TOTAL

SUBTOTAL	
Sales tax (see tax table below)	
Shipping charge (see chart)	
TOTAL	

U.S. SHIPPING CHARGES
Books are mailed book rate and take 4-6 weeks for delivery.

Up to $20	$2.00
$20.01 to $30	$3.00
$30.01 to $40	$4.00
$40.01 to $50	$5.00
$50.01 to $60	$6.00
Over $60	$7.00

FORM OF PAYMENT

☐ VISA ☐ MasterCard ☐ American Express ☐ Check

Card #: |_|_|_|_|_|_|_|_|_|_|_|_|_|_|_|_|

Expiration date: ____________________

Signature: ____________________ Date: ____________________

Mail this order form to:

Tate Publishing Division
Ashton-Tate
20101 Hamilton Avenue
Torrance, CA 90502

TAX TABLE

CA	6.0%*	MO	4.225%
CO	3.6%	NC	3.0%
CT	7.5%	NJ	6.0%
DC	6.0%	NY	4.0%
FL	6.0%	NYC	8.25%
GA	5.0%	OH	5.0%
IL	5.0%	PA	6.0%
MA	5.0%	TX	8.0%
MI	4.0%	VA	4.5%
MN	6.0%	WA	8.1%

* 6.5% for residents of: Contra Costa, Fresno, Los Angeles, San Diego, Santa Cruz, San Francisco, or San Mateo counties.

* 7% for residents of: Alameda, or Santa Cruz counties.